THE HUMAN MIND AND THE MIND OF GOD

Theological Promise In Brain Research

James B. Ashbrook

UNIVERSITY PRESS OF AMERICA

LANHAM • NEW YORK • LONDON

University Press of America,™ Inc.

4720 Boston Way
Lanham, MD 20706

3 Henrietta Street
London WC2E 8LU England

Printed in the United States of America

Library of Congress Cataloging in Publication Data

Ashbrook, James B., 1925-
The human mind and the mind of God.

Includes indexes.
1. Brain--Religious aspects--Christianity. 2. Man (Christian theology) 3. Christianity--Philosophy.
I. Title.
BT702.A84 1984 230 84-15303
ISBN 0-8191-4225-5 (alk. paper)
ISBN 0-8191-4226-3 (pbk. : alk. paper)

All University Press of America books are produced on acid-free paper which exceeds the minimum standards set by the National Historical Publications and Records Commission.

To the Library Staffs

Colgate Rochester/Bexley Hall/Crozer

The United Library Garrett-Evangelical Theological Seminary/ Northwestern University

for encouraging

a seeker of strange information

for delighting in

collaborative endeavors

Table of Contents

Tables

Figures

ACKNOWLEDGMENTS

No endeavor of any magnitude can be undertaken alone. Nor can it mature rapidly. I first referred to the suggestiveness of the human brain as an analytic tool at the end of my book HUMANITAS (1973). That involved the convergence of the experimental approach of the West and the experiential approach of the East. I applied the hemisphere structure to issues associated with RESPONDING TO HUMAN PAIN (1975), and then, in CHRISTIANITY FOR PIOUS SKEPTICS (1977), to theological issues such as using the Bible, speaking of God, praying for the Spirit, and living for Christ.

During a leave in 1976-77, I participated in the Neurosciences course at the Medical School of the University of Rochester. Simultaneously, I talked regularly with Garth Thomas, then Director of the Center for Brain Research. Although he remained "unconvinced that facts extracted from one level of organization of experience can have anything compelling to contribute to another level," he did assist me in learning the grammar of neuropsychology and tolerated my speculations. Through contact in a short-course on "Frontiers in the Neurosciences," sponsored by the National Science Foundation (1981), Robert B. Livingston, professor of Neuroscience, University of California at San Diego, urged me to continue developing the mind as a metaphorical tool.

Two Doctor of Ministry students contributed to early applications of the metaphor: Karl Johnson related lateralization and holography to pastoral functioning (1976), and James Flurer applied lateralization to spirituality and sports meditation (1980).

Since 1978 I have explored theological promise in brain research in seminars on "The Working Brain and The Work of Theology." Students have added greatly to my understanding. In particular, Mary Lou Anderson analyzed 17th, 18th, and early 19th century music. Later she examined Italian Renaissance landscape painting and the creation stories in Genesis. Regretfully, other demands precluded her contribution being available in this book. However, she has continued discussing the issues and supporting the project, for which I am most appreciative.

I have profited from presentations to the Eastern and Mid-Atlantic Regions of the Association of Clinical Pastoral Education, to the Eastern Region of the American Association of Pastoral Counselors, to Southeastern Baptist Theological School on the occasion of my presenting the Page Lectures, to various church groups, to Colgate Rochester/Bexley Hall/Crozer for public lectures and faculty discussion, and to my colleagues at Garrett-Evangelical Theological Seminary.

Those who have contributed to the work are numerous. Some have critiqued the ideas; others have brought research to my attention; still others have read portions of the argument; all have encouraged the undertaking as an "evocative synthesis," to quote one colleague. Byzantinist Susan Ashbrook Harvey has encouraged, critiqued, and contributed to this endeavor with loving and meticulous enthusiasm. I, of course, am alone responsible for the finished product.

Keith McBarron's exquisite illustrations enable me to present some material in visual form. Without them the ideas would lose some of their impact.

Secretarial support has been necessary, constant, and competent: in the early stages in Rochester, Debra Watkins and Mary Beth Curten; in the later stages in Evanston, Linda Koops and Joan Svenningsen. Without Joan, especially, I would not have been able to manage a leave from teaching, a change of locations, and still continue work on the manuscript. Anita Lauterstein not only contributed skill in computer technology but also careful attention and sensitivity to nuances of style and accuracy. The fact that we unexpectedly discovered that she had walked through my oriental garden only added to a special sense of a working alliance. William Preston exercised thorough and thoughtful editorial clarifications. Colgate Rochester/Bexley Hall/Crozer and Garrett-Evangelical Theological Seminary each provided extra time to pursue the task. I am particularly grateful to Garrett- Evangelical and the Institute for Research in Pastoral Psychology for special assistance in bringing the project to print.

Through these years my wife, Pat, has exercised patience during periods when she did not understand, engaged me in discussion at points where she did understand, and helped our living increasingly balance work and love and play. I think I am beginning to understand the mind of God in our togetherness, in our shared engagement in the community, and in our separate work in the world.

Grateful acknowledgement is made for the following:

Chapter One "Juxtaposing the Brain and Belief" first appeared in article form in the *Journal of Psychology and Theology*, 1984, Volume 12, Number 3. The copyrighted article, with minor revisions, is used here with the permission of the *Journal*.

Chapters Two and Three are expanded from James B. Ashbrook, "Neurotheology: Thc Working Brain and The Work of Theology," (c) by the Joint Publication Board of *Zygon: Journal of Religion & Science*, Volume 19 No. 3 (September 1984) and used by permission.

Quotations from BYZANTINE CHRISTIANITY: Emperor, Church and the West (1970) by Harry J. Magoulias used by permission of The Wayne State University Press.

Charles Scribner's Sons for permission to quote from Cyril Mango, BYZANTIUM (1982).

Extracts from R.W. Southern, THE MAKING OF THE MIDDLE AGES. Copyright (c) by Yale University Press, (1953) 1980, used by permission.

Extracts from WESTERN SOCIETY & THE CHURCH IN THE MIDDLE AGES (Pelican Books, 1970). Copyright (c) R.W. Southern, 1970. "Reprinted by permission of Penguin Books Ltd."

Extracts from A SCHOLASTIC MISCELLANY, edited and translated by Eugene R. Fairweather (Volume X: The Library of Christian Classics). Printed in the U.S.A. November 5, 1956 by The Westminster Press. Used by permission of The Westminster Press and SCM Press, Ltd.

Copyright (c) 1980 by David R. Cartlidge and David L. Dungan, DOCUMENTS FOR THE STUDY OF THE GOSPELS. Extracts used by permission of Fortress Press.

The Blaisdell Institute/Claremont Graduate School for material from Paul Ricouer, "Manifestation and Proclamation," The Blaisdell Institute 12 (Winter) 1978.

Excerpt(s) from THE JERUSALEM BIBLE, copyright (c) 1966 by Darton, Longman & Todd, Ltd. and Doubleday & Company, Inc. Reprinted by permission of the publishers.

Scripture quotations from the Revised Standard Version of the Bible, copyrighted 1946, 1952, (c) 1971, 1973 by the Division of Education and Ministry of the National Council of the Churches of Christ in the U.S.A., used by permission.

Table 9 adapted from Philip Sherrard, BYZANTIUM (New York: Time-Life Books, 1966), page 76.

Tables 14-16 used by permission of M.P. Bryden, LATERALITY: functional asymmetry in the intact brain (New York: Academic Press, 1982).

Gulbenkian Museum of Oriental Art, University of

Durham, School of Oriental Studies for photographs of mid-17th century maps of the cosmos (India).

The illustrations by Keith McBarron are adapted from the following:

The brain from STRUCTURE OF THE HUMAN BRAIN: A Photographic Atlas by Stephen J. DeArmond, Madeline M. Fusco, and Maynard M. Dewey (New York: Oxford University Press, 1974), page 5 Lateral surface of the brain-actual size.

St. Sophia (exterior) and (interior) from Steven Runciman, BYZANTININE STYLE AND CIVILIZATION (Baltimore: Penguin Books, Inc., 1975), figures 37 and 40 are photographs by Josephine Powell, Hirmer, Phototech, Marburg. The minarets in the exterior view were removed on the photograph.

Ground Plan and Elevation St. Sophia from figures 272 Section of Hagia Sophia (after Gurlitt) and 273 Plan of Hagia Sophia (after v.Sybel) in HISTORY OF ART. 2nd rev. ed., by H.W. Janson and used by permission of Harry N. Abrams, Inc.

West Facade of Chartres Cathedral, courtesy of French Government Tourist Office.

Ground Plan, Chartres Cathedral, from Plate 33 in THE GOTHIC CATHEDRAL: Origins of Gothic Architecture and the Medieval Concept of Order, Bollingen Series 48, by Otto von Simson. Copyright (c) 1956, 1962, and used by permission of Princeton University Press.

Interior, Chartres Cathedral, from Illustration 2 in CHARTRES CATHEDRAL: Illustrations, Introductory Essay, Documents, Analysis, Criticism, edited by Robert Branner (New York: W.W. Norton & Company, 1969).

Begun in Rochester, New York 1976
Continuing in Evanston, Illinois 1984

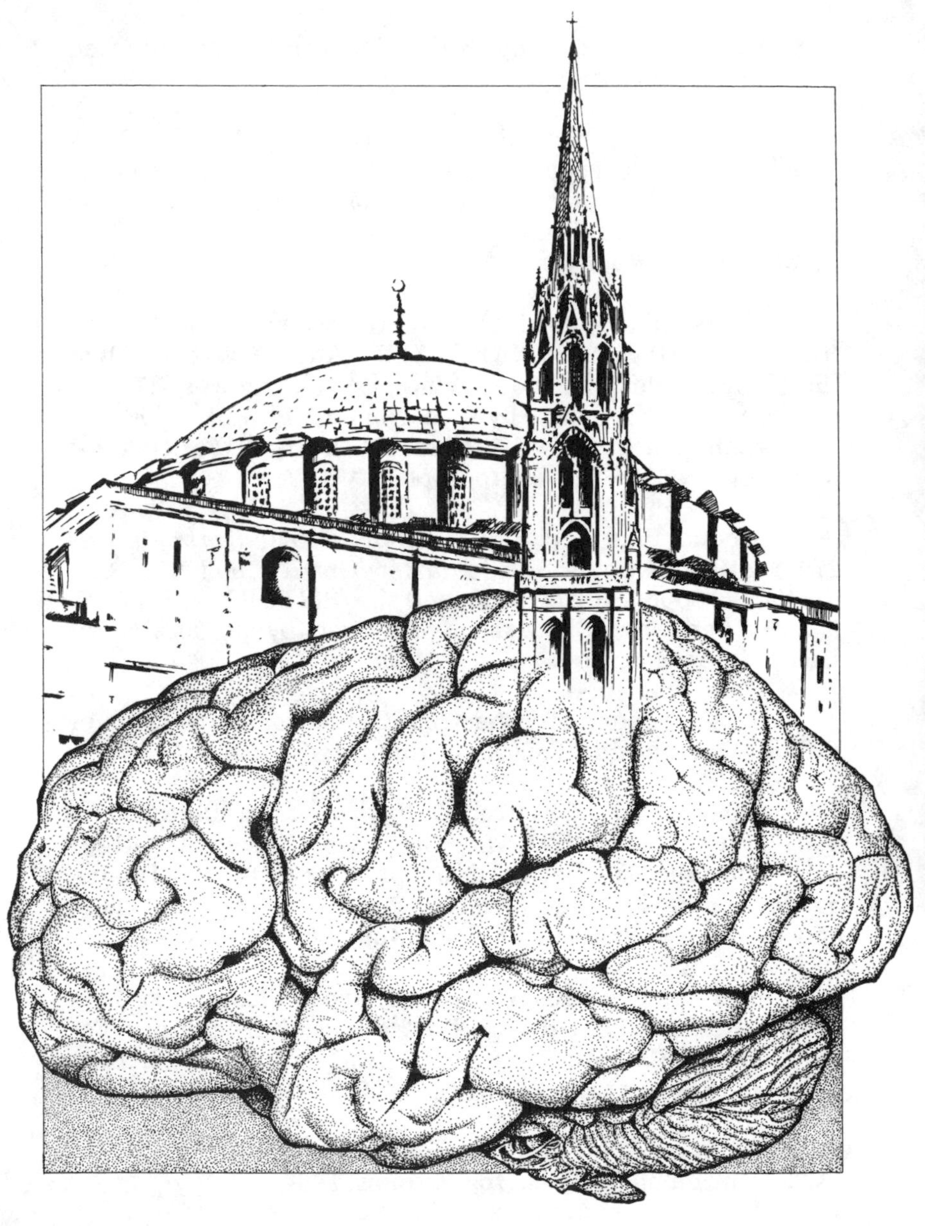

Figure 1 Brain, Dome, Spire

INTRODUCTION

Who can know the mind of God?

So St. Paul asked Isaiah's rhetorical question (1 Corinthians 2:16; Isaiah 40:13). And he answers, No one! The mind of God is past our understanding. Instead we Christians are given "the mind of Christ." While that answer quiets the heart, it fails to satisfy my mind.

I am a Christian skeptic, a believing unbeliever, one who participates in that which I question, an heir of Athens as much as Jerusalem. From a Pauline perspective this book can be dismissed as the foolishness of the Greeks. That means I address the question of God and temporarily bracket a relationship to Christ (1 Corinthians 1:18-24). I follow the progression of Paul's thinking from God-talk to commitment to Christ, yet I alter his conclusion, namely, that we can only know the mind of Christ since the mind of God is inaccessible. Brain research provides a way to approach theological issues somewhat apart from, though parallel to, Christological issues.

As a skeptic I want to understand conceptually, to be able to anchor my faith empirically, to put my

Once when my thoughts were turned toward the existence of things, and my mind was greatly uplifted, my bodily senses were subdued as in those who are weighed down by sleep. . . it seemed a great being of unmeasurable size began to call my name. It said to me, 'What do you wish to hear and to see, and when you have understood, to learn and to know?'

I said, 'Who are you?'

'I am Poimandres, (i.e., bearer of) the True Mind; I know what you wish; I am with you everywhere.'

I said, 'I want to learn about the existence of things, and to understand the nature of these things, and to know God. Oh, how I want to hear these things.'

He replied, 'Hold in your mind whatever you want to learn, and I will teach you.' He had no sooner said this than he changed his appearance, and in an instant all things were opened to me, and I saw a boundless vision . . .

'Do you know what this vision means?'

'Well,' I said, 'I shall know.'

'That light is I, Mind, your God...'

'What does this mean?'

'Know this. The (capacity) in you to see and hear is the Logos of the Lord, and the Mind is the Father, God. They are not distinguished from each other. Their union is life. . . You see in the

> Mind the archetypal form, the primal beginning of the beginning which never ends. . . the Mind, God, was both male and female; it was life and light, and it begot by Logos another Mind, the world-creator. . . The Father of all, Mind, who was life and light, brought forth a (Human Being) in his own likeness whom he loved as his own child. . . having the image of the Father, God truly loved his own image, and he made him lord of all creatures."[4]

This text sets forth a vision of an archetypal creation of the cosmos much like an architect's model of a building. A secondary creator-God or demiurge, which is created by the God who is both male and female, shapes creation because the high God cannot have anything to do with evil creation directly. But based upon the archetypal model of the cosmos, which is in Mind, the demiurge and the Logos spin out a world that takes on order and form.

Poimandres expressed the gnostic pessimism regarding the material world. Authentic existence required an enlightenment which freed people from the prisonhouse of the unredeemable, bodily, finite world. In contrast, in fact in exactly a reverse valuation, I view the mind of the human brain as full of promise, the reality which we are to engage and affirm. Knowledge comes from discerning meaning-and-matter, mind-and-brain, rather than mind apart from matter. The human brain holds a central key to the human mind and the mind of God. For it is, as Poimandres asserted, in the everywhere present, everywhere ordering, everywhere seeing and hearing of world-creation, cosmos, that Mind as the archetypal matter of meaning presents itself to us.

So I pick up the analogical approach of the Greek view of Mind but anchor Mind in current research on the brain. This is a cross-disciplinary approach, correlating what is being learned in neuropsychology with what is understood in historical theology.

Because I write about the mind of God I begin with the human mind. The human mind is mysterious enough in itself, much more so the mind of God. Yet I put these two mysteries side-by-side. In so doing the concept "mind" serves as a bridge between theology and neuropsychology.

In nonbehavioral investigations the brain has been taken primarily as an image or metaphor. Theologians have responded intuitively to early popularization of the psychology of consciousness.[5] They have applied active and receptive modes of consciousness to symbol and myth, [5] ritual,[7] aesthetics,[8] theology,[9] Bible study,[10] pastoral care,[11] and education.[12] Historical investigation has received scant attention. Julian Jaynes has been virtually alone with his work on The Origin of Consciousness in the Breakdown of the Bicameral Mind. [13]

In these endeavors the use of the brain for analytic purposes has been minimal. Perhaps rightly so. To generalize between levels of organization has been questioned. Understandably, specialists in one area of knowledge shy away from making inferences about other areas. However, we can distinguish between reducing and relating levels of organization to one another. Mind allows us to relate levels as disparate as biochemical, cortical, cultural, and cosmic. Just as the mind reveals the human meaning of the brain, so God discloses the religious meaning of the mind.

The phrase "working brain" suggests what mind can mean by identifying how the brain works. The term refers to that reality which includes both the materiality of brain and the integrated meaningfulness of mind. It marks the interface between sensory input and personal experience. Thus, I use mind as an analytic metaphor to link the human mind and the mind of God. The analytic features sharpen the image of mind with knowledge of how the brain functions. The metaphoric qualities are implied by the idea of "the mind of God." These ideas offer perspective, suggesting what is of more than passing significance. Together, human mind and mind of God let us speculate about what is real and how reality works. The mind of God and the mind of humanity are related.[14]

Contrary views of reality abound. One way understands it by abstracting out from the flux of things distinct parts and precise steps. Another way understands by attending to flowing patterns and immediate wholes. Despite the ambiguity in the rich data of neuropsychological research, the brain offers a powerful metaphor consistent with these ways of dealing with reality. Complementary orientations have their parallels in theology.

Specifically, I address the following issues:

—what does brain research contribute to understanding theology?

—how do the specialized functions of the left and right hemispheres correspond to contrasting patterns of belief?

—can central images of faith, such as the Medieval cathedral spire and the Byzantine dome, be understood as relying more on left mind or right mind processes?

—what implications might such correlations have for us?

What to Expect

In Part I, I explore the use of mind as a metaphor of meaning. First I juxtapose the brain and patterns of belief. Then I lay out more fully what we know about the brain. It is characterized by asymmetry. The two halves of our one head each play unequal roles in all brain activity. The left half works step-by-step, while the right half functions all-at-once. No activity can be isolated in a single area. All activity utilizes the whole head. The one brain depends upon both minds.

Even so we can distinguish these contrasting ways of working and relate them to parallel theological emphases. Interpretive proclamation of God's intent is a left mind pattern; celebrative manifestation of God's presence is a right mind pattern. Such correlations allow us to use the human mind as an analytic metaphor with which to understand God's mind, God's ways of being God. With the metaphor we can also analyze how cultures evolve and people function.

In Part II on "architectures of mind," I apply the metaphor to the work of theology in two historical periods: Byzantine and Medieval. Each shared the common Judaeo-Christian heritage. Each developed its own distinct features. Each paralleled the other for almost a thousand years. Both perceived reality as an expression of the mind of God and organized their lives accordingly. I use the Dome of St. Sophia and the Spire of the Cathedral of Chartres as cultural expressions in which we can glimpse their contrasting perceptions of God. The buildings provide central images for our understanding of ways our minds work and ways our hearts beat in the experience of faith.

Finally, in Part III on "many minds—many meanings," I identify the odd mind of humanity by examining the experience of Pentecost in Acts. Here are clues to make real what truly matters in our faith. For while I deal with Byzantine and Medieval architectures of the mind of faith, this book is not about religious architecture per se. Rather it is about left and right ways of making real genuine human community.

One word about the notes. I regard them as substantive in themselves. They undergird the analysis. As such they are extensive. Many issues are elaborated and/or qualified there. I have added a glossary of terms for the brain and for theology as an aid to less familiar material.

A final comment. I deal only with the Christian West prior to the Renaissance/Reformation. I believe the approach can be applied to these more recent periods. Further, I believe it can illumine cross-cultural investigation, especially the richness of Asian and African cultures. I hope others will nurture these extensions.

I have hypothesized that theology is more understandable because of what we are learning about the human mind. I find that true and misleading both. The more we understand the brain the more mystery we discover. The mystery of meaning-within-matter continues to elude us, entice us, and enlighten us all at the same time.

Although the book comes to an end in order to go to press, I continue exploring theological promise in brain research. I experience the task as like trying to grab mercury resting in the palm of my hand. The moment I try to grab it, it keeps slipping out of its conceptual container. The human mind cannot contain the mind of God. Yet, the metaphor of mind has helped me engage expressions of faith and patterns of belief in fresh and exciting ways. It continues leading me in paths of promise even as it continues leaving me short of promised fulfillment.

NOTES

1. Cf. such increasingly typical comments as those of Robert Hogan: "psychology needs to get back to the problems that initially inspired the discipline: the nature of consciousness, the nature of religious experience, the body-mind problem, basic issues in epistemology, in how we experience the world. . . we need to become more tolerant of crazy ideas and wiggly sorts of notions. We have to suppress the critical editorial function and sort of enlarge or reward or prop up the imaginative and playful faculty of people's mind . . . Generally, we need to loosen up" (American Psychological Association Monitor, April 1979, 5); R. W. Sperry, "Bridging Science and Values: A Unifying View of Mind and Brain," American Psychologist, April 1977:237-245.

2. For the Greeks especially "(t)here was no material world devoid of mind, and no mental world devoid of materiality; matter was simply that of which everything was made. . . and mind was simply the activity by which everything apprehended the final cause of its own changes" (R. G. Collingwood, THE IDEA OF NATURE [London: Oxford at the Clarendon Press, 1945], 111).

3. Ibid., 3.

4. David R. Cartlidge and David L. Dungan, DOCUMENTS FOR THE STUDY OF THE GOSPELS (Philadelphia: Fortress Press, 1980), 243-246.

5. Robert E. Ornstein, THE PSYCHOLOGY OF CONSCIOUSNESS. Second edition (New York: Harcourt Brace Jovanovich, Inc., [1972] 1977); Bob Samples, THE METAPHORIC MIND: A Celebration of Creative Consciousness. With an introduction by George Leonard (Reading, MA: Addison-Wesley Publishing Company, [1976] 1978); Marilyn Ferguson, THE BRAIN REVOLUTION: the frontiers of mind research (New York: Taplinger Publishing Company, 1973); Carl Sagan, THE DRAGONS OF

EDEN: speculations on the evolution of human intelligence (New York: Random House, 1977).

6. Urban T. Holmes, III, THE PRIEST IN COMMUNITY: Exploring the Roots of Ministry (New York: The Seabury Press, 1978); idem., MINISTRY and IMAGINATION (New York: Crossroad Books. The Seabury Press, 1976); Eugene G. D'Aquili, "The Myth-Ritual Complex: A Biogenetic Structural Analysis," Zygon, Sept. 1983, 18, 3:247-269.

7. Eugene G. D'Aquili and Charles D. Laughlin, Jr., "The Neurobiology of Myth and Ritual." In E. G. Aquili, et. al., THE SPECTRUM OF RITUAL: A Biogenetic Structural Analysis (New York: Columbia University Press, 1979), 152-182; Luis Maldonado and David Power, eds., SYMBOL and ART in WORSHIP. English Language Editor Marcus Lefebure (New York: The Seabury Press, 1980); George S. Worgul, Jr., FROM MAGIC to METAPHOR: A Validation of the Christian Sacraments. Forward by Piet Fransen, S. J. (New York: Paulist Press, 1980); Victor Turner, "Body, Brain, and Culture," Zygon, Sept. 1983, 18, 3:221-245.

8. Samuel Laeuchli, RELIGION and ART in CONFLICT: Introduction to a Cross-Disciplinary Task (Philadelphia: Fortress Press, 1980).

9. James B. Ashbrook, "A Theology of Consciousness: With All Your Mind," Review and Expositor, Spr., 1979, 167-178; Paul W. Walaskay, "A Pathway to God," The Christian Century, March 7, 1979, 246-249; James B. Ashbrook and Paul W. Walaskay, CHRISTIANITY FOR PIOUS SKEPTICS (Nashville, Tenn.: Abingdon Press, 1977); Eugene P. Wratchford, BRAIN RESEARCH AND PERSONHOOD: A Philosophical Theological Inquiry (Washington, D.C.: University Press of America, 1979).

10. Walter Wink, TRANSFORMING BIBLE STUDY: A Leader's Guide (Nashville, Tenn.: Abingdon Press, 1980).

11. Don S. Browning, THE MORAL CONTEXT OF PASTORAL CARE (Philadelphia: Westminster Press, 1976); James B. Ashbrook, RESPONDING TO HUMAN PAIN (Valley Forge, PA.: Judson Press, 1976), 67-74, 81; Howard W. Stone, "Left Brain, Right Brain," Theology Today, October 1983: 292-301.

12. Gloria Durka and Joan Marie Smith, eds., AESTHETIC DIMENSIONS OF RELIGIOUS EDUCATION (New York: Paulist Press, 1979).

13. Julian Jaynes, THE ORIGIN OF CONSCIOUSNESS IN THE BREAKDOWN OF THE BICAMERAL MIND (Boston: Houghton Mifflin Co., 1977).

14. James B. Ashbrook, "The Working Brain: A New Model for Theological Exploration," Religion in Life, Spr. 1979, 6-16.

Part I MIND AS METAPHOR: an analytic bridge

(People) ought to know that from the brain and from the brain only, arise our pleasures, joys, laughter and jests, as well as our sorrows, pains, griefs and tears. Through it, in particular, we think, see, hear, and distinguish the ugly from the beautiful, the bad from the good, the pleasant from the unpleasant . . . It is the same thing which makes us mad or delirious, inspires us with dread and fear . . . These things that we suffer all come from the brain, when it is not healthy.

Hippocrates, <u>On the Sacred Disease</u>*

*Hippocrates. With an English translation by W.H.S. Jones. Vol. II (New York: G.P. Putnam's Sons, 1923), XVII, 175.

Chapter One

THE BRAIN AND BELIEF

Can knowledge of the brain contribute to theology?

Conversely, can theology contribute to neuropsychology? What correlations might exist between the way the brain works and traditional patterns of belief?

An answer to these questions requires juxtaposing what is known in neuropsychology with what is known in historical theology. The loose interface between personal meaning and sensory data supplies a key to their correlation. Here we deal with "mind." And the concept of mind relates specifics of neuropsychology and speculations of theology to each other. This chapter sketches those specifics and summarizes those speculations.

The Brain[1]

The brain is so complex that almost everything we say about it must be qualified.[2] With that caveat we can say simply that the brain is divided:

(1) our one head has two nervous systems: one connects us to outside reality, the other deals with internal processes;[3]

(2) our one head has two spheres: the left sphere which works step-by-step, and the right sphere which functions all-at-once;

(3) each hemisphere has two areas: the back or posterior region which brings information in and the front or anterior area which sends intentions out;

(4) each system (back/front) and each sphere (left/ right) perform different tasks; though they are distinguishable, they overlap.

A neurotheological approach—for want of a simpler label—starts with the fact that the brain is divided. Our one head has two minds that function as one.[4]

Left hemisphere activity can be summarized with confidence: active speech, complex language, and the processing of separate and unconnected things. It works in a computer printout style, line-by-line, character-by-character. In other words it takes the lead over the right hemisphere in step-by-step processing.[5] Because such activity is associated with logic and language the pattern is termed analytic. The left brain observes and explains the world with an eagle-eyed vigilance.

Right hemisphere activity cannot be summarized with the same certainty.[5] On its own the right half cannot say what it knows. It takes the lead over the left hemisphere in processing activities for which words are poor translations. Whereas the left side specializes in conceptualizing, the right side specializes in immediate experiencing.

The right half sees images, senses patterns, and feels the personal significance of what goes on. Instead of processing data in logical steps, it may take in everything at once or start anywhere with anything simply as it appears. The right hemisphere reacts milliseconds faster than the left in an all-at-once process. The simultaneous and paradoxical features of its activity have led to its being known as holistic. The right brain experiences and synthesizes the world. It discerns changing impressions within an unchanging context. Quite simply, the right brain responds rapidly to the world around.

Although each hemisphere differs in the way it works, the distinctives are seldom all-or-none. Each side is capable of handling many similar tasks. Complex functions require complex input. Thus, they share what is common to both left and right hemispheres as well to what is unique to each.[7]

Parallels, many of cosmic proportions, have been associated with these differences.[8]

In philosophy we find contrasts between: knowledge by experience (experiment) and reasoning (theory);[9] tacit and explicit knowledge;[10] ecstatic and technical reason;[11] inward regularities with conservation and outer variations with acquisition;[12] eternity and time;[13] presentational symbolism, which uses visual and auditory imagery, and discursive symbolism, which is presented in a linear order with primarily a generalized reference.[14]

In personality theory distinctions have been elaborated between: a communion which includes relatedness (i.e., contact, being at one with other organisms, openness, cooperation, and nonrepression) and an agency which seeks achievement (i.e., self-protection, self-assertion, self-expansion, isolation, aloneness, and repression);[15] primary process, which expresses unconscious drives governed by the pleasure-principle, and secondary process, which uses conscious logic governed by the reality-principle;[16] interpersonal dimensions of love and power;[17] dialectical and demonstrative theories;[18] analogical communication, which lacks boundaries and is characteristic of metaphoric and nonverbal communication, and digital communication, which uses a conventional or arbitrary mode characteristic of linguistic communication.[19]

Mythology sets forth symbolic contrasts with the broadest sweep of all:[20] sun and moon, light and dark, good and evil, heaven and hell, yang and yin.

Wild speculation has led to what Michael Kinsbourne termed "dichotomania," an avalanche of sharply contrasted attributes as though those are distinct entities.[21] It is important to disabuse literal correspondence between anatomical structures and cognitive functions. Even so, although mental processes do not fall into neat divisions between left and right sides, such contrasts are intriguing. At the very least the double brain makes for many minds.

Many minds contribute to divided minds. And with divided minds we split reality into good and bad, right and wrong, desirable and undesirable. Just consider such contrasts as these: neurotic and healthy,[22] deficiency and growth,[23] concrete and abstract,[24] bound and free,[25] sin and salvation,[26] profane and sacred,[27] life and death,[28] among many. Which "mind" is negative and which positive depends upon which mind-set is valued most.[29] For a left brain orientation, health and the capacity for abstraction are ideal. For a right brain bias, abstraction contributes to neurosis and death. We can neither make simple nor absolute distinctions between hemisphere activity and their importance. The context, what is fitting at the moment, determines what is more desirable or less desirable.

Even recognizing the distortion which accompanies comparisons, we continue to struggle with contrasts. It comes as no surprise that Lancelot Whyte claimed European thinkers fall into two camps: "the one seeking order, similarities, and unity (often called 'mystical' or 'religious') and the other seeking differences among particulars (the 'tough' thinkers or scientists). The first seek comfort in feeling a unifying order, the second in defining particulars."[30] Antagonism between the camps has prevented each from seeing that the other represents what it itself has inhibited even as it has assumed the other unconsciously. Those seeking order are identifying particular similarities and those defining differences are creating unifying particulars.

Apparently, people develop one approach at the expense of the other. These tendencies coalesce into major ways of dealing with reality.[31] We can use them to understand experience without having to give them the status of absolute reality.

> One approach abstracts from data objectively. It takes isolated pieces, establishes sequences, and develops procedures based upon standard notations. Since each sign carries specific meaning, which meaning is defined by conventional definitions, "reality" is perceived as stable. The approach usually produces common conclusions—a convergence—as to what is "right."

> Another approach attends to data subjectively. It intuits patterns, identifies totalities, and synthesizes many dimensions into what is personally meaningful. Every symbol carries multiple meanings, all influenced by the context. Because impressions seldom stay the same, "reality" is perceived as an ever-changing scene. The approach generates different conclusions—a divergence—as to what is "real."

These styles of thinking help us understand how contrasts arise and why they persist. I suggest that the features summarized in Table 1 offer clues to theological differences.

By virtue of its ability to abstract, a left half approach simplifies the world. That is, it selects data in accord with its rational scheme. This results in the paradox of analytically identifying complexity at the

Table 1. **Cognitive Contrasts With Suggested Hemisphere Activity**

	Left Hemisphere	Right Hemisphere*
Demonstrated Contrasts		
	expression	perception of patterns
	linguistic	kinesthetic
	propositional	visual
	discrete process	diffuse process
	logical	synthetic
	verbal	visuospatial
Suggested Contrasts		
in philosophy:		
	knowledge by argument	knowledge by experience
	explicit knowledge	tacit knowledge
	technical reason	ecstatic reason
	regularities	variations
	time	eternity
	discursive symbolism	presentational symbolism
in personality theory:		
	agency (achievement)	communion (relatedness)
	secondary process	primary process
	power	love
	demonstrative theories	dialectical theories
	digital communication	analogic communication
in mythology:		
	sun	moon
	light	dark
	good	evil
	heaven	hell
	yang	yin

Table 1. **Cognitive Contrasts With Suggested Hemisphere Activity** (continued)

	Left Hemisphere	Right Hemisphere*
Suggested Contrasts		
European thinkers:		
	seek differences among particulars	seek order, similarity, and unity
identified emphases:		
	abstract from objective	attend to subjective
in split reality:**		
	healthy	neurotic
	actualized	alienated
	abstract	concrete
	free	bound
	salvation	sin
	sacred	profane
	life	death

*Right hemisphere attributes can be identified with less confidence than left hemisphere attributes.

**These designations under left and right hemisphere are reversible depending upon the value orientation of the person or group. They are listed here from the perspective of a left brain bias.

same time it arbitrarily reduces complexity. It establishes fixed entities in the midst of changing circumstances. The right half's ability to attend contributes to ever-fresh experience. Its responsiveness discloses a reverse paradox to that of a left half vigilance, namely, its attention to the immediate context both resists complex schematization and contributes infinite variation. It generates many patterns within an unchanging context. While the left side can handle nonverbal synthesis and the right can handle analysis, generally, each half does so reluctantly and awkwardly. In most instances, the kind of task influences which side takes charge.

Patterns of Belief

Just as the brain is divided so belief has been divided. People have experienced and interpreted the way God works in terms very like the way the brain works, particularly people in the West. Thus, theologians have distinguished God's creating or world-affirming activity and God's redeeming or world-transforming activity. And these two expressions have contributed to two emphases about the Godhead.[32]

Philo of Alexandria, for instance, claimed: "While God is indeed one, his highest and chief powers are two, namely, goodness and sovereignty. Through his goodness he begat all that is, through his sovereignty he rules what he has begotten. And in between the two there is a third which unites them, Logos: for it is through reason (logos) that God is both ruler and good."[33]

Behind this Hellenistic distinction between goodness and sovereignty lies a more Hebraic unity. Consciousness of God's creating activity appeared after the experience of God's redeeming activity. In what is called the Historical Credo, Israel's oldest confession of faith, God's saving act begins with Exodus:[34]

> My father was a wandering Aramean. He went down into Egypt. . . The Egyptians ill-treated us. . . we called on Yahweh. .

. (who) heard our voice and saw our misery. . . and Yahweh brought us out. . . and gave us this land. . .
(Deuteronomy 26:5-11 JB)

From that experience the Hebrews saw God's power everywhere. In contrast to purposeful power in nature per se, they experienced life within the plan of the One who is Lord of history itself:

His wisdom made the heavens,
his love is everlasting!. . .
He struck down the first-born of Egypt,
his love is everlasting!
And brought Israel out,
his love is everlasting!
(Psalm 136:5-12 JB)

Thus says God, Yahweh,
he who created the heavens and spread them out, who gave shape to the earth of what came from it, who gave breath to its people and life to the creatures that move in it: "I, Yahweh, have called you to serve the cause of right. . ."
(Isaiah 42:5-7 JB)

In effect, the emphasis upon the creative activity of God underscored the universal imperative of the prophets' insistence on righteous (e.g., Amos 4:12)

God's perceived activity in redeeming and creating were combined into a single affirmation:

. . . thus says Yahweh,
who created you, Jacob,
who formed you, Israel:
Do not be afraid,
for I have redeemed you."
(Isaiah 43:1ff JB)

The One who brought order to primordial chaos was the same One who pushed back the waters of the Red Sea to lead Israel out of bondage (Isaiah 51:9-10). In their deliverance from slavery that motley band of nomads came to see the activity of God throughout the universe on behalf of all humanity.

When Yahweh confronted Moses at the burning bush, this twofold emphasis of redemption and creation was revealed (Exodus 3:13-14).[36] That Oneness of Being escapes definition. Nameless Name does not really name. The name "Yahweh" discloses reality undefined and unexplained. "I Am Who I Am" transcends every name as Alpha and Omega (Revelation 21:6), the beginning and the end.

Yet the Reality that "is" also was ever and always the Reality that "acts." "I have witnessed the way the Egyptians oppress my people, so come, I send you to Pharoah to bring them out of bondage" (Exodus 3:9-10). The very Name of God reveals the very nature of God: "I Am The Reality That Acts. I Act to relieve suffering (Exodus 3:7-8) and to create community" (Exodus 20:1-20; 21:1ff; 34:1-35:29).

In Genesis (1:1-2:4a; 2:4b-3:24) the two accounts of creation suggest something of the distinction between redeeming and creating. God alone is common to the orderly speaking of the first and the concrete acting of the second.[37] Both are present in the earliest days of Israel, each with a different origin and discernible history.[38]

The blessing of creation, which parallels right brain responsiveness, and the redeeming of that creation, a left brain vigilance, are maintained as double emphases through both the Old and New Testament.[39] Like the two halves of the brain, neither can be subsumed under the other. Again, like the brain in which each side utilizes the whole cortex, neither can these emphases be separated. Creation and redemption are complementary. Even so, just as the left hemisphere tends to dominate the right hemisphere, so, too, does the doctrine of redemption tend to subordinate that of creation.[40]

Such a characterization suggests two aspects of the mind of God. "I Am" reflects creative presence, an attending process of affirming what is. "I Act" conveys ruling power, an abstracting process of identifying what ought to be. In essence, a creating aspect and a redeeming aspect. The ultimately Real of creation combines with the urgently Right of redemption.[41]

Formally stated, Paul Ricoeur identified two shapes of religious consciousness: the phenomenology of manifestation and the hermeneutics of proclamation.[42] As manifestation, God has been perceived in mystical-priestly-metaphysical-aesthetic ways. That is, people see and sense what God discloses in nonconceptual ways. In proclamation, God has revealed prophetic-ethical-historical-doctrinal emphases. In other words, people hear and heed what God declares explicitly.

The "family resemblances" represent what David Tracy called "trajectories" of belief.[43] They distinguish what is foreground and background in the gestalt of understanding God's ways of being God. As such they provide contrasts of "focal meaning" comparable to brain contrasts of cognitive processing. The human mind perceives differences in the divine mind.

The trajectory of proclamation focuses on the word which emerges from the awesome presence of the Wholly Other.[44] This is the "I Act" mind-set. Theology is organized around basic acts of speech, such as stories and instructions. Because God is a jealous God, one who demands uncompromising obedience, prophetic faith stands against complacent culture. The world as it is—observed from the vantage point of the Transcendent Other—is negated.

More specifically, that means wisdom is folly, religion sickens, and culture distorts what is true. The proclamation of God's judgment, the kerygma, calls for the transformation of society, of nature, and of the cosmos itself. In technical language, that is known as "descacralization." The "radical non-participation" in everyday life makes the negative aspects of our ambiguous world explicit. Because of humanity's fall the true order has not-yet been realized.

Various ideas have been used to suggest the redeeming activity of God: prophetic, kerygmatic, Protestant Principle, Word-event, the cross, agape, eschatological, doctrine, dogma, Thomistic cosmology as an "argumentative rationality,"[45] political, ethical, and historical. This unusual assortment has one feature in common, namely, each proclaims a critical judgment on ordinary reality. The world is limited and limiting, separated and alienated from its ground and maker. Rational interpretations and ethical imperatives outweigh aesthetic appreciation. The recital of historical liberation downplays the rhythmic rituals of nature.

In contrast, the trajectory of manifestation lifts up the sacred, the awesome, the overwhelming power of what is purely and truly "given." This is the "I Am" mind-set. It shows itself in sacred mysteries without passing over "completely into articulation."[46] In symbolic faith the world itself is experienced as the center of the Really Real. That immediacy may be a rock, a mountain, a tree, a rite, a ritual, an archetype, an icon, a myth. The world as it is—experienced from within in the power of the Immanent One—is affirmed. That can mean philosophical wonder, the extraordinariness of the simple, and "erupting illuminations" of "the liberating rhythms" of human passages.[47] God's graciousness is manifested in the concrete, whether that be the body, the sexual, and the sensual of personal reality; the communal, the traditional, and the organized of social reality; or the natural, the ecological, and the mystical of cosmic reality. Opposite elements come together in such a way that their union, for instance male and female or sun and moon, reveals the sacred union of heaven and earth.[49] To immerse oneself in an ambiguous world bears witness to its created goodness. Thus the world as "graced" has been realized always-already as the Really Real.

Many terms have been used to suggest this creating activity: sacramental, apologetic, Catholic Substance, incarnation/resurrection, eros, realized eschatology, "the feeling of absolute dependence,"[50] Augustinian ontology as "an immediate rationality,"[51] the mystical, the aesthetic, "the always-already presence of the horizon of mystery,"[52] folk religion, and indigenous Christianity. Here we find the non-linguistic quality of intensified imagination.

Historically, people have emphasized one activity of God at the expense of the other. Because of those predispositions these focal meanings exaggerate contrasting minds of God or, more accurately, ways in which God has been perceived.

> One mind-set proclaims Truth from outside the world, objectively. It negates nature, society, and the universe by disclosing the inadequacy of reality and declaring a transcendent reality. It looks to an end of what has been by proclaiming the coming of what ought to be. It demands obedience to the original image in which humanity is created. People are to hear the Word of God.
>
> Another mind-set manifests meaning from inside the world, subjectively. It affirms the natural, the communal, and the cosmic by disclosing the Real in every concrete experience. It celebrates the worthwhileness of what is by showing forth the presence of what is always-already at work. It calls forth trusting dependence upon the Truly One. People can see or sense the presence of the Holy.

A theology of redemption focuses upon the meaning and means of what is urgently Right. It calls for integrity. A theology of creation lifts up the meaning and means of what is ultimately Real. It calls for involvement. Involvement with integrity and integrity through involvement—together the two theologies reflect the full mind of God.

Tracy rightly observed that an historical description of Christianity shows it to be "a religion which includes both a prophetic-ethical-historical defamiliarizing focus and power and a mystical-metaphysical-aesthetic transformed and transformative enveloping ground."[53] When the redeeming mind-set is lost, manifestation turns into the magical, the mechanical, and the private. When the creating mind-set is lost, proclamation hardens into legalism, rationalism, and literalism.[54] As Ricoeur noted, "without the support and renewing power of the sacred cosmos and the sacredness of vital nature, the word itself becomes abstract and cerebral."[55] Word and symbol are intertwined, both halves of one mind.

These perceptions of God sharpen primary emphases in the ways people construe reality. Table 2 correlates these theological contrasts with the working brain. By virtue of proclaiming truth objectively through the use of language, theologies of proclamation parallel left brain process. Because of manifesting meaningfulness subjectively by focusing on symbolic expressions, theologies of manifestation parallel right brain process.

The "Mind" as Bridge

I am proposing that the concept of "mind" can bridge the brain and patterns of belief.[56] In the loose interface between sensory input and personal experience[57] we find clues which allow us to move back and forth between the mystery of the human mind and that of the mind of God. With these clues we can analyze and assess what we do as human beings. Mastery may elude us but an approach to mystery is available.

The brain itself is a model of successive regularities. Taken alone it can be viewed as an entity, an autonomous center which coordinates and governs lower levels of neural and endocrine activity. The mind, in contrast, is an image of emergent features. It cannot be understood by itself. Mind reflects an expanding universe of influences which affects its functioning and is affected by its character. Thus the brain can be viewed both as a whole and a part.[58] In itself the brain is an organized whole, complex yet integrated. We can analyze predictable regularities through its parts.

Table 2. **Theological Contrasts With Suggested Activity of God**

	Redeeming Activity	(Re)Creating Activity
biblical		
	Exodus	Easter
	prophetic	priestly
	Word-event	Image-event
	the cross	the resurrection
	eschatological-apocalyptic	realized eschatology
theological		
	wrath	love
	judgment	mercy
	kerygmatic	apologetic
	not-yet	always-already
	Protestant Principle	Catholic Substance
philosophical		
	logos	eros
	Thomistic cosmology	Augustinian ontology
	doctrine	experience
	verbal	preverbal
intention		
	historical	metaphysical
	political	mystical
	ethical	aesthetic
	loyal obedience	trusting dependence
focal meaning		
	proclamation	manifestation
sensory modality		
	hearing	seeing/sensing
hemisphere dominance		
	left brain's step-by-step	right brain's all-at-once

Emergent features of mind, on the other hand, cannot be predicted from lower levels of analysis. They are unpredictable in prin ciple.[59] Between the predictable brain and the unpredictable mind lies the challenge of juxtaposing neuropsychology and theology. How the whole emerges from the parts defies explanation[60] even as it invites exploration.

Neuroscientist Robert Livingston argues that scientists have been "too shy about making inferences."[61] They prefer the security of the brain's regularities to the uncertainties of the mind's emergent features. In contrast, theologians have been quick to generalize, confident about the mind's unpredictability. Sometimes this is called the work of the Holy Spirit: "The wind blows wherever it pleases. . . but you cannot tell where it is going" (John 3:8 JB). I am opting for suggestive inferences.

My approach is analogical. Just as mind is the human significance of the brain,[62] so God is the theological significance of mind. The brain gives more content to what mind can mean than theology ordinarily includes. Without reducing mind to brain, the working brain helps anchor the meaning of mind in the empirical realm. At the same time, without equating mind with God, the functioning mind allows intimations of what matters most to the humanness of human beings. With this tool we can investigate "matter"--material matter and what matters theologically. To state the parallel cautiously, trajectories of belief are the meaning of mind.

As an analogy, the metaphor crosses neuropsychology and theology without assuming literal correspondence.[63] I juxtapose these disciplines "as if" they belong together. They may not correspond except through an act of faith or an exercise in imagination. The metaphorical value of the human brain, however, can serve as "a pathway to God."[65] The approach is a new form of an empirical-natural theology.

Historically, natural theology meant undergirding faith in the vision of God with knowledge of objective conclusions arrived at by philosophers according to the rational structure of reality.[65] Thomas Aquinas' Summa theologia stands as its most elegant expression. Charles Hartshorne, who extended the work of Alfred North Whitehead, may represent the most elegant contemporary exponent.[66] Natural theology emphasizes the rational structure of reality.

In contrast to philosophical theology,[67] empirical theology has dealt with the existence of God, or purposive Being, by focusing on basic categories and logical structures of "lived experience." It has generalized from "the commonly shared features" of the world-as-nature and the world-as-history.[68] Empirical theology deals with what can be observed and shaped by the imagination.

As an analytic metaphor, the working brain integrates rational, natural, and empirical values. It searches for what is common in the separate disciplines. This correlational,[69] mutually critical,[70] approach between the mind of God and the human mind assumes that identity is greater than nonidentity, similarity greater than dissimilarity, and continuity greater than discontinuity. "The Word was made flesh, he lived among us, and we saw his glory. . . " (John 1:14 JB).

To assume that brain and belief are associated is not simply the wild speculation of a psychologist theologian. Santiago Ramon ý Cajal (1852-1934), an acknowledged "maestro" of the microscopic study of the brain, joined brain and universe this way:[71]

> As long as the brain is a mystery, the universe, (which is) the reflection of the structure of the brain, will also be a mystery.

That suggests that what goes on in the head and in the universe constitute a "coherent whole." As Roger N. Walsh put it: "they cannot be separated."[72] To study them independently creates "an artificial and distorting duality" which hides their "underlying unity and interconnectedness." Alan Watts reasoned that "(h)uman beings are aware of a world because, and only because, it is the sort of world that breeds knowing organisms. Humanity is not one thing and the world another. . . An intelligent (human being) argues. . . an intelligent universe."[73] Little wonder that Gardner Murphy described humanity as "a universe in miniature."[74]

Mystics and religious thinkers have believed something like that for centuries. What is outside the head is revealed in what is inside the head. We are created in the image of our Creator.

John Calvin opened his Institutes on the Christian Religion with a similar contention. He wrote: "Our wisdom . . . consists entirely of two parts; the knowledge of God and of ourselves. But as these are connected together by many ties, it is not easy to determine which of the two precedes, and gives birth to the other."[75] In linking knowledge of God and humanity, however, he also contrasted them.

Origen, the great Christian theologian of Alexandria, in the third century, and Bernard of Clairvaux, in the twelfth century, each spoke of the mystical marriage of the Logos and the soul.[76] Logos suggests the structure of the universe as ordered and orderly. Soul connotes the core of a human being. In some mysterious way, such thinkers believed, the universe revealed itself in humanity, macrocosm-in-microcosm, mind-in-mind.

William James (1842-1910) regarded the difficulty of stating the connection between brain and mind as "the ultimate of ultimate problems."[77] Neurosurgeon Wilder Penfield (1891-1976) expressed similar wonder when he asked: "Can the brain explain (the human being)? Can the brain achieve by neural action all that the mind accomplishes?" He answered that it could not.[78]

This is intriguing yet speculative. What we do know, however, is that the way the brain works affects the way humanity struggles and believes. James put the issue sharply:

> Is the Kosmos an expression of intelligence, rational in its inward nature, or a brute external fact pure and simple? If we find ourselves, in contemplating it, unable to banish the impression that it is a realm of final purposes, that it exists for the sake of something, we place intelligence at the heart of it and have a religion. If, on the contrary, in surveying its irremediable flux, we can think of the present only as so much mere mechanical sprouting from the past, occurring with no reference to the future, we are atheists and materialists.[79]

A neurotheological approach sheds new light on the puzzling patterns of belief. More theological data becomes more understandable as a result. We can avoid the trap of splitting belief into simplistic proclamation or simple manifestation. God's creating and redeeming express one mind. The analytic metaphor reinforces our conviction that the contrasts are neither exclusive nor competitive. Neuropsychological research holds promise for theological reflection.

We have seen that the brain signals two processes: step-by-step and all-at-once. Theology and belief also present two patterns: redemptively setting things right and creatively making things real. As an organized whole, the brain reveals and creates regularities analogous to the interpretations and imperatives of proclamation. As part of a larger whole, the mind unfolds and generates emergent features similar to the experiences and symbolizations of God's manifestation of God. If not related, the features of the brain and belief are at least relatable.

That which is most fully us is that which is most truly real. The goodness and sovereignty of God are reflected in our one brain with its two ways of working. Mind is the human meaning of the brain as God is the theological referent of mind—our human mind and the mind of God.

In the next chapter I detail what is known about how the brain works. Then, in Chapter Three, I organize the data into prototypical mind-sets which suggest that God can be of different minds.

NOTES

1. The following works have been consulted as background. Basic and accessible references are indicated by an "*."

Colin Blakemore, MECHANICS OF THE MIND (New York: Cambridge University Press, 1977).

Jason Brown, MIND, BRAIN, AND CONSCIOUSNESS: the neuropsychology of cognition (New York: Academic Press, Inc., 1977).

Nigel Calder, THE MIND OF MAN: An investigation into current research on the brain and human nature (New York: The Viking Press, [1970] 1973).

Jeanne S. Chall and Allan F. Mirsky, eds., EDUCATION AND THE BRAIN: The Seventy-seventh Yearbook of the National Society for the Study of Education. Part II (Chicago: The University of Chicago Press, 1978).

Julian M. Davidson and Richard J. Davidson, eds., THE PSYCHOBIOLOGY OF HUMAN CONSCIOUSNESS (New York: Plenum Publishing Corp., 1980).

S.J. Dimond, THE DOUBLE BRAIN (London: Churchill-Livingstone, 1972).

S.J. Dimond and J.G. Beaumont, eds., HEMISPHERE FUNCTION IN THE HUMAN HEAD (New York: John Wiley & Sons, 1974).

Stuart J. Dimond and David A. Blizard, eds., EVOLUTION AND LATERALIZATION OF THE BRAIN (New York: The New York Academy of Sciences, 1977).

John C. Eccles, FACING REALITY: Philosophical Adventures by a Brain Scientist (New York: Springer-Verlag, 1970).

John C. Eccles, THE UNDERSTANDING OF THE BRAIN (New York: McGraw-Hill Book Company, 1973).

Michael S. Gazzaniga, THE BISECTED BRAIN (New York: Appleton-Century-Crofts, 1970).

*Michael S. Gazzaniga and Joseph E. LeDoux, THE INTEGRATED MIND (New York: Plenum Publishing Corp., 1978).

David H. Hubel, et. al. THE BRAIN. A Scientific American Book (San Francisco: W.H. Freeman and Company, 1979).

Philip R. Lee, et. al. SYMPOSIUM ON CONSCIOUSNESS (Baltimore: Penguin Books, [1976] 1977).

Robert B. Livingston, SENSORY PROCESSING, PERCEPTION, AND BEHAVIOR (New York: Raven Press, 1978).

A.R. Luria, HIGHER CORTICAL FUNCTIONS IN MAN. Prefaces to the English Edition by Hans-Lukas Teuber and Karl H. Pribram. Second Edition, Revised and Expanded. Translated by Basil Haigh (New York: Basic Books, Inc., Publishers, [1966] 1980).

*A.R. Luria, THE WORKING BRAIN: An Introduction to Neuropsychology. Translated by Basil Haigh (New York: Basic Books, Inc., Publishers, 1973).

Peter Nathan, THE NERVOUS SYSTEM (Baltimore: Penguin Books, Inc., 1969).

*Robert E. Ornstein, ed., THE NATURE OF HUMAN CONSCIOUSNESS. A Book of Readings (San Francisco: W.H. Freeman and Company, 1973).

Karl H. Pribram, LANGUAGES OF THE BRAIN: Experimental Paradoxes and Principles of Neuropsychology (Englewood Cliffs, NJ: Prentice Hall, Inc., 1971).

Steven Rose, THE CONSCIOUS BRAIN (New York: Alfred A. Knopf, 1974).

Peter Russell, THE BRAIN BOOK (New York: Hawthorn Books, Inc., 1979).

F.O. Schmitt and F.G. Worden, eds., THE NEUROSCIENCES: Third Study Program (Cambridge: Massachusetts Institute of Technology Press, 1974).

Sally P. Springer and Georg Deutsch, LEFT BRAIN, RIGHT BRAIN (San Francisco: W.H. Freeman and Company, 1981).

Gordon Rattray Taylor, THE NATURAL HISTORY OF THE MIND (New York: E.P. Dutton, 1979).

William R. Utall, THE PSYCHOBIOLOGY OF THE MIND (New York: Halsted Press, 1978).

E.A. Weinstein and R.P. Friedland, eds., HEMI-INATTENTION AND HEMISPHERE SPECIALIZATION: Advances in Neurology Series. Vol. 18. (New York: Raven Press, 1977).

*M.C. Wittrock, et. al., THE HUMAN BRAIN (Englewood Cliffs, NJ: Prentice-Hall, Inc., 1977).

2. The brain's complexity applies to both structure and functioning. As Livingston (n.1 above, 29) reports: "In a relatively short time, sensory processing mechanisms (which underlie perception and behavior) have advanced from being intuitively straightforward and based largely on concepts of

interactions to a highly sophisticated congeries involving transactions. Transactions occur among multiple, mutually interdependent systems in simultaneous action. In the case of sensory systems (which is but a partial case of the larger brain-mind system) the pertinent transactions operate integratively among a cascade of levels of increasing complexity." To state "simply" is tantamount to misstating.

3. To speak of two nervous systems—one dealing with the outer environment and one with the inner environment—oversimplifies the structure and function of The Nervous System (see Nathan, THE NERVOUS SYSTEM [n.1 above]). The most conspicuous system is composed of two parts: the peripheral nervous system (PNS), which processes sensory input on the boundary between the surface and the outside, and the central nervous system (CNS), which consists of the spinal cord and brain. Together this system controls the entire body and its interaction with the environment. It possesses afferent (sensory) nerves, which keep the body in contact with the world around, and efferent (motor) nerves, which carry out the body's response to the world.

   The less conspicuous system is known as the autonomic nervous system (ANS). This system is connected more to the viscera nervous system and internal processes than to the muscles and external activity as are the central and peripheral systems. The ANS is found only in vertebrates and cannot be classified as either CNS or PNS. It has connections with both systems. It, too, is composed of two parts: the adrenosympathetic system, which alerts the body to dangerous or interesting outside stimuli, and the parasympathetic system, which relaxes the bodily processes in adapting to the outside environment.

4. Considerable debate surrounds the issue of "two minds" (Michael S. Gazzaniga, "One Brain - Two Minds," American Scientist [1972] 60:311-317).

Some argue for double and bimodal consciousness (e.g., Arthur J. Deikman, "Bimodal Consciousness," Archives of General Psychiatry, 25 [Dec. 1971], 481-489. In Ornstein [n.1 above], 67-86; David Galin, "The Two Modes of Consciousness and The Two Halves of the Brain." In Lee [n.1 above], 26-53; Roger W. Sperry, "Hemisphere Deconnection and Unity in Conscious Awareness," American Psychologist, 1968, 23:723-733). Others restrict "mind" to consciousness and language (esp., Eccles [n.1 above]). A few identify "mind" or "consciousness" with volitional activity generated from subcortical sources such as the upper brain stem (e.g., Wilder Penfield, THE MYSTERY OF THE MIND: A Cortical Study of Consciousness and The Human Brain [Princeton, NJ: Princeton University Press, 1975]). Still others regard "mind" as linked with language, which is operative in both integrated and double consciousness (e.g., Gazzaniga and LeDoux, [n.1 above]). Springer and Deutsch [n.1 above, 203] provide a balanced review of the evidence for the structural and functional asymmetry of consciousness. They identify inconsistent findings and warn against the temptation to speculate. While hemispheric differences can be exaggerated, they "have become even more impressed with the reality of hemispheric differences and with their potential for helping us understand the brain mechanisms underlying higher mental functions."

5. Michael S. Gazzaniga, "Cerebral Dominance Viewed as a Decision System." In Dimond and Beaumont (n.1 above), 367-382. Early evidence about left-right hemispheric differences was identified as verbal-nonverbal (visual-spatial) distinctions. Subsequent investigations have refined the conceptualization of these differences. The distinction is more accurately based "on different ways of dealing with information" (Springer and Deutsch [n.1 above], 45). Each side appears to use different strategies or approaches to handling incoming information. The left hemisphere is best thought of as analytic; the right hemisphere as

holistic (J. Levy-Agresti and R.W. Sperry, "Differential Perceptual Capacities in Major and Minor Hemispheres," *Proceedings of the National Academy of Science*, U.S.A. 61 [1968]: 1151; J. Levy, "Psychobiological Implications of Bilateral Asymmetry." In Dimond and Beaumont [n.1 above], 121-183).

6. J.E. Bogen, "The Other Side of the Brain: An Appositional Mind." *Bulletin of the Los Angeles Neurological Societies*, 34, No. 3, July, 1969, 135-162. In Ornstein (n.1 above), 101-125.

7. Springer and Deutsch (n.1 above), 59.

8. Bogen (n.6 above); Ornstein (0/5), 36-39; Springer and Deutsch [n.1 above], 184-188. A comprehensive synthesis of such views is Charles Hampden-Turner's MAPS OF THE MIND: charts and concepts of the mind and its labyrinths (New York: Collier Macmillan Publishing Company, Inc., 1982).

9. Roger Bacon. Cited in Etienne Gilson, HISTORY OF CHRISTIAN PHILOSOPHY in the MIDDLE AGES (New York: Random House, 1955), 310-311.

10. Michael Polanyi, PERSONAL KNOWLEDGE: Toward a Post-critical Philosophy. Rev. ed. (New York: Harper Torchbook, [1958] 1964); idem., THE TACIT DIMENSION (New York: Doubleday, 1966).

11. Paul Tillich, SYSTEMATIC THEOLOGY, vol. 1 (Chicago: University of Chicago Press, 1951).

12. Gregory Bateson, MIND AND NATURE: A Necessary Unity (New York: E.P. Dutton, 1979).

13. J. Robert Oppenheimer, SCIENCE and the COMMON UNDERSTANDING (New York: Simon & Schuster, 1954), 69. Quoted in Lawrence LeShan, THE MEDIUM, THE MYSTIC and the PHYSICIST (New York: The Viking Press, 1974), 64.

14. Susanne K. Langer, PHILOSOPHY IN A NEW KEY: A Study in the Symbolism of Reason, Rite, and Art (New York: Penguin Books, Inc., 1942).

15. David Bakan, THE DUALITY OF HUMAN EXISTENCE (Boston: Beacon Press, 1971).

16. C. Brenner, AN ELEMENTARY TEXTBOOK OF PSYCHOANALYSIS (Garden City, NY: Doubleday Anchor Books, 1957).

17. Timothy Leary, INTERPERSONAL DIAGNOSIS OF PERSONALITY (New York: Ronald Press, 1957).

18. Joseph F. Rychlak, A PHILOSOPHY OF SCIENCE FOR PERSONALITY THEORY (Boston: Houghton-Mifflin, 1968).

19. Paul Watzlawick, Janet Helmick Beavin, and Don D. Jackson, PRAGMATICS OF HUMAN COMMUNICATION: A Study of Interactional Patterns, Pathologies, and Paradoxes (New York: W.W. Norton & Company, Inc., 1967); Pribram (n.1 above).

20. Alan W. Watts, THE TWO HANDS OF GOD: The Myths of Polarity (New York: P.F. Collier, 1969).

21. Cited by Galin. In Lee (n.1 above), 46. Also see Daniel Goleman, "Split-Brain Psychology: Fad of the Year," Psychology Today, Oct., 1977, 88-90+.

22. Andras Angyal, NEUROSIS AND TREATMENT: A Holistic Theory. Edited by E. Hanfmann and R.M. Jones (New York: John Wiley & Sons, 1965).

23. Abraham H. Maslow, TOWARD A PSYCHOLOGY OF BEING (Princeton: D. Van Nostrand, 1962).

24. Kurt Goldstein, HUMAN NATURE: in the light of psychopathology (New York: Schocken Books, [1940] 1966); THE ORGANISM: A Holistic Approach to Biology. With a Foreword by K.S. Lashley (Boston: Beacon Press, [1939] 1963).

25. Martin Luther.

26. St. Paul.

27. Mircea Eliade, THE SACRED AND THE PROFANE: The Nature of Religion. Translated from the French by Willard R. Trask (New York: Harper Torch Books, [1957] 1961).

28. Norman O. Brown, LIFE AGAINST DEATH: The Psychoanalytic Meaning of History (New York: Columbia University Press, 1959).

29. Hampden-Turner (n.7 above), 152-155), drawing upon Charles Osgood's research with the semantic differential in which almost all evaluative words could be plotted upon a two-axis diagram of Bad-Good and Active-Passive, distinguished between One Dimensional Morality and Synergized Morality. One Dimensional Morality dichotomized values with the dogmatic rhetoric of false choices, such as, concrete versus abstract or profane versus sacred. The results are split-off values leading to repression, violence, and psychic disturbances. The Synergistic Conception of Morality takes account of values in each end of the value continuum (i.e., the semantic differential), thereby "dovetailing" the values, say, of abstract-and-concrete or profane-and-sacred, in ways that make for growth and development.

30. Lancelot Whyte, Contemporary Psychology, xviii, July 1973, 330.

31. "Reality" is a mental construct created by the brain. It does not exist independent of the observer. As such, "reality" constitutes the combined input of: (1) objective data taken in through sensory processing and available to other observers; (2) subjective data as: (a) organized through perceptual processing and accessible to the observer/reporter, (b) interpreted through expectancy patterns which establish the meaning of what is supposedly out-there; and (3) the intersubjectiv-

ity and consensual validation among observer reporters of what is and what it means.

32. Paul D. Hanson, THE DIVERSITY OF SCRIPTURE: A Theological Interpretation (Philadelphia: Fortress Press, 1982); Van A. Harvey, A HANDBOOK OF THEOLOGICAL TERMS (New York: Macmillan Publishing Company, 1964), 62-64, 201-202.

33. Philo, quoted from De Cherubim, 27. In H. Kraft, EARLY CHRISTIAN THINKERS: An Introduction to Clement of Alexandria and Origen (New York: Association Press, 1964), 19-20.

34. Gerhard von Rad, THE PROBLEM OF THE HEXATEUCH and other essays. Trans. by E.W. Trueman Dicken. Intro. by Norman W. Proteous (Edinburgh: Oliver and Boyd, [1965] 1966), 3-8. Also see Claus Westermann, CREATION. Trans. by John J. Scullion, S.J. (Philadelphia: Fortress Press, [1971] 1974), 116.

35. von Rad, ibid., Chapter VI "The Theological Problem of the Old Testament Doctrine of Creation," 131-143. Also see Bernard W. Anderson, CREATION VERSUS CHAOS: The Reinterpretation of Mythical Symbolism in the Bible (New York: Association Press, 1967), Chapter I "Creation and History," 11-42: "According to biblical faith, our historical existence is enfolded within the plan and purpose of the God who is not a phenomenon of history but the Lord of history, who is not a power immanent in nature but the sovereign Creator—the God whose purpose and presence were made known in Israel's historical experience and in the fullness of time, according to Christian faith, in Jesus Christ" (41-42).

36. See THE INTERPRETER'S DICTIONARY OF THE BIBLE (Nashville: Abingdon Press, 1962): E-J, "God, Names of," 407-417, by B.W. Anderson; and K-Q, "Name," 501-508, by R. Abba.

37. Westermann (n.34 above), 17. Even in the first account of creation the Hebrew word bara' for God's act of creation includes an older layer referring to "making or separating or forming," which is the view of the second narrative, and the later preemptive meaning which presents creation as coming "through God's word" (115). See Anderson (n.35 above), 124-126, on verbs of creation in Second Isaiah with their use in the two creation accounts.

38. See DICTIONARY OF BIBLICAL THEOLOGY. 2nd edition, revised and enlarged (New York: Crossroads, [1967] 1973), Creation, 98-102; Redemption, 481-484.

39. Westermann (n.34 above), 121-123.

40. von Rad (n.34 above), 142.

41. Ashbrook and Walaskay, CHRISTIANITY FOR PIOUS SKEPTICS (0/9), 116-126.

42. Paul Ricoeur, "Manifestation and Proclamation," The Journal of the Blaisdell Institute, 12 Winter 1978, 13-35.

43. David Tracy, THE ANALOGICAL IMAGINATION (Chicago: The University of Chicago Press, 1981), 202-229, 376-389, 398-404.

44. Ricoeur (n.42 above), 21.

45. Thomas stated: "The human intellect cannot reach by natural virtue the divine substance, because, according to the way of the present life the cognition of our intellect starts with the senses." Quoted by Paul Tillich, THEOLOGY OF CULTURE. Edited by Robert C. Kimball (New York: Oxford University Press, 1959), 16, 18.

46. Ricoeur (n.42 above), 14.

47. Tracy (n.43 above), 383. He interprets critical wonder as the power of the whole "now disclosed through the critical mediations of reason reflecting upon the original experience of wonder in existence only to yield through philosophical reflection to a mediated sense of fundamental trust in the ultimate reality of God as well as an attendant trust in all reality as graced. Reflection upon that uncanny sense of wonder discloses the uncanny giftedness of all creation. It transforms the stuttering self into a creature alive to and with a fundamental trust in the ultimate reality manifesting itself/himself/herself as none other than an incomprehensible, a pure, unbounded, powerful love decisively re-presented as my God in the event of Jesus Christ" (379).

48. Ricoeur (n.42 above), 20.

49. Eliade (n.27 above), 20-29, 95-113.

50. Frederich Schleiermacher, ON RELIGION: Speeches to Its Cultural Despisers (New York: Harper, 1958).

51. Augustine stated: "Where I have found the truth, there I have found my God, the truth itself." Quoted by Tillich (n.45 above), 12, 16.

52. Quoted in Tracy (n.43 above), 379; "Alternatively, with Schubert Ogden or Hans Kung, 'fundamental trust'" (see Schubert Ogden, THE REALITY OF GOD [New York: Harper & Row, 1966] 37-38; Hans Küng, ON BEING A CHRISTIAN [New York: Doubleday, 1976], 57-83 (Tracy [n.43 above], 400, n.20).

53. Tracy (n.43 above), 215.

54. Ibid., 217.

55. Ricoeur (n.42 above), 35.

56. The idea or concept of "mind" has a long and rich history. See Robert Maynard Hutchins, editor in chief, GREAT BOOKS OF THE WESTERN WORLD.

THE GREAT IDEAS: A Syntopicon. Volume II Man to Nature (Chicago: Encyclopaedia Britannica, Inc., 1952), chp. 58 Mind, 171-204; James B. Ashbrook, "The Functional Meaning of the Soul in the Christian Tradition," The Journal of Pastoral Care, Spring (1958), 1-16.

G.W.F. Hegel struggled with the beauty of Greek religion, the morality of Kantian philosophy, and what he understood as the love of the Christian Gospel by utilizing the German concept of "Geist," a term which means "mind" or "spirit," as "the inseparable connection between mind and spirit, between the human and the divine" (G.W.F. HEGEL: EARLY THEOLOGICAL WRITINGS. Translated by T.M. Knox. With an Introduction & Fragments translated by Richard Kroner [Philadelphia: University of Pennsylvania Press, (1948, 1971) 1979], 33). His work on THE PHENOMENOLOGY OF MIND ("Hegel's Philosophy of Mind." Translated from THE ENCYCLOPAEDIA OF THE PHILOSOPHICAL SCIENCES. With Five Introductory Essays by William Wallace [Oxford: The Clarendon Press, 1894]) strikes the uninitiated reader as strange. His thought and style reflect extremes of rational (Section II Mind Objective) and metaphorical patterns (Section I Mind Subjective). He called it "his voyage of discovery" and it has been called "the journey of the mind to God" (Kroner, 44), the knowledge of God or (Section III) Absolute Mind or the final goal of the journey.

Susanne K. Langer, in her magnum opus, MIND: An Essay on Human Feeling. Volumes I, II, III (Baltimore: The John Hopkins Press, 1967, 1972, 1982), traced the concept with her philosophical lens and a vast range of historical and contemporary knowledge. Hanna Arendt analyzed the nature of thought in her scintillating work on THE LIFE OF THE MIND: Volume One: Thinking; Volume Two: Willing (New York: Harcourt Brace Jovanovich, [1971] 1977, 1978).

An approach to "mind" which combines philosophical/behavioral ideas/data is THEORIES OF THE MIND, edited by Jordan M. Scher (New York: The Free Press of Glencoe, 1962): Mind as Brain; Mind as Participation; Mind as Method.

My use of "mind" as a bridge between human and divine, body and spirit, matter and meaning, represents a middle range methodology. Thus, the distinction and choice of "it" as "an analytical metaphor" brackets philosophical insights in order to focus upon the interface between subjective experience and objective sensory data (see n.63 below).

57. Taylor (n.1 above); R.W. Sperry, "Bridging Science and Values" (0/1).

58. Arthur Koestler, THE ACT OF CREATION: A study of the conscious and unconscious in science and art (New York: A Laurel Edition, Dell Publishing Co., Inc., 1967), esp. Chp. XIII Partness and Wholeness. The distinction is not unique to Koestler; the application to brain-mind is mine. See Karl H. Pribram, "Transcending The Mind/Brain Problem," _Zygon_, June 1979, vol. 14, no. 2, 103-124.

59. Livingston (n.1 above) 2.

60. Uttal (n.1 above) 694.

61. Livingston (n.1 above) 2.

62. Polanyi argued against reducible levels of analysis, contending that the mind, though rooted in the body, is free in its actions. Consequently, "body and mind are profoundly different singly, and not two aspects of the same thing." Inquiry, thus, presumes that "two faculties of the mind are at work jointly. . . the deliberately active powers of the imagination, and the other a spontaneous process of integration which we may call intuition" ("Logic and Psychology," _American Psychologist_, Jan., 1968, 27-43). See also "The Structure of Consciousness," _Brain_, 1965 (Part 4), 779-810.

63. In THE MYTH OF METAPHOR (New Haven: Yale University Press, 1962), Colin Murray Turbayne warned against "using metaphor and being used by metaphor." Two features are re-presented as one. Like a screen or filter, the metaphor suppresses some features and emphasizes others (21). He rejected the use of metaphor because of its metaphysical danger, namely, confusing the mask about the events of reality with the fact of the events of reality itself.

Aristotle had indicated that "a good metaphor implies an intuitive perception of the similarity in dissimilars." In THE RULE OF METAPHOR: Multi-disciplinary studies of the creation of meaning in language (Translated by Robert Czerny, Kathleen McLaughlin, and John Costello, S.J. Toronto: University of Toronto Press, 1975), Paul Ricoeur explored the hermeneutics of metaphor in the need to shift referents in describing reality (6). Metaphor requires the dual functions of rhetoric/proof/persuasion and poetics/mimesis (representation of reality)/catharsis (purification) (12-13). It is "a semantic event that takes place at the point where several semantic fields intersect" (98). Two transfers of context are made: a "metaphysical transfer of the sensible to the non-sensible," and a "metaphorical transfer of the literal to the figurative" (281). There is a circularity of movement between "the abstractive phase" of conceptualizing of traits of reality and "the concretizing phase" of making referents appear (298). Ricoeur concluded that "(w)hat is given to thought in this way by the 'tensional' truth of poetry is the most primordial, most hidden dialectic—dialectic that reigns between the experience of belonging as a whole and the power of distanciation that opens up the space of speculative thought" (313).

In order to insure the as if feature of this use of brain, I avoid labelling it as a model. That would imply too much similarity. In order to encourage the "concretizing" use of the analogy, I use the adjective "analytic" to suggest some similarity. My approach, thereby, is apologetic. I am explaining theology as an area worthy of attention and defending belief in God as an intelligible conceptualization.

64. Walaskay, "A Pathway to God" (0/9).

65. See Maurice R. Hollway, AN INTRODUCTION TO NATURAL THEOLOGY (New York: Appleton-Century-Crofts, Inc., 1959), viii. These conclusions were derived from what was regarded as "self-evident principles and factual experience." The philosophical knowledge of God provided the foundation for communicating what was "wholly incommunicable." This rational base was implicit in human reason "in the formation of the act of faith" (4). It proceeded by presenting problems, advancing difficulties, dealing with evidence, identifying principles, re-examining the original difficulties, and through summary synthesis formulating a thesis which provided a rational foundation for a conviction of faith.

66. See John B. Cobb, Jr., A CHRISTIAN NATURAL THEOLOGY Based On The Thought of Alfred North Whitehead (Philadelphia: Westminster Press, 1965). Charles Hartshorne went behind the Greek dichotomies of finite/infinite in exploring the possibility of rational or natural theology, i.e., "a theory of divinity appealing to 'natural reason' — that is critical consideration of the most general ideas and ideals necessary to interpret life and reality" (A NATURAL THEOLOGY FOR OUR TIME. La Salle, IL: Open Court, 1967). For him, God and God "alone is both finite and infinite, and likewise: both relative and absolute, conditioned and unconditioned, mutable and immutable, contingent and necessary. He is individual, but the individual with strictly universal function, the all-encompassing and yet not merely universal principle of existence . . . the ultimate principle is individual, not a mere or universal form, pattern system, matter, or force—or that, conversely, the ultimate individual is

strictly universal in its scope or relevance" (36). Thus, God is "the all-inclusive yet individual actuality, and the all-inclusive yet individual potentiality" (86). Hartshorne's position is not "a proof of the reality of God' but rather "a disproof of both empirical atheism and empirical theism" (87). Empirical arguments finally rest on the belief of the believer. Because "God is the inclusive concrete reality, he is least of all exhaustible by any concept or conscious human percept" (131).

67. For instance, in his Gifford lectures, THE ROAD OF SCIENCE AND THE WAYS TO GOD (Chicago: The University of Chicago Press, 1978), physicist Stanley L. Jaki argued that "steps to God" are "stepping stones to science" (33-49). As "'hybrid' essence," humanity "can, for all (its) materiality, transcend all matter and achieve an intricate grasp of its totality, a grasp not material though rooted in material data" (261). The supreme queerness of the universe is "the ability of the mind to master what is not mind by finding it to be a coherent whole, a universe . . . By relating that queerness to the ultimate ground of all being, cosmic queerness becomes that cosmic singularity which points to the Ultimate in intelligibility and being" (278). The metaphysical answer of God "will greatly strengthen the scientist's trust in the existence of an objectively existing, rationally ordered universe which can be investigated by the human mind, a pursuit which is (humanity's) exclusive privilege and responsibility. This trust, privilege, and responsibility constitute the backbone of the scientific enterprise," beyond which <u>no</u> progress can be made (326-327). Thus, he argued for an inspiration of natural theology which "can only come from unreserved commitment to the very same inner logic which gives life to theism as well as to science" (331).

68. Bernard S. Meland, "The Empirical Tradition in Theology at Chicago." In B.S. Meland, ed., THE FUTURE OF EMPIRICAL THEOLOGY (Chicago: The University of Chicago Press, 1969), 54.

Huston Smith conceived of empirical theology as working with facts as they are shaped by the theory of a given theological circle. He went on to identify "religious empiricism" as working with facts "on a looser, more common sense level," asking "what there is in (humanity's) common understanding and belief" (Huston Smith, with Samuel Todes, "Empiricism: Scientific and Religious." In Meland, ibid., 144). Facts neither tell us what to do nor how to believe. What an empirical approach can do is "discover suggestive facts for the religious imagination to work with." But "after it has done its most, it must wait upon insights and disclosures that are revelatory. It can be a noble partner but not sole master. For as in science observations are idle without theories that infuse them with meaning, so in theology observations indicate nothing by themselves. They must be shaped by the religious imagination in ways that cannot, in full, be empirically delivered" (146).

69. Other correlational approaches include Tillich's questions and answers (i.e., Reason and Revelation, Being and God, Existence and the Christ, Life and the Spirit, History and the Kingdom of God) and Tracy's tradition and situation (BLESSED RAGE FOR ORDER [New York: Seabury, 1975], 45-48). Tracy outlined a correlation spectrum from identity, continuity, similarity, analogy, non-identity to confrontational (n.43 above, 88, n.44).

70. The idea of "mutually critical correlations" between sociological and theological views of the Church was developed by H. Richard Niebuhr. See Tracy (n.43 above] for an expansion of the position (21-28, n.31). The phrase itself is Edward Schillebeeckx's (quoted by Tracy, 88, n.44).

71. Cajal, quoted by William Feindel. In Penfield (n.4 above) xxvi.

72. Roger N. Walsh, TOWARDS AN ECOLOGY OF BRAIN (New York: S.P. Medical & Scientific Books, 1981).

73. Watts (n.20 above) 4-5.

74. Gardner Murphy. Quoted in Ira Progoff, DEPTH PSYCHOLOGY AND MODERN MAN (New York: Julian Press, 1959), 34.

75. John Calvin, INSTITUTES ON THE CHRISTIAN RELIGION. Vol. 1. Translated by Henry Beveridge (Grand Rapids, Michigan: Eerdmans Publishing Co., 1962), 37.

76. Paul Tillich, A HISTORY OF CHRISTIAN THOUGHT. Edited by Carl E. Braaten (London: SCM Press LTD, 1968), 63, 68.

77. William James, quoted by William Feindel. In Penfield (n.4 above) xxviii.

78. Penfield (n.4 above) xxii, 5.

79. William James, THE PRINCIPLES OF PSYCHOLOGY (New York: Henry Holt and Company, [1890] 1904, Vol. I), 8.

Chapter Two

THE WORKING BRAIN

We can characterize how the brain works by identifying which half takes the lead over the other.[1]

Both sides have the potential to engage in similar activities, but each develops specialized capacity. The result is that different work is left to the other side most of the time.

One experiment dramatized this left brain/right brain functioning. Jerre Levy and Colwyn Trevarthen investigated how each brain made decisions in matching visual objects, such as a pair of glasses, a pair of scissors, and a cake on a plate.[2] These stimuli were flashed to each hemisphere separately, and the subjects were to select the best match from a series of choices, such as a needle lying across two spools of thread, a spoon lying across a fork, and a round box-like hat. .

The results were clear. The right brain detected similarities of structure, that is, scissors looked like a fork-and-spoon as did a cake and a hat. It operated, in other words, according to "visual similarity" or how objects appeared. The left brain detected similarities of function, that is, a fork-and-spoon went with a cake for eating and a needle-and-thread with scissors for sewing. It made decisions according to "conceptual categorisation." Under special conditions the right brain could make decisions conceptually but it did so awkwardly.

Furthermore, whether a person used the right brain strategy of how things appear or the left brain one of how things function depended on the person's <u>expectation</u> of the task. Which side takes the lead is more a matter of disposition than aptitude. "How" one acts—that is, by appearance or function—seems "to depend on constraints imposed by values, knowledge, expectations, and intentions." Rather than their specialized abilities, the two brains work according to what a person expects a task to need. These are "metacontrol programs" which operate differently from "what a hemisphere does and how it responds once it is in control."[3]

The contrast between left and right was presented more simply in a drawing by a young patient who had had the fibers connecting the two hemispheres cut.[4] When asked to draw a man, he drew a boy with clear left and right side differences. On the right side of his head he pictured a girl's face and on the left side of the body (which is controlled by the right brain) a pair of eyes. On the left side of his head he wrote "LUV" and on the right side of the body (which the left brain controls) the initials "H" and "B." The girl's face equaled ("=") "luv." The right brain saw a face and the left brain supplied the label "luv."

A great amount of evidence supports both left and right brain patterns.[5] I describe it in detail. Whenever the detail becomes too much, remember that the right brain sees faces and responds by how things appear, while the left brain works conceptually and detects according to how things function.

The Left Brain

The general features of the left brain are well documented for right-handed people.[6]

The individual deliberately takes charge of whatever goes on.[7] The hemisphere orients us by means of concepts.[8] This makes reasoning logical and sequential. Causal factors are specified. Attention is narrow.[9] Strategy moves step-by-step. People deal with reality in a common sense way.

Those with an impaired left hemisphere are disturbed in thinking and feeling alike.[10] Their verbal ability suffers, whether they speak or write.[11] They do not learn. They give no evidence of being able to reason.

Two moods have been linked with left half damage.[12] One is depression, the other a sense of catastrophe. Patients give the impression of being done in by what's happening or else they seem on the verge of disaster. They are aroused easily or else fail to become aroused enough. They exaggerate their mood and their problems. Because of anger, humorlessness, sadness, and aggression they experience things being much worse than others see them. Researches call this pattern "tarnishing," a dulling or spoiling or tainting of what is.

What we know about normal people clarifies the part which the left half plays in cognitive activity: the personality is keen;[13] attention is focused;[14] distracting or irrelevant stimuli are ignored;[15] speech is precise. These attributes of keenness, focus, and concentration are summarized by the word vigilant.[16] The left brain maintains an eagle-eyed vigilance. Because sequential processing, language, orientation to time, and planning all correlate with is activity, I call the process intentional thinking.

The left brain comes at the world as an analytic observer.[17] That means it explains everything. Even when it doesn't understand, it still acts as though it does.[18]

Consider the following series of observations made by a split-brain patient.[19] They illustrate this tendency to rationalize—to make up a coherent story about what it sees. Different picture objects were flashed simultaneously to each brain: a snow scene from the left visual field to the right hemisphere and a chicken's claw from the right visual field to the left hemisphere. He was asked to point to the appropriate object in an array of pictures in front of him. The pictures included a toaster, a hammer, a snow shovel, a chicken's head, an apple, and so on. His left hand pointed to the snow shovel; his right to the chicken's head. Each side chose a picture related to the one it had seen.

But listen to how he explained his choices. When asked what he had seen, he replied, "I saw a claw and I picked the chicken." Then, without a moment's hesitation he continued, "and you have to clean out the chicken shed with a shovel."

What had happened? The left brain easily told why it picked the chicken after seeing the claw. But it included in its explanation the right brain's choice of the snow shovel. It had no knowledge of the snow scene. It simply guessed, yet in guessing it incorporated the shovel it could not ignore into a supposedly reasonable statement. The vigilant eye must account for everything it sees.

In addition to observing we find an abstracting feature. Language itself is the prime expression. Something is taken from a concrete referent and used in place of the thing itself.[20] Words are twice removed from the initial stimuli. Sights, sounds, and sensations are re-presented from primary to secondary processes and then re-represented in symbols.[21] The symbols or words themselves become objects which the left brain observes. Reality no longer lies in the world itself but rather in ideas about the world.

Whether dealing with auditory,[22] visual,[23] or tactile[24] information, the left brain handles it rationally. Sounds are analyzed conceptually and re-presented linguistically. Senses are refined according to sequences which are capable of becoming conscious. Sights are simplified in a way that makes them permanent. In this way they take on standard form.

In brief, the left brain creates a rational reality. From what it observes it builds an orderly world, a world that makes sense and can be explained logically. According to Michael Gazzaniga and Joseph LeDoux, it develops "an attitudinal view of the world involving beliefs and values." This idiosyncratic view becomes "a dominant theme."[25] Everything is reasonable in its own eyes.

With the vigilance of an eagle-eye the left hemisphere sharpens attention. It takes the lead from the right in anything which requires or permits step-by-step analysis. This applies to input and output alike.

> The back of the hemisphere works with concepts, that is, separate, discrete, abstract labels. It comprehends this conceptual reality in a coherent way. That means it observes from a fixed position, in a stable structure, through inductive reasoning.
>
> The front of the hemisphere organizes what we intend to happen, that is, consciously, deliberately, purposefully. It acts according to the logic of principles, through formal procedures, with deductive reasoning.

The intentional strategy of the left brain brings everything together in controllable form. Input is analyzed; output is exact. Table 3 summarizes major features of the working brain.

Table 3. **Major Features of The Working Brain**

General Features	Left-Brain	Right Brain
*source of responses:	the individual	the environment
*oriented to:	concepts	impressions
*type of thinking:	logical	associative
*attentional direction:	narrow focus	broad range
*interest value:	specific & realistic	tangible & symbolic

Specific Features

	Left-Brain	Right Brain
*input	Analytic, i.e., (i) observer - detached perspective - sequential & serial method (ii) temporal analysis - abstracts parts - categorizes with concepts - generalizes	Impressionistic, i.e., (i) participant - personal position - simultaneous & parallel method (ii) spatial synthesis - attends to patterns - identifies with images - unifies
*output:	Exact, i.e., (i) deliberate responses - slow - controlled - convergent - fixed structure, i.e., procedures & principles (ii) language style - formal - conceptual	Expressionistic, i.e., (i) varied responses - rapid - spontaneous - divergent - flexible approach, i.e., trial-and-error & pragmatic (ii) language style - informal - imaginative
*controls:	right side ear/eye & hand/foot	left side ear/eye & hand/foot

Takes the Lead in:

	Left-Brain	Right Brain
	Rational Strategy item-by-item step-by-step	Relational Strategy all-at-once leaps of imagination

The Right Brain

We can describe what the right brain does with less certainty yet with increasing confidence.[26]

The right hemisphere responds rapidly[27] to what comes in from the outside.[28] Because of it we are immersed in a pulsating environment. Time seems shortened, either rushing by or standing still. Space also feels different, intensified in ways that make it expand or contract. Because of this general responsiveness right half patterns are always varied.[29] Little remains fixed. Impressions are immediate, expressions heightened, emotional richness greater, passion more intense. The result is that we ascertain the core of situations more faithfully.[30]

Various activities have been linked with the right brain: processing images,[31] music, [32] rhythms;[33] recognizing faces,[34] main features,[35] emotional meanings,[36] and nonverbal wholes.[37] Verbal distinctions are few[38] and visual distinctions many.[39]

People with an impaired right hemisphere show disturbances in perceiving as well as feeling. Vision suffers most, whether images or sensations. Often the loss is subtle, though sometimes it is dramatic. Patients fail to see the left half of their visual field.[40] If they look at a clock, for instance, the numbers from 7 to 11 simply do not exist. Further, such impairment prevents them from holding together the complex aspects of a situation, which makes any sense of closure impossible. Puzzles remain unsolved. Pictures are not completed. Reactions are rigid and concrete.

Patients fail to synthesize complex input.[41] They simply cannot process two levels of meaning, so they react only to concrete meanings. To "work one's head off" means to actually lose one's head. Their speech, therefore, sounds like "a kind of talking computer that decodes literally."[42]

Patients also react inappropriately.[43] They take something which is personally sensitive as funny and something which is emotionally light as serious. They laugh too much or too little. They are either very high or amazingly indifferent. They ignore how something is said and miss what is not said.

Right half damage has been associated with hysterical optimism.[44] Elation gets exaggerated. The joy of high mood reactivity leads to denying that problems exist. With normal people pleasure ranges from "relaxed harmony to ecstasy," with long periods of "a positive background state of feeling." Patients, however, overestimate elation and underestimate negative circumstances. They minimize their obsessiveness, their dependency, their sadness, their lack of humor. In contrast to left brain "tarnish," researchers call this "polishing," a smoothing over of the rough and a shining up of the dark.

Research with nonimpaired people clarifies what the silent half contributes to cognitive activity: faster reaction time;[45] immediate impressions of the felt-meaning of situations; visual recognition;[46] a dream-like state[47] which weaves everything into a mosaic that integrates the diverse elements.[48] Quite simply, the right brain responds directly to what is around.[49] Because perception, recognition of faces, and orientation in space are linked with its activity, I identify what the right brain does as intouch thinking.

A study of ways people code and retrieve information illustrates right brain process.[50] Eighteen subjects were divided into three groups, each with different instructions for remembering the words "robot," "clock," and "umbrella." When these words were flashed on a screen, one group was to say each word silently in a strategy of verbal rehearsal. A second group was to create images associated with the words in a step-at-a-time visual rehearsal. The third group had to use a single all-at-once visual approach that imaged each word and placed them all in a single scene. For instance, a robot held a clock in its right hand and an umbrella in its left.

Results showed two kinds of information recall: either a serial process of comparing items one at a time (whether word-by-word in the first group or image-by-image in the second) or a parallel process of comparing all items simultaneously with a single image. Serial coding retrieved information item-by-item; parallel coding retrieved information all-at-once. Studies in cognitive development[51] suggest that the imaging-parallel system operates prior to the linguistic system. Thus, early memories of childhood are inaccessible in words but can be recalled visually. The nonverbal, parallel process constitutes a separate source of knowledge. Once language develops people may code experience verbally or visually or both.[52]

Significantly, sensory processing by the right brain is tied with the limbic system,[53] the center for motivations such as hunger, sex, anger, and fight-or-flight. These responses relate to self-preservation and the continuation of the species. Further, seeing and feeling go together.[54] Either we approach situations or avoid them. Which we do depends on whether or not they contribute to our own security and self-esteem. The convictions we hold result from this assessment.

Because the right brain responds so actively little becomes repetitious. In technical language we do not habituate. We remain immersed in a flow of consciousness without attaching a label to it. Without labels we encounter situations more fully.[55] Everything appears to us as for the first time. Even the familiar impresses us freshly, as in returning home after a vacation.

Although the right half lacks voluntary speech, it does exhibit complex language.[56] Grammar is like that of an average five year old; vocabulary similar to that of a fourteen year old. While a five year old knows a lot, she or he can only express it simply.

In a series of investigations Gazzaniga and Steven Hillyard[57] found that the right hemisphere could not distinguish the active from the passive voice, the present from the future, the singular from the plural, nor a negative statement from a positive one. It lacked the links between subject, object, and verb.

Such evidence suggests the right brain is a concrete synthesizer,[58] regardless of auditory,[59] visual,[60] or tactile[61] input. It hears sounds according to their intonation,[62] emotional meaning,[63] and melody.[64] It expresses itself in vivid language.[65] It integrates senses into naturally flowing patterns. It sees immediate impressions and imaginative constructions. In brief, it responds to the broad features of situations from the inside, as it were.[66]

Gazzaniga and LeDoux have modified this conclusion.[67] They construed this all-at-once style as the right half's "superior capacity for response production." That means, the right brain responds more rapidly and more often than the left brain. Furthermore, they found that every right hemisphere advantage "critically involved the hands as the mode of either stimulus per- involved the hands as the mode of either stimulus per- ception or response production." It appears the right half holds a relative advantage in visual perception and decisive advantage in manual perception. It knows something more by handling it than by simply seeing it.

One neurologist likened right brain activity to "a traveller in a foreign land who always relies on an interpreter."[68] One is constantly taking-in, but in putting-out one is reduced to gestures and simple words. Only the interpreter—the left hemisphere—can make intentions explicit.

In summary, the right hemisphere takes the lead in activity which eludes being classified. This includes input and output alike. It exhibits broad attention, waiting for the world to activate its responsiveness.

> The back half processes impressions as an everchanging kaleidescopic-stereophonic-mosaic of patterns. Because it stands inside a changing scene, everything is personal. Nothing remains objective. Impressions are associated in

terms of their tangible or symbolic features.

The front of the hemisphere intuits the felt-meaning of the whole. It grasps what is going on, what to do with an object like a fork, for instance, even though it cannot put that into words.[69] Because of its responsiveness it relies on a trial-and-error approach to whatever works.

The intouch strategy of the right brain opens everything up in an imaginative way. Input consists of impressions; output takes on qualities of personal expressiveness (see Table 3). The right brain processes in terms of relational patterns rather than with individual and distinct item recognition.

Sensory Features

The integration of either the rational or the relational style suffers with cerebral damage, regardless of location. Both brains are sophisticated, each "active, responsive, highly intelligent, thinking, conscious, and fully human with respect to its cognitive depth and complexity."[70] Even so, a dominant or preferred style suggest that differences in aptitude or disposition encourage people to seek out "environments in which the more developed mode is utilized more."[71]

More needs to be said about the major features of these two processes, however. The early distinction between verbal and nonverbal information was too simplistic.[72] Focus has shifted to strategies or styles of information processing. "How" a brain deals with sensory input and motor output is more crucial than "what" the input and output are in themselves. This shift permits us to juxtapose sensory-motor systems and cultural expressions, regardless of linguistic elements.[73] Activities with similar processing features are associated functionally with the same part of the brain, namely, with either a synthesis of basic ("primitive") wholes or an analysis of "constituent parts."[74] The correspondences are "not categorical," but they do refer "in the most general and basic terms to the manner in which understanding grows."[75]

Language frees us from the symmetry of nature.[76] The asymmetry or unequal halves of the brain suggests the priority of the rational over the relational.[77] Language translates raw input into abstract codes. These re-representations are maps of reality.[78] In effect, the two brains are map-makers. Each "maps" reality according to its own strategy or style of working.

Like maps, these re-representations are deceiving. They distort "what is" in order to convey "what is there." They delete information in order to simplify complexity. In A. Korzybski's words, a map is not the territory,[79] a menu is never a meal.

As human beings we have developed three primary language maps.[80] Each depends upon a preferred sensory system. These basic ways of re-representing data are: the language of the ear, which is an auditory map; of the eye, which is a visual map; and of the body, which is a sensory or visceral map. In addition, there are the minor sensory maps of the nose, which is the language of smell (the only non-crossing sensory system), and the tongue, which is the language of taste.

As input maps, they reconstruct "reality." The more maps we use the more accurately we know the territory. The fewer maps we use the less adequately we know the territory. The more distorted or deficient our knowledge of The Way Things Are[81] the more disturbed or deficient our responses. Under those conditions we take our "perceived" worlds as the "real" world.

Proponents of the neurolinguistic approach to human behavior claim that our primary language can be identified by the words we use. Phrases such as "What do you think" or "How does it add up?" or "What do you suppose?" reflect auditory language. Other phrases such as "How do you feel?" or "What do you sense?" or "Can you get a handle on the issue?" suggest bodily or visceral language. And phrases like "What do you see?" or "Can you imagine what's there?" or "Is it clear?" convey visual language. Each language—ear, body, eye—differs in the way it organizes reality. People use the conventional language of their culture but think with the primary language of their preferred sensory system.

These implicit ways of mapping are influenced by the basic process strategies (see Table 4). "How" a primary language is used, namely, conceptually or metaphorically, suggests which brain is in charge. From the previous evidence, I associate the following representational activity with left brain rationality:

- in the bodily system muscle tension produces deliberate responses that are slow, controlled, specialized, and refined;
- in the visual system observations are made from a fixed perspective which conveys a sense of a realistic, objective, and permanent reality;
- in the auditory system sounds are converted into concepts or signs which contribute to precision; language is ideational, with narrow meanings, which makes for abstract prose.

The right brain relational activity can be identified in a similar fashion:

- in the bodily system muscle relaxation produces natural responses that are rapid, spontaneous, patterned, and varied;
- in the visual system perceptions are made from a personal position which creates a symbolic, changing, and unique reality;
- in the auditory system sounds are heard directly, which makes whole units; language is pictorial, with broad meanings, which generates metaphorical prose and poetry alike.

Table 4. **Features of the Sensory Systems**

	Left Brain	**Right Brain**
Sensing		
	tension	relaxation
	deliberate responses	natural responses
	- slow	- rapid
	- controlled	- spontaneous
	- convergent	- divergent
	- refined sensations	- sensory patterns
	- stable parts	- varied wholes
Seeing		
	observation	participation
	perspective	perception
	- fixed position	- personal position
	- realistic	- symbolic
	- objective	- subjective
	permanence	impressions
	- common sense	- changing scenes
	- basic elements	- changing elements
	* separate	* distinct
	* isolated	* connected
	* repeatable	* unique
	fixed visualization	flowing imagination
Hearing		
	sounds translated into concepts	sounds heard apart from concepts
	- particular	- global
	speech or writing	speech or writing
	- ideational	- vivid
	- narrow meanings	- broad meanings
	- prosaic/abstract	- metaphoric/imaginative
Overall		
	intentional vigilance	intouch responsiveness
	- differences	- connections
	- isolated senses	- combined senses
	input	input
	- conceptual/abstract	- concrete/perceptual
	output	output
	- rational/specialized	- relational/synthesized

Left brain language is characterized by an analytic style—complete sentences with subject, object, and verb. So it is formal, detailed, exact, orderly. Because of these sequential features, it is objective in form and conceptual in content. In effect, the eye and the body serve the right ear of the left hemisphere.

Right brain language can be recognized from its flowing style. Words are informal, vivid, suggestive, imaginative: drama, story, paradox, parable are its modes.[82] Because it expands and embraces at the same moment, it is personal in form and metaphorical in content. In effect, the ear serves the left eye and the body of the right hemisphere.

The preferred system is enriched and supported by the other two. When the primary system breaks down or needs supplementing, one of the other systems serves as an auxiliary back-up. The third system usually is neglected. Most of the time we get along with one map. Occasionally, we draw on the auxiliary system for input. Only under extreme necessity do we turn to the third map.

Both Brains

Neither brain works by itself. Full functioning requires both.[83] Even so, evidence suggests a division of labor. Under normal conditions one side takes the lead, responding milliseconds faster than the other. Further, when one half is activated, the other is suspended.[84] When a task, such as writing a letter, requires a rational strategy, the left brain is activated and the right is quiet. Conversely, when a task, such as matching a set of colored blocks with a given pattern, utilizes a relational strategy, the right brain is active and the left is quiet. When one side is "on," the other side is "off."[85]

The cutting of the corpus callosum, the fibers which connect the two sides, suggests what happens when the halves do not cooperate. The fewer the connections, the greater the confusion. Split brain consciousness leaves people "more at the mercy of uncontrollable surges of hemispheric preponderance and to that extent [people are] handicapped in [their] ability to select strategies to fit a given situation." They are left with "an extreme and rigid right- or left-hemispheric approach."[86]

The work of Gazzaniga and LeDoux with one split-brain patient clarifies the picture of hemisphere conflict.[87] Under controlled conditions the patient's right brain could respond to questions presented only to it. Results showed that his right hemisphere possessed a sense of self, since it knew its name; experienced feeling, since it could describe its mood; held a hierarchy of values, since it could express likes and dislikes; retained a sense of temporality, since it understood the future based on its knowing what day tomorrow is; and exhibited intentionality, since it had goals and aspirations as suggested by its naming an occupational choice different from the one named by the left hemisphere. It had "its own independent response-priority-determining mechanisms, which is to say, its own volitional control system."

When the left and right brains compete for attentional dominance, their inputs create difficulties. Without information flowing back and forth the patient is deprived of needed data. Even though he or she is no less conscious, they lose the richness of the territory and struggle with conflicting information. At times they are "informed by the logico-analytical control system of the left hemisphere and at times by the global-synthetic strategies characteristic of the right."[88]

We do not need to have our corpus callosum cut to experience competition for attentional dominance. It happens to everyone. Sometimes we are responding to too many demands, sometimes to conflicting demands, sometimes to too few demands. Split brain consciousness is a metaphor of the human condition. We can be of two minds—a house divided against itself (Matthew 12:25).

With the full flow of information the two processes of item-by-item and relational attributes "combine to program a unitary pattern of behavior."[89] People use whatever combinations of strategies and systems best handle the task. Neither half excludes the other. One leads with the other contributing. Every act is an act of the whole head.

Cautions

Speculations about hemisphere specialization require three crucial qualifications: one related to hand dominance, one associated with gender differences, and one involving the evidence itself.

As to hand dominance, the generalization applies only to left hemisphere right hand dominance. Recent studies[90] show that only one fourth of the population are thoroughly right handed and slightly more than one third exhibit marked left hemisphere dominance. About one out of ten people have a complete absence of left hemisphere dominance for language. John L.M.B. Dawson argued that handedness reflects not only genetic factors but socialization pressures.[91] More conformist cultures show a smaller percentage of left hand or mixed hand dominance than more permissive cultures. And there are fewer left handed women than men because women are the recipients of greater socialization pressure than men.

Levy has summarized the research on gender differences.[92] Males exhibit strong asymmetry with extreme separation between verbal and nonverbal processes. This results in males being field independent, contextually less sensitive, and more adept at extracting formal principles relevant to spatial or logical organization. Females, in contrast, show weak asymmetry with a mixture of verbal and nonverbal processes. This makes for field dependence, contextual sensitivity, and a responsiveness to subtle experiential variations that interfere with formal structuring of abstract variants. To state the qualification precisely, male and female brains are organized[93] and develop[94] differently.

The comparative patterns modify the popular generalization of left and right brains. Males perform better in verbal reasoning and with formal language, while females show better reading skills and verbal fluency. Conversely, females show less mathematical reasoning because the content is purely denotative (that is, it has no metalinguistic features such as tone of voice or concrete referents that affect its meaning), whereas males exhibit difficulty in integrating experiential representations that bear close resemblance to original perceptual experiences. In brief, men tend to be oriented to the physical world and abstract invariants; women tend to be oriented to the social world and concrete variants. Further, women exhibit more variable patterns than men.

A small study of a sex difference in the shape and surface of the connecting fiber tract of the corpus callosum hints at one source of these differences.[95] These fibers feed information back and forth between the hemispheres so rapidly that, except in highly unusual instances, we experience a single consciousness. In every case the back part of splenium of the female callosum was more bulbous and larger than the male counterpart. Here is data suggesting extensive interhemisphere transfer of visual information in women. It corroborates the hypothesis that female brains are less specialized than male brains for visuospatial functions.[96]

Males excel in processing shapes and females in processing sounds.[97] Males show more proficiency in various spatial activities and females in language related tests.[98] Male brains tend to be more asymmetrical, suggesting more specialized functioning by each hemisphere, than female brains.[99]

In females, language tends to be represented in both hemispheres. This impedes spatial ability and strengthens interpersonal skills. In contrast, males have language restricted to the left hemisphere which allows the right hemisphere to develop spatial ability critical for environmental activity. Male dominated cultures, therefore, tend to manifest wide-ranging environmental interaction with the likelihood of exaggerated and one-sided disequilibrium in psychic activity.[100]

Those whose brains are less specialized and more integrated are early maturers.[101] That is, the maturational rate is such that they use conceptual means earlier and more easily. As early maturing adolescents, they perform better on tests of verbal ability, such as fluency, articulation, and perceptual speed, than on tests of spatial abilities. The reverse pattern appears in late maturers. They perform better on tests of spatial abilities than on verbal skills. Although rate of maturation is distributed along a physiological continuum and so is not gender specific, as a group girls tend to mature earlier than boys.

What is genetically determined and culturally conditioned are hard to separate. Gender differences represent about one quarter of a standard deviation,[102] which means that distinguishable differences are of such modest proportions and involve such complex variables that there can be more difference between any two males or any two females than between any particular male and any particular female.[103]

As a very cautious generationalization, men's hemispheres tend to specialize, each handling analytical and perceptual processes separately. In contrast, women's hemispheres tend to function as "generalists," each half processing linguistically.[104] These are not so much "absolute categories of reality" as "dynamic rather than static phenomena."[105]

The evidence for two brains comes from varied sources, with varying degrees of decisiveness:

- from impaired brains:[106] i.e., those individuals born with only one hemisphere; those with some portion of the cortex damaged by stroke, tumor, or trauma; those who have had either one hemisphere removed (hemispherectomy) or one or both hemispheres surgically interferred with (lobotomy or hemispherotomy); those who have had the activity of one hemisphere temporarily suspended in what is called spreading cortical depression which results from the injection of sodium amytal in the carotid artery to determine speech lateralization prior to surgery; those who have had the fibers connecting the two hemispheres severed (the great commissure of the corpus callosum, the anterior commissure, the posterior commissure, and the optic chiasm) in a split-brain operation;

- from intact brains: i.e., those individuals who function normally and for whom distinguishable hemisphere specializations have been sought in ways that neutralize the contribution of the opposite side to the particular activity considered.

Evidence from people with impaired brains is more subject to uncertain interpretation. Widespread cerebral deficits can affect any and all activity. Evidence from those whose brains are normal also calls for cautious interpretation. In addition to hand dominance and gender difference, there is the necessary input of every cortical region in all mental activity. Furthermore, the subcortical areas of the brain stem contribute both input and integration.[107]

Even so, evidence for asymmetry is strong. We need not be reduced to shyness or silence. We can say something, and something substantial, about two brains. That substantive something provides empirical clues to understand "phenomena at more complex levels of analysis."[108] One brain works with two minds.

NOTES

1. Jerre Levy, "Varieties of Human Brain Organization and the Human Social System," Zygon, vol. 15, no. 4 (December 1980):351-375; Judith S. Schlesinger, "Laterality and Myth Continued," American Psychologist 31 (December 1980):1147-1149; Thomas G. Bever, "Cerebral Asymmetries in Humans Are Due To The Differentiation Of Two Incompatible Processes: Holistic and Analytic," Annals New York Academy of Sciences (1975):251-262.

2. Jerre Levy and Colwyn Trevarthen, "Metacontrol of Hemisphere Function in Human Split-Brain Patients," Journal of Experimental Psychology: Human Perception and Performance 2 (1976):299-312; Jerre Levy, "Psychobiological Implications of Bilateral Asymmetry." In Dimond and Beaumont (n. 1/1), 164-166. Such tasks use a tachistoscope.

3. Jerre Levy, "Performance, Capacity, and Hemispheric Dominance for Processing and Behavior: Metacontrolling Programs in the Central Nervous System," Cognition and Brain Theory, 1982, 5(3):199-210.

4. Levy (n.2 above), 181; Roger Sperry, "Some Effects of Disconnecting the Cerebral Hemispheres," Science (1982) 217:1223-1226.

5. Michael S. Gazzaniga, "Cerebral Dominance Viewed as a Decision System," (n. 1/5), 367-382. Early evidence about left-right hemispheric differences was identified as verbal-nonverbal (visual-spatial) distinctions. Subsequent investigations have refined these differences. More accurately, the distinction is based "on different ways of dealing with information" (Springer and Deutsch, LEFT BRAIN, RIGHT BRAIN [n.1/1], 45). Each side uses different strategies to handle incoming information. The left hemisphere is best thought of as analytic; the right hemisphere as holistic. See Jerre Levy-Agresti and

Roger W. Sperry, "Differential Perceptual Capacities in Major and Minor Hemispheres," Proceedings of the National Academy of Science, U.S.A. 61 (1968):1151; Jerre Levy, "Psychobiological Implications of Bilateral Asymmetry." In Dimond and Beaumont (n. 1/1), 121-183.

6. Robert E. Hicks and Marcel Kinsbourne, "Human Handedness." In Marcel Kinsbourne, ed., ASYMMETRICAL FUNCTION OF THE BRAIN (New York: Cambridge University Press, 1978), 523-549; Luria, THE WORKING BRAIN (n. 1/1), 78-79.

7. G. Berlucchi, "Cerebral Dominance and Interhemispheric Communication in Normal Man." In Schmitt and Worden (n. 1/1), 68; Donald E. Broadbent, "Division of Function and Integration of Behavior." In Schmitt and Worden (n. 1/1), 34-40.

8. Eccles, THE UNDERSTANDING OF THE BRAIN (n. 1/1), 216.

9. Luria, THE WORKING BRAIN (n. 1/1), 197-199.

10. Levy (n. 2 above), 147.

11. Aaron Smith, "Dominant and Nondominant Hemispherectomy." In M. Kinsbourne and W.L. Smith, eds., HEMISPHERE DISCONNECTION AND CEREBRAL FUNCTION (Springfield, IL: Thomas, 1974), 16.

12. H. Hécaen, "Clinical Symptomatology in Right and Left Hemisphere Lesions." In V.B. Mountcastle, ed., INTER-HEMISPHERIC RELATIONS AND CEREBRAL DOMINANCE (Baltimore: The John Hopkins Press, 1962), 217, citing L. Peria, G. Rosadini, and G.F. Rossi, "Determination of Side of Cerebral Dominance with Amobarbital," Archives of Neurology 4 (1961): 173-181. Evidence and interpretation about personality and emotional correlates of lateralization are controversial. Marcel Kinsbourne (Psychology Today [May, 1981], 92) cited evidence which

suggests that damage to the left hemisphere results in pessimism and unjustified feelings of gloom, guilt, and despair, while damage to the right hemisphere is accompanied by cheerfulness and indifference to disturbance. He then interpreted the evidence to mean that the left hemisphere is happy and the right sad. The work of David M. Baer and Paul Fedio ("Quantitative Analysis of Interictal Behavior in Temporal Lobe Epilepsy," Archives of Neurology 34 [August 1977]:451-467) and Arnold J. Mandell ("Toward A Psychobiology of Transcendence: God in the Brain." In J.M. Davidson and R.J. Davidson, eds., PSYCHOBIOLOGY OF CONSCIOUSNESS [New York: Plenum Press, 1980], 379-464) provide a contrasting interpretation. Mandell identified "syndromes of temporal lobe disinhibition." Rather than the emotion associated with hemisphere damage coming from the opposite side, it reflects an intensification of the personality features of the damaged side. The disinhibition from damage, combined with lateralization bias, "leads to intensification of the spectrum of personality features that have as feeling components of cognitive style . . . two aspects of mood: pessimism and obsessiveness (in the left) and optimism with hysteria (in the right); in the extreme, depression and elation" (417). The "ideational traits" of the left temporal lobe patients, i.e., "ruminative, intellectual tendencies: religiousity, philosophical interests, and sense of personal destiny" present a left brain pattern. Similarly, the "emotional tendencies" of right temporal lobe patients, i.e., "anger, sadness, elation, circumstantiality, viscosity (i.e., a tendency to repetition) and hypermoralism" suggest a right brain pattern (Baer and Fedio, "Quantitative Analysis" [n.12], 458-466).

13. G.S. Ferris and M.M. Dorsen, "Agenesis of the Corpus Callosum," Cortex 11 (1975):95.

14. Luria, THE WORKING BRAIN (n. 1/1), 197-199.

15. Eccles, THE UNDERSTANDING OF THE BRAIN (n. 1/1), 143-144.

16. S.J. Dimond and J. Graham Beaumont, "Experimental Studies of Hemisphere Function in the Human Brain." In Dimond and Beaumont (n. 1/1), 66-69.

17. Gazzaniga, THE BISECTED BRAIN (n. 1/1), 107.

18. Robert D. Nebes, "Hemispheric Specialization in Commissurotomized Man," Psychological Bulletin 81 (January 1974):1-14.

19. Gazzaniga and LeDoux, THE INTEGRATED MIND (n. 1/1), 146-150, 155.

20. Robert D. Nebes, "Dominance of the Minor Hemisphere in Commissurotomized Man for the perception of part-whole relationships." In Kinsbourne and Smith (n. 11 above), 155-156; Marcel Kinsbourne, "Mechanisms of Hemispheric Interaction in Man." In Kinsbourne and Smith (n. 11 above), 266-267.

21. J.Z. Young, "Why Do We Have Two Brains?" In Mountcastle (n. 12 above), 23.

22. Robert Efron, "Temporal Perception, Aphasia and Deja Vu," Brain 86, n.3 (1963):403-424; Thomas G. Bever, "Discussion Paper: Some Theoretical and Empirical Issues That Arise If We Insist on Distinguishing Language and Thought," Annals New York Academy of Sciences 263 (1975):76-83; Thomas G. Bever, Richard R. Hurtig, and Ann B. Handel, "Analytic Processing Elicits Right Ear Superiority in Monaurally Presented Speech," Neuropsychologia 14 (1976):175-181; Eran Zaidel, "Auditory Vocabulary of the Right Hemisphere Following Brain Bisection or Hemidecortication," Cortex 12, no. 3 (September 1976):191-211.

23. Marlene Oscar-Berman, Sheila Blumstein, and David DeCusa, "Iconic Recognition of Musical Symbols in the Lateral Visual Fields," Cortex 12, no.2 (September 1976):241-248; Amiram Carmon, "Spatial and Temporal Factors in Visual Perception of Patients With Unilateral Hemispheric Lesions." In Kinsbourne

(n.6 above), 86-98; V. Krynicki, "Hemisphere differences in the recognition of and evoked potential to random sided forms," (Unpublished dissertation research, 1974), cited by Bever (n.1 above), 255-256.

24. E. Zaidel, cited by Harold W. Gordon, "Auditory specialization of the Right and Left Hemispheres." In Kinsbourne and Smith (n.11 above), 134.

25. Gazzaniga and LeDoux, THE INTEGRATED MIND (n. 1/1), 155.

26. Luria, THE WORKING BRAIN (n. 1/1), 238; Jerre Levy, "Language, Cognition, and the Right Hemisphere," American Psychologist 38 (May 1983): 538--541; and Ellen Perecman, ed., COGNITIVE PROCESSING IN THE RIGHT HEMISPHERE (New York: Academic Press, Inc., 1983).

27. Gazzaniga and Le Doux, THE INTEGRATED MIND (n. 1/1); Howard Gardner, THE SHATTERED MIND: The Person After Brain Damage (New York: Vintage Books, [1974] 1976), 321-322.

28. Doreen Kimura, "The Asymmetry of the Human Brain," Scientific American (March 1973):72-73.

29. S.J. Dimond and J.G. Beaumont, "Experimental Studies." In Dimond and Beaumont (n. 1/1), 74-75; Marcel Kinsbourne, "Mechanisms." In Kinsbourne and Smith (n. 1/1), 278-286.

30. Gardner (n.27 above), 321-322.

31. Gazzaniga and LeDoux, THE INTEGRATED MIND (n. 1/1), 122; Ronald R. Kelly and Kenneth D. Orton, "Dichotic Perception of Word-Pairs With Mixed Image Values," Neuropsychologia 17 (1979):363-371; Allan Paivio, IMAGERY AND VERBAL PROCESSES (New York: Holt, Rinehart & Winston, 1971); Allan Paivio and K. Csapo, "Concrete Image and Verbal Memory Codes," Journal of Experimental Psychology 80 (1969):279-285.

32. Harold W. Gordon, "Hemispheric Asymmetries in the Perception of Musical Chords," Cortex 6 (1970):394; Gardner (n.27 above), 301-302.

33. Gardner (n.27 above), 356; Brenda Milner, "Laterality Effects in Audition." In Mountcastle (n.12 above), 182-188; Lauren Julius Harris, "Sex Differences in Spatial Ability: possible environmental, genetic, and neurological factors." In Kinsbourne (n.6 above), 423-425.

34. Berlucchi (n.7 above), 67; Levy (n.5 above), 156, 159; R.D. Hillard, "Hemispheric Laterality Effects on a Facial Recognition Task in Normal Subjects," Cortex 9 (1973):246-258; R.K. Lin, "Looking at Upside-Down Faces," Journal of Experimental Psychology 81 (1968):141-145.

35. Gazzaniga, THE BISECTED BRAIN (n. 1/1), 58; Colwyn Trevarthen, "Functional Relations of Disconnected Hemispheres with the Brain Stem, and with Each Other: monkey and man." In Kinsbourne and Smith (n.11 above), 155-156.

36. Norman Geschwind, "Disconnection Syndromes in Animals and Man. I," Brain 88 (June 1965):256; Gardner (n.27 above), 372; Bryan Kolb and Laughlin Taylor, "Affective Behavior in Patients with Localized Cortical Excisions: Role of Lesion Site and Side," Science (October 1981)214:89-91; Springer and Deutsch, LEFT BRAIN, RIGHT BRAIN (n. 1/1), 171; Sheila Blumstein and William E. Cooper, "Hemispheric Processing of Intonation Contours," Cortex 10 (1974):146-158; Ruth Campbell and Michael Heap, "The Divided Self and the Divided Brain," New Scientist (19 April 1979):191-193.

37. Berlucchi (n.7 above), 67; Nebes (n.20 above), 155-156.

38. Gazzaniga, "Cerebral Dominance Viewed as a Decision System" (n.5 above), 376; Michael S. Gazza-

niga and Roger W. Sperry, "Language After Section of the Cerebral Commissures," Brain 90 (1967):131--148; Gazzaniga, THE BISECTED BRAIN (n.1/1); Roger W. Sperry, "Lateral Specialization in The Surgically Separated Hemispheres." In Schmitt and Worden (n.1/1), 11-12.

39. Visual distinctions include visualizing points in space, enumerating stimuli from rapid scanning, perceiving depth forms, and orientation of lines. Jerre Levy, Colwyn Trevarthen, and Roger W. Sperry, "Perception of Bilateral Chimeric Figures Following Hemispheric Deconnection," Brain 95 (1972):61-78.

40. Vernon B. Mountcastle, "The World Around Us: Neural Command Functions for Selective Attention," Neurosciences Research Program Bulletin, vol. 14, Supplement (April 1976):8-9. The right-field stimulus appears to "extinguish" the left-field stimulus when presented together, thereby competing for attentional focus (Springer and Deutsch, LEFT BRAIN, RIGHT BRAIN [n.1/1], 173-177).

41. Gerald Goldstein, "The Use of Clinical Neuropsychological Methods in the Lateralization of Brain Lesions." In Dimond and Beaumont (n.1/1), 287.

42. Gardner (n.27 above), 295-296, 370.

43. Hécaen, "Clinical Symptomatology." In Mountcastle (n.12 above), 217; Peria, et. al. (n.12 above); Gardner (n.27 above), 371-372; Howard Gardner, Paul K. Lin, Laurie Flamm, and Jen Silverman, "Comprehension and Appreciation of Humorous Material Following Brain Damage," Brain 98 (1975):399-412.

44. Baer and Fedio (n.12 above); Mandell (n.12 above), 417, 424.

45. Sperry (n.38 above); 11-12.

46. Levy, Trevarthen, and Sperry (n.39 above); Mortimer Mishkin, "A Possible Link Between Interhemispheric Integration in Monkeys and Cerebral Dominance in Man." In Mountcastle (n.12 above), 101-107; Oliver L. Zangwill, "Thought and the Brain," British Journal of Psychology 67 (1976):314; Ralph N. Haber, "How We Remember What We See," Scientific American 222 (May 1970):104-112; Nelson Butters, Ina Samuels, Harold Goodglass, and Betty Brody, "Short-term Visual and Auditory Memory Disorders After Parietal and Frontal Lobe Damage," Cortex 6 (1970): 440-459.

47. Oliver L. Zangwill, "Consciousness and the Cerebral Hemispheres." In Dimond and Beaumont (n.1/1), 273, based upon his observing the testing of a split-brain patient in Sperry's laboratory in July 1970; Paul Bakan, "The Right Brain is the Dreamer," Psychology Today (November 1976):66-68.

48. Gardner (n.27 above), 379; J. Semmes, "Hemisphere Specialization: A possible clue to mechanism," Neuropsychologia 6 (1968):23; Doreen Kimura, "The Asymmetry of the Human Brain," Scientific American 228 (March 1973):70-78; N. Butters, M. Barton, and B.A. Brody, "Role of the right parietal lobe in the mediation of cross-modal associations and reversible operations in space," Cortex 6 (1970):174-190.

49. Levy-Agresti and Sperry (n.5 above).

50. John G. Seamon, "Coding and Retrieval Processes and the Hemispheres of the Brain." In Dimond and Beaumont (n.1/1), 184-203.

51. Jerome S. Bruner, "On Cognitive Growth: I." In J.S. Bruner, R.R. Oliver and P.M. Greenfield, eds., STUDIES IN COGNITIVE GROWTH (New York: John Wiley & Sons, Inc., 1966); Michael S. Gazzaniga, "One Brain - Two Minds?" American Scientist 60 (1972):311-317; Ulric Neisser, "Cultural and Cognitive Discontinuity." In Anthropological Society of Washington, ANTHROPOLOGY AND HUMAN BE-

HAVIOR (Washington, D.C.: Gaus, 1962); all cited by Seamon (n.50 above), 201.

52. H.P. Bahrich and B. Boucheer, "Retention of Verbal and Visual Codes of the Same Stimuli," Journal of Experimental Psychology 78 (1968): 417-422.

53. Paul D. MacLean, "A Mind of Three Minds: Education the Triune Brain." In Chall and Mirsky (n.1/1), 325-342.

54. Geschwind (n.36 above), 256.

55. Dimond and Beaumont (n.29 above), 74-75; Gazzaniga and LeDoux, THE INTEGRATED MIND (n.1/1), 136-137.

56. Eran Zaidel, "Auditory Vocabulary of the Right Hemisphere Following Brain Bisection of Hemidecortication," Cortex 12 n.3 (1976):191-211. See Alan Searleman, "A Review of Right Hemisphere Linguistic Capabilities," Psychological Bulletin 84 (1977):503-523; Eran Zaidel, "A Response to Gazzaniga: Language in the Right Hemisphere, Convergent Perspectives," American Psychologist, May 1983:542-546.

57. Michael S. Gazzaniga and Steven A. Hillyard, "Language and Speech Capacity of the Right Hemisphere," Neuropsychologia 9 (1971):273-280.

58. Levy, "Cerebral Asymmetries." In Kinsbourne and Smith (n.11 above), 180; Nebes (n.18 above), 13.

59. Kelly and Orton (n.31 above), 363-371; Bever (n.1 above), 254-258.

60. Paivio (n.31 above).

61. Hans-Lukas Teuber, "Effects of Brain Wounds Implicating Right or Left Hemisphere in Man: Hemisphere Differences and Hemisphere Interaction in Vision, Audition, and Somesthesis." In Mountcastle (n.12 above), 136.

62. Brenda Milner, "Laterality Effects in Audition." In Mountcastle (n.12 above), 187-188.

63. K.M. Heilman, R. Scholes, and R.T. Watson, "Auditory Affective Agnosia: Disturbed Comprehension of Affective Speech," Journal of Neurology, Neurosurgery, and Psychiatry 38 (1978):69-72.

64. Doreen Kimura, "Left-Right Differences in the Perception of Melodies," Quarterly Journal of Experimental Psychology 16 (1964):355-358.

65. Zaidel, "Auditory Vocabulary of the Right Hemisphere" (n.56 above); Kelly and Orton (n.31 above).

66. Mountcastle (n.40 above), 41.

67. Gazzaniga and LeDoux, THE INTEGRATED MIND (n.1/1), 48.

68. Cited by MacLean (n.53 above), 337.

69. Nathan, THE NERVOUS SYSTEM (n.1/1), 276.

70. Levy, "Language, Cognition, and the Right Hemisphere" (n.26 above). The quotation was a summary of right hemisphere functioning to emphasize its active, meaning-extracting, capacity. I use it to summarize the capacity of the left as well.

71. Levy and Trevarthen (n.2 above).

72. Bever (n.1 above), 256; Springer and Deutsch, LEFT BRAIN, RIGHT BRAIN (n.1/1), 46.

73. Bever (n.1 above), Harold W. Gordon, "Auditory Specialization of the Right and Left Hemispheres." In Kinsbourne and Smith (n.11 above), 134; Marcel Kinsbourne, "Hemisphere Specialization and the Growth of Human Understanding," American Psychologist 37 (April 1982):411-420.

74. Bever (n.1 above); 252-254, 260.

75. Kinsbourne (n.73 above), 419.

76. M.C. Corballis and I.L. Beale, THE PSYCHOLOGY OF LEFT AND RIGHT (Hillsdale, NJ: Erlbaum, 1976).

77. Jean L. Marx, "The Two Sides of the Brain," Science 220, 29 April 1983:488-490.

78. Richard Bandler and John Grinder, THE STRUCTURE OF MAGIC I: A Book About Language and Therapy (Palo Alto, CA: Science and Behavior Books, Inc., 1975).

79. A. Korzybski, SCIENCE AND SANITY (Lakeville, Conn.: The International Non-Aristotelian Library Publishing Company, 4th Edition, 1933).

80. John Grinder and Richard Bandler, THE STRUCTURE OF MAGIC II: A Book about Communication and Change (Palo Alto, CA: Science and Behavior Books, Inc., 1976), 3-26.

81. The phrase was used by P.W. Bridgeman, THE WAY THINGS ARE (Cambridge: Harvard University Press, 1959).

82. Paul Watzlawick, THE LANGUAGE OF CHANGE: Elements of Therapeutic Communication (New York: Basic Books, Inc., Publishers, 1978).

83. Zaidel, "A Response to Gazzaniga," (n.56 above), 545.

84. Galin, "The Two Modes of Consciousness and The Two Halves of the Brain." In Lee (n.1/1), 42-45.

85. Ibid., 53-66; David Galin and Robert Ornstein, "Lateral specialization of cognitive mode: An EEG study," Psychophysiology 9 (1972):412-418.

86. Kinsbourne and Smith (n.11 above), 288-289.

87. Gazzaniga and LeDoux, THE INTEGRATED MIND (n.1/1), 142-145; Michael S. Gazzaniga, "Right Hemisphere Language Following Brain Bisection: A 20-Year Perspective," American Psychologist 38 (May 1983):525-527.

88. Kinsbourne and Smith (n.11 above), 286-288.

89. Kinsbourne (n.73 above), 413.

90. Luria, THE WORKING BRAIN (n.1/1), 78-79; Hicks and Kinsbourne (n.6 above); Theodore Rasmussen and Brenda Milner, "The Role of Early Left-Brain Injury in Determining Lateralization of Cerebral Speech." In Dimond and Blizard (n.1/1), 355-369; H. Hécaen and J. De Ajuriagueira, LEFT-HANDEDNESS: Manual Superiority and Cerebral Dominance. Trans. E. Ponder (New York: Grune & Stratton, 1964); Springer and Deutsch, LEFT BRAIN, RIGHT BRAIN (n.1/1), 103-120.

91. John L.M.B. Dawson, "An Anthropological Perspective on the Evolution and Lateralization of the Brain." In Dimond and Blizard (n.1/1), 424-447.

92. Levy (n.1 above), 367-371.

93. Jo Durden-Smith, "Male-Female-Why?" Quest 80 (October 1980):15-19, 93-99.

94. Carol Gilligan, IN a DIFFERENT VOICE: Psychological Theory and Women's Development (Cambridge: Harvard University Press, [1982] 1983).

95. C. deLacoste-Utamsing and R.L. Holloway, "Sexual Dimorphism in the Human Corpus Callosum," Science (1982)216:1431-1432.

96. Harris (n.33 above); R.W. Goy and B.S. McEwen, eds., SEXUAL DIFFERENTIATION OF THE BRAIN (Cambridge: MIT Press, 1980); M.A. Wittig and A.C. Peterson, eds., SEX-RELATED DIFFERENCES IN COGNITIVE FUNCTIONING: Developmental Issues (San Francisco: Academic Press, 1979).

97. M. Coltheart, E. Hull, and D. Slater, "Sex Differences in Imagery and Reading," *Nature*, 1975, 253:438-440.

98. E. Maccoby and C. Jacklin, THE PSYCHOLOGY OF SEX DIFFERENCES (Stanford, CA: Stanford University Press, 1974).

99. J.A. Wada, R. Clark, and A. Hamm, "Cerebral Hemisphere Asymmetry in Humans," *Archives of Neurology*, 1975, 32:239-246.

100. Harris (n.33 above).

101. D.P. Waber, "Sex Differences in Cognition: A Function of Maturation Rate?" *Science* (1976) May:572-573.

102. Springer and Deutsch, LEFT BRAIN, RIGHT BRAIN (n.1/1), 129.

103. J.S. Hyde, "How Large Are Cognitive Gender Differences? A Meta-analysis using w^2 and d," *American Psychologist* (1981)36:892-901.

104. Thomas R. Blakeslee, THE RIGHT BRAIN: A New Understanding of the Unconscious Mind and Its Creative Powers (Garden City, NY: Anchor Press/Doubleday, 1980), 99-101.

105. M.K. Martin and B. Voorhies, FEMALE OF THE SPECIES (New York: Columbia University Press, 1975).

106. Moyra Williams, BRAIN DAMAGE, BEHAVIOR, AND THE MIND (New York: John Wiley and Sons, 1979).

107. W. Penfield and L. Roberts, SPEECH AND BRAIN - MECHANISMS (Princeton: Princeton University Press, 1959), 21.

108. Kinsbourne (n.73 above), 419.

Chapter Three

SEVERAL MINDS

Initially, I juxtaposed neuropsychology and theology.

Each discipline enriched the other: the former by identifying the regularities of step-by-step and all-at-once processes, the latter by suggesting the emergent meanings of proclamation and manifestation. Next, I drew together what is known of how the brain works. Now, before moving to the historical-cultural analysis, I relate these cognitive processes and focal meanings with each other. The result is the mind as an analytical metaphor, a tool with which to identify and assess how humanity reflects and expresses God.

I propose four prototypes of the mind as the bearer and maker of meaning. Theologies of proclamation parallel left brain activity because of sequential language. The redeeming mind of the left brain, thereby, can be either a simple conceptual mind or a complex analytic one. Theologies of manifestation parallel right brain activity because of relational meaningfulness. Similarly, the creating mind of the right brain can be distinguished in either a simple concrete mind or a complex imaginative one. These several minds sharpen ways that people construe reality.

In proposing this map of the mind, both human and divine, remember we are really dealing with one head, one brain, one mind. Its unity overshadows its divisions. Neither the left mind nor the right functions alone. Although one side leads and the other follows, taking turns according to the task at hand, each draws upon the whole cortex, the other side, in order to do its work.

Remember further that I am identifying patterns of relations between brain processes, trajectories of belief, and historical-cultural expressions.

> I assume that beliefs reflect brain processes.
>
> I assume that these combine as people create highly coherent realities, or what in effect are socio-historical and cultural-theological universes of meaning.
>
> I assume that the several minds, though not discrete in themselves, are distinct patterns of approach to meaning.
>
> I assume that these value orientations—theological convictions to use a less neutral construct—represent the interweaving of cognitive processes and social influences.

Most fundamental of all, I relate, though not equate, the human mind and the mind of God. They are reciprocal. To the degree the brain is limited in its functioning to that degree the perceived mind of God is limited.

Basic Background

Before I describe the several minds it is necessary to say just a little about the input-output systems as a whole. The sequences of what comes in and how it goes out help establish the suggested configuration of each of the four minds.

Basically the brain works with data that ranges from simple input to complex output.[1] The back of the brain—its posterior regions—takes in information, codes it, and combines it—in that order. The anterior, or front of the brain, transforms that information into general data, simplifies it, and acts upon it—in that order. The sequence, then, is straight-forward: the Receiving System moves from coding data to combining it; the Using System proceeds from regulating data to doing something with it. What "comes in" is developed from the simple to the complex; what "goes out" progresses from the complex to the simple. Regardless of whether the left or right hemisphere takes the lead, the sequences of simple-to-complex and complex-to-simple are the same.

The cortex grows and decays in the same sequence. Coding areas develop first and are the last to go. Complex areas mature last and under normal conditions decline first. After complex activity disappears simple activity continues. Apart from development and decay these areas are suggestive of processing preferences. Mental activity discloses what Michael Polanyi identified as "an ascending sequence of principles," a "rising series of relations" of consciousness and responsibility.[2] Although such levels of consciousness and responsibility are difficult to isolate with accuracy, configurations of orientation and organization can be discerned.

Based on the input/output systems of left and right brain, I propose a fourfold typology of mind-states.[3] The tendency to receive life through sensory input may show itself as either a naming mind or an immersed mind. The tendency to act upon life through motor output appears as either an analyzing mind or an imaginative mind. Each reflects fully functioning consciousness.

I will describe each of these "minds" as metaphors of meaning. That is, they crystallize a universe of relationships among levels of complexity which range from cognitive processes through socio-historical patterns to cultural-theological expressions. Genetic inheritance, social influence, and cultural circumstances combine to shape the central features of each. Once I have elaborated these prototypical minds we can then use the metaphor to assess various historical mind-states.

TWO MINDS/FOUR MIND-SETS

The Redeeming Mind of the Left Brain

The hermeneutics of proclamation is a technical way of referring to the redeeming activity of God. As Ricoeur demonstrated, the "emergence of the word from the numinous is . . . the primordial trait that rules all the other differences" between the trajectory of proclamation and manifestation.[4] For this mind Word and Deed are primary.

Whether the medium of communication is speaking or writing, the interpreted word is the basic feature. The ear, the auditory sensory system of the left brain, takes the lead since instruction and transformation are more important than appreciating and affirming. "Hear, O Israel . . ." (Deuteronomy 5:1) or "You have heard it said . . . but I say unto you . . ." (Matthew 5:21:22). Theology, as the articulated conceptions of God, is "organized around certain fundamental discourses,[5] such as, the story of Exodus, the teaching of the Torah, and the prophetic sayings. Each deals with imperatives which arise out of the tradition.

Like the word and its interpretation, the direction of history also organizes cognitive processes. Whether the end is apocalyptic destruction of all that distorts God-given reality or realized fulfillment of all that discloses God-given reality, history means uprooting. Life is a pilgrimage, a going out from an encapsulated Ur of the Chaldeans (Hebrews 11) or a deliverance from Egyptian slavery, a movement toward a yet-to-be realized consummation (Psalm 68; Ephesians 4:18).

Consider the ritual behavior which accompanies this mind-state. Instead of the repetitive cycle of the natural order—spring, summer, fall, winter—the rhythm is historical remembrance. People recite the special events that interrupt the cycle of the seasons.[6] It is the passover meal (Exodus 12:8) in which the Jews tell how Yahweh brought <u>them</u> "out of Egypt" (Deuteronomy 6:20-25). It is the worship of Christians on the first day of the week because that is when God raised Christ from the dead (Matthew 28:1). Special days are recalled because of special events that carry meaning beyond the moment.

This pattern of cognition is rational. Its logic rejects a sacred environment by questioning the apparent validity of every structure. Nothing is regarded as ultimately significant, not nature (Isaiah 44:9-20), not the family (Matthew 10:34-36; Mark 3:31-33), not established government (Deuteronomy 5:2-3 and the covenant--centered institutions of the confederacy),[7] not even religion itself (Jeremiah 7:1-11; Hebrews 9:1-14; Revelation 21:22). It demands obedience to what is still to come, calling for integrity in thought and action. It insists upon what is urgently right: the day of "righting" all relationships.[8] Here is the left mind with its right ear and right hand.[9] It is aroused to redeem humanity from its denial of what is right and to establish what is meant to be.

I distinguish two mind-sets in this rational mind—a naming mind and an analyzing one. Both construe reality as fixed and stable. Further, it suggests the vigilance of the adrenosympathetic nervous system which alerts the body to what is both interesting and dangerous in the environment.[10] God speaks and God acts.

A Naming Mind

If the left mind takes in more than it puts out, I call it A Naming Mind. The following features are evident.

First, reality is received in terms of concepts. That means input is labelled, specified, and named. This reduces ambiguity and permits what is known technically as habituation. The context is less important than the concepts. In biblical imagery it is Yahweh God bringing before Adam all the wild beasts and birds "to see what he would call them; each one was to bear the name the man would give it" (Genesis 2:19-20 JB). This is an anthropocentric universe with humanity at the center (Genesis 2:4b-3:24).[11]

Second, just as input is conceptualized so it is organized according to abstract explanations. In other words what comes in is processed objectively, taken out of its network of relationships and put into a formal schema. Simple cause-and-effect sequences and separate spheres construct a rational reality. In biblical imagery it is God shaping order out of disorder—distinguishing light and darkness, earth and sky, water and land, fish and birds, plants and animals, and conscious humanity "at the pinnacle of the creation pyramid" (Genesis 1:1-2:4a).[12]

Because of the conceptual-abstract way of thinking, words are regarded as reality. In its simpler form the left mind takes everything literally. The map is the territory. Those in exile could not sing the Lord's song in a strange land (Psalm 137:1-5).

Think of the naming mind as active. It looks for differences and sets them up as distinct entities and distinct spheres. It stabilizes flux by ignoring the passing and isolating the permanent, item-by-item.

An Analyzing Mind

If the left mind puts out more than it takes in, I regard it as An Analyzing Mind. The following features are evident.

First, reality is shaped analytically. That means it develops a rational schema with fundamental principles, standard procedures, and carefully developed plans. In biblical imagery it is spelling out The Covenant between Yahweh God and the Israelites at Sinai (Exodus 19ff; Leviticus). The regulations about stealing, cursing, coveting, farming, and real estate or about borrowing, sacrificing, courtesy to strangers, and truth-telling or about building and furnishing the sanctuary, investing priests, offering sacrifices for sins, and separating the clean from the unclean,[13] all reflect the organization of reality for responsible accountability.

Second, the analytic approach is processed systematically. Assumptions are explicit. Rationale or theory is crucial. Language has a structure which frees ideas from being enmeshed in immediate social structures.[14] The systematic elaboration postpones satisfaction or fulfillment until everything is in place. In biblical imagery it is the prophetic discernment of the Lord Yahweh showing Amos a man standing by a wall, plumbline in hand, "Look, I am going to measure my people Israel by plumb-line: no longer will I overlook their offences" (Amos 7:7-9 JB). Life is assessed as it is meant to be (Hosea 4:1-3).

Because of the analytic-systematic way of thinking, the elaboration of precise steps results in correct procedures. In this more complex yet simplified form the left mind incorporates input into explicit pieces of information. Precision reduces the surplus meaning with which facts are surrounded. Among the many maps of the territory one follows the only map that maps accurately.

The analyzing mind develops a sharp ear and a focused eye. It works with differences in order to build true reality. It redeems what is out of order by putting it in proper order. It reforms and re-formulates what appears to be according to what actually is intended.

The Creating Mind of the Right Brain

The phenomenology of the sacred is a technical way of identifying the creating activity of God. Its non-linguistic quality, an unmediated presence if you will, clearly distinguishes the trajectory of manifestation from that of proclamation. For this mind-set numinous power and natural symbols are primary.

Awesome presence never passes over completely into articulation. In Mircea Eliade's phrase, God is ever appearing in hierophanies or sacred mysteries.[15] One's imagination is intensified, seeing and hearing and sensing something "more than" ordinary in the ordinary. "The heavens declare the glory of God, the vault of heaven proclaims his handiwork" (Psalm 19:1 JB). The transcendent appears through such natural symbols as sky, earth, air, fire, and water. Thus earth and sky manifest the union of male and female.[16] Water speaks of death and rebirth.[17] Fire destroys even as it creates.[18] Ritual behavior expresses more of the rhythmic pattern of nature's cycles than the remembrance of historical events.[19] The eye and the body, the visual and kinesthetic sensory systems of the right brain, take the lead since imaginative meaningfulness preempts exact certainty.

This pattern is relational. Life is known by its connectedness (cf. Genesis 35:9-15 and Jacob's becoming Israel). It flows out everywhere and anywhere. By celebrating the worthwhileness of all that is, a stone, a tree, a circle, a cross, a labyrinth, a festival, each calls for personal involvement. Everything is hallowed (John 1:1-4)—the natural world (Psalm 104; Job 38ff), the family (Genesis 1:28; 9:1; Deuteronomy 5:16; Ecclesiasticus 7:27-28), established government (2 Samuel 5:1-3 and Israelite monarchies; Mark 12:17; John 19:11; Romans 13:2-7), [20] the religious institution itself (1 Corinthians 12:27). It assumes trust in what is here right now. "Ever since God created the worlds his everlasting power and deity—however invisible—have been there for the mind to see in the things he has made" (Romans 1:20 JB). And what Paul had pointed to in the natural world becomes more explicit in the Pauline poetry of Colossians (1:15-17 JB) where Christ "is the image of the unseen God for in him were created all things in heaven and on earth: everything visible and invisible, Thrones, Dominations, Sovereignties, Powers—all things were created through him and for him. Before anything was created, he existed, and he holds all things in unity." Here is the right mind with its left ear and left hand[21] responding to the inexhaustible manifestations of meaning. God creates a cosmos that vibrates with visions of the real.

I distinguish two mind-sets in this relational mind—an immersed mind and an imaginative one. Both process reality as appearing and reappearing presence. Further, it suggests the responsiveness of the parasympathetic nervous system which relaxes bodily processes in adapting to the environment.[22] God creates and re-creates.

An Immersed Mind

If the right mind takes in more than it puts out, it is An Immersed Mind. The following features are evident.

First, reality is received perceptually. That means input is direct, tangible, unnamed, all-of-a-piece. Because of its ambiguity one needs the context to know what is being conveyed, whether that is a gesture or a word. In biblical imagery it is shepherds going to Bethlehem, the city associated with the Davidic tradition, to understand what had appeared to them and then returning to and remaining in the same context (Luke 2:8-20).

Second, since reality is received directly, it is organized concretely or wholistically. Because of nuances words require knowing the context to be understood. In fact words serve a double purpose: "They convey information" and "they also express the social structure, embellish and reinforce it."[23] In biblical imagery it is the experience of Yahweh as the good Shepherd and generous host (Psalm 23:1-4, 5-6) which becomes the sacramental context of baptism and eucharist.

Because of the perceptual-concrete way of thinking, the tangible or symbolic is taken as reality. In its simpler form the right mind experiences being immersed in an encompassing environment. Mosaic impressions are the territory. God-and-government together.

Think of the immersed mind as receptive. It sees commonalities and experiences a coherence between outer forms and inner meanings. Within its assumptive context it permits variations, all-at-once.

An Imaginative Mind

If the right mind puts out more than it takes in, I consider it An Imaginative Mind. The following features are evident.

First, reality is shaped imaginatively. That means personal values, pragmatic procedures, and plans emerge as a uniquely woven tapestry. Multiple causations reveal a relational reality. In biblical imagery it is knowing that "the earth is the Lord's" (Psalm 24:1 KJ) and that humanity's dominion derives from that relationship (Psalm 8).

Second, the imaginative approach is processed wholistically. Assumptions are implicit. Connections are basic. Language opens itself to multiple meanings—metaphorical, figurative, suggestive.[24] In biblical imagery it is affirming that "we are already the children of God but what we are to be in the future has not yet been revealed; all we know is that when it is revealed we shall be like (God) because we shall see (God) as (God) really is" (1 John 3:2 JB).

Because of the imaginative-wholistic way of thinking, impressions are varied. In this more complex yet unified form the right mind transforms everything into images. For instance, "I am the rose of Sharon" (Song of Songs 2:1). "I am the way, the truth, and the life" (John 14:6). Lady Julian of Norwich saw that God as "(o)ur

Mother by nature and grace—for he would become our Mother in everything—laid the foundation of his work in the Virgin's womb with great and gentle condescension."[25] Meister Eckhart declared that "The eye with which I see God is the same eye with which God sees me . . . one vision or seeing, and one knowing and loving."[26] Everything bears larger meanings, surplus nuances, intimations that put us into multiple realities. All the mosaics of the territory are real. As Eckhart put it: "God never tied (our) salvation to any pattern. Whatever possibilities inhere in any pattern of life inhere in all, because God has given it so and denied it to none."[27]

The imaginative mind cultivates sensitive eyes and ears. It processes relationships by generating a trustworthy reality. It shows forth what is in all its subtlety and splendor.

Let me summarize the functioning mind-states (Table 5). Vigilant in intent, the redeeming mind stresses obedience to the proclamation of word-and-deed. It may deal more with naming the urgently right or with systematically analyzing the one right way. In parallel fashion, the responsive creating mind opens up trust by celebrating the manifestations of awesome power in natural symbols. It may stay immersed in a single mosaic of the ultimately real or integrate many mosaics in an ever-emerging wholeness. The rational mind redeems what has been lost. This mode is the "I Act" of power. The relational mind creates what is being realized. This mode is the "I Am" of presence. Together they re-present and express metaphorically the one mind of God and the one mind of Humanity. Just as God acts to make real what is right, so we are meant to make real what is right.

ASSESSING ADEQUACY

Ordinarily, which mind dominates appears to involve two issues—which is fastest and which cares the most.[28]

The hemisphere which can deal with the perceived task the quickest fires first. The other hemisphere stays

Table 5. **Functioning Mind-States**

The Redeeming Mind of the Left Brain	The Creating Mind of the Right Brain
vigilant	responsive
rational	relational
Theological Emphases	
word and history	awesome power and natural symbolism
proclamation and redemption	manifestation and creation
obedience and integrity	trust and involvement
Simple Input	
A Mind That Names	An Immersed Mind
*conceptual orientation	*perceptual orientation
- labels	- direct
- little ambiguity	- much ambiguity
- independent of context	- dependent on context
*abstract operation	*concrete operation
- objective	- personal
- simple cause-and-effect	- multiple causation
*the map is the territory	*the mosaic is the territory
- differences sharpened	- similarities identified
- permanence established	- patterns vary
Complex Output	
A Mind That Analyzes	An Imaginative Mind
*analytic approach	*associative approach
- underlying principles	- personal values
- standard procedures	- pragmatic procedures
- developed plans	- emerging plans
*systematic intent	*wholistic intent
- explicit assumptions	- shared values
- basic rationale	- basic constellations
- precision	- metaphoric
- delayed satisfaction	- present satisfaction
*the right map maps the territory	*many mosaics present the territory
- proper order	- meaningful ordering
- true reality	- trustworthy reality
- the urgently right	- the ultimately real

"off." This is called "resolution (of the problem-solving task) by speed."[29] The left half handles item analysis better, the right relational patterns. Further, the hemisphere which gets reinforced also tends to take over. This has been called "resolution (of the problem-solving task) by motivation."[30] Although the evidence derives from experiments with monkeys, David Galin speculated that it applies to humans as well.[31] The capacity of the left brain to manipulate the environment because of its step-by-step processing may contribute to its being used and viewed as "dominant." By the age of three labelling and languaging take center stage. The rational mind acts more assertively than the relational mind.

Under normal circumstances each mind acts as the whole mind. No matter which brain takes the lead full consciousness is present. Sometimes we rely on only one sensory system such as hearing or seeing; other times we use other systems such as sensing or smelling. The fully functioning mind engages both brains as it draws upon every sensory system. As the experience of Pentecost suggests, the people heard and saw and felt (Acts 2:1-4). Every mind, any mind, each mind, can enter into and be the bearer of God (cf. Revelation 21:12,21).

Consider an example of consciously utilizing the whole head. Mstislav Rostropovitch is one of the leading cellists in the world. On the eve of becoming director of the National Symphony in Washington, a reporter interviewed him.[32] He talked so fast he stumbled over words, his lips trembled, his eyes lit up, he bubbled like a child, totally absorbed in describing his excitement.

Rostropovitch spoke of the orchestra as a collective instrument, which is a right mind orientation. "The sound fascinates me, the timbre. I want to play orchestra music as I hear it, which is how I play the cello." Then he drew an analogy between rational performance and relational creation.

"After a certain point I could not have gone further with the cello if I hadn't conducted, hadn't heard, seen, and felt outside my own instrument." One "must move outside (one's) own discipline in order to make a leap in imagination." He combined the auditory, visual, and kinesthetic re-presentational systems as well as differentiated them.

To cross the chasm between what is "one's own" and what is "more than one's own," as Rostropovitch described it, requires experience with what is "other than one's own." In the language of neuropsychology that means the whole brain with all its input-and-output. To stay with one mind-set only reinforces what has been. The known remains set; the unfamiliar grows less inviting. The emerging whole is lost. The unintended effect is a less than adequate mind.

A shift between the two brains and among the sensory systems generates unsuspected possibilities. Comparisons enhance commonalities, with contrasts enriching differences. The strange quickens the familiar because of fresh perception. The familiar clarifies the strange by putting it into a frame of reference. Synergy results. Sensory systems combine and recombine in a kaleidoscopic, stereophonic symphony of harmonizing diversity beyond the capability of any single brain or system. The receiving mind takes in what is there both perceptually and conceptually; the initiating mind fits pieces together in ways that matter. Full consciousness activates the whole head.

Without sensory input, whether isolated sensations or concrete impressions, the redeeming mind hardens into a sterile rationalism and the creating mind spins a web of illusory relationships. Similarly, without cognitive output, whether analytic sequences or synthesized expressions, the redeeming mind withers into literalism and the creating mind fosters a misplaced concreteness.

In detailing the polar tension between proclamation and manifestation Ricoeur's concern parallelled this neuropsychological perspective. From a theological point of view the uttered word of proclamation needs the renewing power of presence if the word is not to become merely "abstract and cerebral."[33] Only the incarnation, concrete sensory input to make the analogy explicit, "ceaselessly reinterpreted gives this word something to say." That immediate "something," in Ricoeur's view, is addressed to "our imagination and our heart" as much as to "our understanding and will . . . in short, to the whole human being."

Ricoeur sought to avoid pitfalls which would collapse proclamation and manifestation into each other or else separate them from each other. Like the two halves of the head, these poles do not constitute "a simple identity" nor "a sterile antinomy" nor yet "an unmediated dichotomy."[34] He argued for "some mediation" between the phenomenology of the sacred and the hermeneutics of the kerygmatic. Humanity requires sacred presence, that otherness of meaning which manifests itself in privileged places and people, in special times and rituals.[35] Like the left brain's observing and explaining right brain activity, proclamation derives its power from the fact that it reflects, reconstitutes, and reaffirms the sacred wholeness of our human setting. Word and manifestation are reconciled, re-united, according to Ricoeur and those of us within the Christian tradition, in the affirmation that "the Word became flesh and we beheld his glory" (John 1:14 JB).

By including all the sensory systems in both their active and receptive modes we have an analytical tool for assessing the adequacy of various states of mind (Table 6). We can identify regressive, functional, and creative patterns. These reflect how the human mind works and by implication how that mind understands God to work.

A mind exhibits <u>regressive</u> features in one of two ways. First, if it is deficient, it uses only one mode and one system. The other mode and other input/output are neglected. The two modes function as completely separate systems. The resulting mind-set makes activity stilted, mechanical, and at times inappropriate. It insists upon the map or mosaic as the sole way the mind works. Second, if it is disturbed, the two modes compete with each other over which takes charge and/ or conflict about the task to be handled.[36] Sensory systems map dissonant information. Repression, avoidance, ambiva-

Table 6. **Assessing Adequacy**

The adequacy of functioning mind-sets can be assessed on a continuum from deficient/disturbed to creative/synergistic

Adequacy		Processing Modes (all-at-once/step-by/step)	Re-presentational Systems (auditory, visual, kinesthetic)
Regressive:			
	deficient	one mode only other mode ignored at times inappropriate	one system/one map
	disturbed	one mode avoided modes compete &/or conflict	systems/maps are denied systems/maps are dissonant
Functional:		modes alternate depending on task modes supplement, complement, &/or contrast	systems/maps converge
Creative:		modes integrated or interchangeable	systems/maps are differentiated & synergistic

lence, or paralysis can characterize the way the mind works.[37]

A mind is <u>functional</u> if the two modes alternate, depending on the task. At least two of the sensory systems map the environment in ways that are congruent and convergent. The result makes for a conventional realism. While the two brains appear polar, the dominant one draws on the other in ways that supplement, complement, or contrast with its own activity.

A mind functions <u>creatively</u> when it combines all input and output synergistically. The two halves and the various sensory systems achieve a reality of which none is capable by itself. Here is the level of shifts in paradigms, such as Martin Luther's insistence on scripture over tradition or quantum physics going beyond Newtonian physics. Both brains and all systems work as one. To use Gregory Bateson's formulation it takes "steps to an ecology of mind."[38]

The key to adequate functioning is partnership, cooperation, non-competing processing between the two halves and their sensory systems. Either half may be preferred in its simpler or more complex form—receptive input or active output. With the full flow of information, however, both rational and relational processes "combine to program a unitary pattern of behavior."[39] People use whatever works best for them in handling a task. Every act utilizes the whole head.

Two Modes/Two Theologies

By analogy God acts to make-whole what is created whole in two ways. And human beings, made in the image of God (Genesis 1:26), participate in that power of whole-making. The functioning minds manifest the shaping of what matters most. As William James expressed the emerging evolutionary conviction: "Mind and world . . . have evolved together, and in consequence are something of a mental fit . . . The special interactions between the outer order and the order of consciousness" suggest that "<u>mental life is primarily teleological</u>; that is to say, that our various ways of feeling and thinking have grown to be what they are because of their utility in shaping . . . (our) 'adjustment of inner to outer relations.'"[40] God is present within the mind of each of us even though our individual minds are incapable of manifesting the full mind of meaning. Only in and through community can the limitations of our minds be discovered and the contributions of our minds be realized.

The evidence of how the brain works helps us avoid traditional struggles between revelation and reason. Revelation reflects the wholistic patterning of right brain process, while reason operates in the sequential logic of left brain process. Neither can be reduced to the other nor need they be in conflict with the other.[41] As in the model of complementarity in quantum physics, the apparently conflicting modes have rationales of their own, neither can be subsumed under the other yet each is dependent upon the other. If fact, the evidence of working brain and functioning minds clearly demonstrates that the rational and relational mind-sets are one mind.

A right mind strategy attends to what is, in its rhythms and cycles, already-always present, fulfilled and fulfilling, affirming The Way Things Are. People celebrate universal experiences of birth-and-death, commitments-transitions-losses, in rituals that transform what could be ordinary into what is special or sacred. The creating of life occurs right here/right now (Psalm 118:24), in the new creation of the old creation (2 Corinthians 5:17), in the everywhere present Promised Land in which God becomes all-in-all (Hebrews 11:8-16). This mode is the "I Am" of presence.

A left mind strategy works on what ought to be, in its structure and function, its direction and development, not-yet achieved, delayed and postponed, identifying The Way Things Are To Be. People communicate their liberation from constricting environments through prophetic utterances and ethical-political acts. The redeeming of life remains not-yet complete/still-to-come, in the eternal pilgrimage of making everything new

(Revelation 21:5) as we become like God (1 John 3:2). This mode is the "I Act" of power.

The left mind power arises from right mind presence. No word fully declares the numinous. Further, a word is necessary to transform natural symbols, such as bread and wine, into disclosures of what matters to the genuinely human (1 Corinthians 11:23-27a). For Christians, Jesus as the Christ, the Logos, the Word, "unites rational structure and creative power." He manifests the New Being without distortion.[42] "Something more" than ordinary is necessary for new being in a new reality. We are to love all with the all that we are (Mark 12:28-34).

The concept of two minds, whether in our human processing or in my use of mind as a metaphor of meaning, is more than basic neuroscience. Although intimately related, brain and mind are not equivalent. No electrical stimulation of the cortex causes a person "to believe or to decide" anything.[43] The brain is a necessary but insufficient condition for human life. Nor does culture, despite its pervasive influence, exert the last word about cosmic connections. I infer from the double processing of the brain/mind a double processing in the human universe, the world of purposes and meanings.

The symbolic transformation of sensory input marks the interface between brain and mind, between a finite context and an infinite cosmos. The regularities of the brain specify how things work, but the emergent features of mind precipitate the infinite ways in how things function. Language represents the fundamental consequence of unequal halves, the division of labor between item analysis and relational framing. It constitutes consciousness, that re-presenting of sensory data for human purposes. Without language there would be no human culture.

Theological implications of language and symbolic transformations of sensory input have generated tensions through the centuries. When, in the nineteenth century, Friedrich Schleiermacher (1768-1834) emphasized the importance of "feeling" and Georg Wilhelm Friedrich Hegel (1770-1831) stressed the importance of "thought," the conflict reminds us that such dichotomies are not restricted to the twentieth century. Paul Tillich suggested that back in the third century C.E. Clement of Alexandria anticipated the argument when he noted "that if animals had a religion, it would be mute, without words." Tillich went on to assert: "Reality precedes thought; it is equally true, however, that thought shapes reality."[44]

In sum, symbolic consciousness—in its thought-ful and feeling-ful expressions—generates human differences and dilemmas. How we deal with these is the issue. The mind as an analytical metaphor enables us to investigate such divine-human consciousness.

CAUTIONS

Just as I qualified the case of brain specialization in Chapter Two, so I caution even more about the speculative nature of the analytical metaphor. Beyond the complexity of hand dominance, gender difference, and the nature of the evidence itself lie two crucial factors: cultural relativism and masculine domination.

First, the matter of cultural relativism. The nature of cultural bias is complicated. The left brain simplifies data. Its abstracting and specializing strategy creates a stable reality in a way that increases knowledge by accumulation. The right brain multiplies data exponentially. Its experiential and imaginative strategy generates an ever-changing scene, resulting in a wisdom that cannot be passed objectively.

Furthermore, the left brain appears more assertive than the right.[45] It exercises more control of information-processing and problem-solving. In fact in development first claim goes to language, propositional needs, and expressive activity.[46] Culture itself derives from such priority of processing. As the prologue of the Gospel According to John and the first chapter of Genesis affirm: in the beginning is the Word. Yet different cultures reflect different assumptions about left mind steps and right mind relations.

The Judaeo-Christian tradition has perceived God in terms of historical activity, most specifically the deliverance from Egyptian oppression and the conquering of the sting of death in the resurrection of Jesus as the Christ. God intends the right order of creation by reordering the disorder of sin and death. This vie is biased on the side of human asymmetry. The redeeming mind directs what is to happen based on the creating mind of what has been made.

Not everyone shares that assumption.

For instance, Zen Buddhists reject the centrality of the conceptual. They believe that abstractions—in whatever form—are responsible for desires, longings, differentiation, intentions, directions, disturbances, and deficiencies. In short, the left mind makes people "anxious" to express themselves.

Zen emphasizes original asymmetry.[47] Such asymmetry destroys every physical and mental form in "the Self-Awareness of the Formless Self." Distinctions of body-brain, brain-mind, and mind-soul disappear. Only "the Self That is not Anything" remains. What is truly inside has neither inside nor outside as "Presence" replaces the "ideas" of transcendence and immanence.

For Zen Buddhists, asymmetry "means the lack of regularity," "the negation of fixed forms," "the manifestation of No Form as the negation of adherence to any perfection of form." Both left mind maps and right mind mosaics are meaningless. Only "what is is." The picture of Bodhidharma, the traditional founder of Zen Buddhism, conveys rough formlessness. He "looks more like a pirate than a saint," according to one interpreter.[48]

The assumption of original asymmetry differs radically from the assumption of human asymmetry. In truth, the asymmetries are reversed. Zen negates complexity, because for Zen, only simplicity participates in a unity deeper than distinctions. Without mind, which means the consciousness of both item and relational processing, people are freed from attachment in order to "take on any form because of not having any form." Only in formless form does serenity remain undisturbed. Only then does nature, the timeless, the intentionless, the directionless, the nonordering "being as we originally are," carry one into an undifferentiated oneness of non-consciousness. The Zen "word" is a Wordless Word.

I point to differences between human and original asymmetry to suggest that each assumption leads to a different theological consciousness. How people value the two modes is predisposed by assumptions about hemisphere specialization. Those assumptions affect not only perceptions about God but also understandings of God as God.

The second qualification concerns masculine domination of cultural expressions. I have already noted that female brains tend to be less lateralized than male brains. Implications of that gender-related, though not gender-specific, phenomenon are speculative. First, women exhibit less specialization of hemispheric activity. The step-by-step and all-at-once processes are not divided as sharply as they are for men. The surrounding world is more available for support and nurturance. In short, less lateralized functioning suggests more integrated experience.

In contrast, more lateralized functioning in men makes a sharper division of labor. One-step-at-a-time strategy contrasts with all-at-once strategy. Males struggle more to name their experience, primarily because their language capacity develops later than their perceptual capacity. Thus the world is experienced and described by them in starker contrasts. Dichotomies and dualities appear more common, and conflicts between the contrasts are reported more often. The world looms as more of a challenge and more of a threat. Specialized functioning, I believe, sets up the condition under which sequential and simultaneous ways of thinking can compete and clash more intensely.

As a consequence, disturbed and deficient features in historical developments may reflect a male-dominated orientation.[49] Regardless of a left mind or a right mind preference, one side has been used to the neglect or rejection of the other precisely because of patriarchy. Competition for attentional dominance, thereby, may have contributed to the clash of cultures, internally as well as externally. Male pride directs energy to activity in the larger world.[50] The masculine mind tends to be a divide-and-conquer mind-set.

As women gain in authority and power I would anticipate a more inclusive approach.[51] A less competitive struggle for mastery and control ought to emerge as these early maturers in language ability and late maturers in perceptual ability soften threatening dichotomies into a richness of differences. Female caring directs attention to relationships. The feminine mind reveals more of a unifying mind-set.[52]

The gender patterns may reflect more biased socialization and stereotyping than what men and women actually can do. A female-dominated culture will exhibit different dilemmas, not necessarily better conditions. Sexism begets distortion in both male and female. My hope would be that as culture grows less sexist and as our understanding of the desirability of utilizing both brains increases, gender-related patterns will modify. Males will have less need to deny dependency and vulnerability; females will exhibit less need to deny power and aspirations. The pride which now tends to be more associated with the male-mind will be transformed into a sustained aspiration for everyone. The care that is associated more with the female-mind will be transformed into a desire to conserve what is valued and valuable. A more genuine humanity will both allow differences and encourage differences.

All this is speculative. I insert it as a caution to underscore the fact that historical forces reflect more male-brain than female-brain processing. What awaits us as more of our humanity is realized can be discerned only dimly.

TRANSITION

I have completed my summary of how the brain works and have elaborated functioning minds as an analytic tool. The concept of mind links the human significance of the brain and theological concepts developed in speaking about God. A left mind pattern utilizes rational vigilance and the imperative instructions of proclamation. In so doing it names and analyzes what is urgently right. A right mind pattern shows the relational responsiveness of numinous presence and natural symbolism. This comes about by its being immersed in and imaginatively integrating what is ultimately real.

Together these two patterns provide a typology of mind with which to assess activity as regressive, functional, and creative. Such generalizations, however, are qualified by the variations revealed in differences between left and right handers, women and men, and cultural convictions.

Even so, the organized regularities of the brain and the emergent features of mind help us understand metaphorically how adequately our minds function and how fully we perceive God's ways of being God. Mind is the meaning of the brain as God is the significance of mind.

In the sections which follow I use the metaphor of mind to analyze historical developments in Byzantine and Medieval cultures.

NOTES

1. Luria, THE WORKING BRAIN (n.1/1), 43-101; A.R. Luria, "The Human Brain and Conscious Activity." In G.S. Schwartz and D. Shapiro, eds., CONSCIOUSNESS AND SELF-REGULATION: Advances in Research and Theory. Vol. 2 (New York: Plenum Press, 1978), 12-19.

2. Michael Polanyi, "Life's Irreducible Structure," Science (1968) 160:1308-1312.

3. Karl Pribram proposed "at least four brains" and "the evidence suggests that even four brains are not enough; we are dealing in fact with more than four" ("Discussion: Interhemispheric Integration in the Visual System." In Mountcastle [n.2/12], 107-111). Two of the brains were analogue and digital, distinguishing "existential discrimination, served by the classical projection systems, and differential discriminations, served by the related 'association' cortex." Further he identified two brains that established stability in space and time, respectively. The "perceptual" brain "maps the everchanging spatial array of our external environment from some of its constant features." The "homeostatic" brain manages the behavior "in the face of changes that take place over time."

   Other four-fold typologies abound and have influenced this analysis. These include: from an intrapsychic and cosmic perspective Carl G. Jung, PSYCHOLOGICAL TYPES: The Psychology of Individuation. Trans. by H. Godwin Baynes (New York: Harcourt, Brace & Co., 1926); James B. Ashbrook, "The Search for a Usable Image: One Way of Conceiving of Man and His World," Foundations, July-September 1970, 207-220; idem., HUMANITAS: human becoming & being human (Nashville, Tenn.: Abingdon Press, 1973), 117-133; from an interpersonal perspective Uriel G. Foa, "Convergences in the Analysis of the Structure of Interpersonal Behavior," Psychological Review, 1961, 68:341-353; Jerry S. Wiggins, "Circumplex Models of Interpersonal Behavior in Clinical Psychology." In HANDBOOK OF RESEARCH METHODS IN CLINICAL PSYCHOLOGY, edited by Philip C. Kendall and James N. Butcher (New York: John Wiley & Sons, 1982), 183-221; Donald J. Kiesler, "The 1982 Interpersonal Circle: A Taxonomy for Complementarity in Human Transactions," Psychological Review (July 1983):185-214; from a social system, general theory of action perspective Talcott Parsons and Edward A. Shils, eds., TOWARD A GENERAL THEORY OF ACTION: Theoretical Foundations for the Social Sciences (New York: Harper Torchbooks, [1951] 1962); and from an anthropological perspective Mary Douglas, NATURAL SYMBOLS: Explorations in Cosmology. With a new introduction (New York: Pantheon Books, [1970, 1973] 1982). Eugene G. d'Aquili hypothesized six neuroanatomical cognitive operators involved in his biogenetic structural analysis of mythmaking and its ritual expression ("The Myth-Ritual Complex: A Biogenetic Structural Analysis," Zygon, vol. 18, no. 3 [September 1983]: 247-269).

4. Ricoeur, "Manifestation and Proclamation" (n.1/42, 21). See Laeuchi, RELIGION AND ART IN CONFLICT (n.0/8), for a careful analysis of the diverse and clashing trends in the Judeo-Christian tradition between the positive passion for truth and the existentialist passion for meaning as these were expressed in various forms of the verbal/visual and idea/icon dilemma. Also see Herbert Read, ICON AND IDEA: The Function of Art in the Development of Human Consciousness (Cambridge: Harvard University Press, 1955).

5. Ricoeur, "Manifestation and Proclamation" (n.1/42).

6. Victor and Edith Turner, IMAGE AND PILGRIMAGE IN CHRISTIAN CULTURE: Anthropological Perspectives (New York: Columbia University Press, 1978); George S. Worgul, Jr., FROM MAGIC TO METAPHOR: A Validation of the Christian Sacraments.

Foreword by Piet Fransen, S.J. (New York: Paulist Press, 1980).

7. I. Rabinowitz, "Government." In THE INTERPRETER'S DICTIONARY OF THE BIBLE: E-J (n.1/36), 451-462.

8. See E. Jenni, "Day of Judgment." In THE INTERPRETER'S DICTIONARY OF THE BIBLE: A-D (n.1/36), 783-784.

9. Robert Hertz, "The Pre-eminence of the Right Hand: A Study in Religious Polarity." In RIGHT & LEFT: Essays on Dual Symbolic Classification. Edited and with an Introduction by Rodney Needham. Foreword by E.E. Evans-Prichard (Chicago: The University of Chicago Press, 1973), 3-31.

10. Nathan, THE NERVOUS SYSTEM (n.1/1), 206-209.

11. Ashbrook, HUMANITAS (n.3 above), 146-158.

12. Ibid., 145.

13. Mary Douglas, PURITY AND DANGER: An Analysis of the concepts of pollution and taboo (London: Routledge & Kegan Paul, [1966] 1980).

14. Basil Bernstein, CLASS, CODES AND CONTROL: vol. 1 Theoretical Studies towards a sociology of knowledge (London: Routledge & Kegan Paul, 1971).

15. Mircea Eliade, COSMOS AND HISTORY: The Myth of the Eternal Return (New York: Harper Torchbook, [1954] 1959); idem., THE SACRED AND THE PROFANE: The Nature of Religion (New York: Harper Torchbooks, [1957] 1961).

16. See Erich Neumann, THE ORIGINS AND HISTORY OF CONSCIOUSNESS. Vol 1. Translated by R.F.C. Hull (New York: Harper Torchbooks, 1962).

17. For water symbolism see B. W. Anderson, THE INTERPRETER'S DICTIONARY OF THE BIBLE: R-Z (n.1/36), 806-810; J.E. Cirlot, A DICTIONARY OF SYMBOLS. Second Edition. Translated by Jack Sage. Foreword by Herbert Read (New York: Philosophical Library, [1971] 1974), 364-367.

18. For fire symbolism see E.M. Good, THE INTERPRETER'S DICTIONARY OF THE BIBLE: E-J (n.1/36), 268-269; Cirlot, A DICTIONARY OF SYMBOLS (n.17 above), 105-106.

19. Luis Maldonado and David Powers (eds.), SYMBOL AND ART IN WORSHIP. English Language Editor Marcus Lefébure (New York: The Seabury Press, 1980); d'Aquili and Laughlin, Jr., "The Neurobiology of Myth and Ritual" (n.0/7); d'Aquili, "The Myth-Ritual Complex" (n.3 above); Victor Turner, THE RITUAL PROCESS: Structure and Anti-Structure (London: Routledge & Kegan Paul, 1969); idem., "Body, Brain, and Culture," Zygon, vol. 18, no. 3 (September 1983):221-246.

20. Rabinowitz, "Government" (n.7 above).

21. Rodney Needham, "The Left-Hand of the Mugwe: An Analytical Note on the Structure of Meru Symbolism." In Needham, RIGHT & LEFT (n.9 above), 109-127; Jerome S. Bruner, ON KNOWING: Essays for the Left Hand (Cambridge, Mass.: Belknap Press, [1962] 1963).

22. Nathan, THE NERVOUS SYSTEM, (n.1/1), 209.

23. Douglas, NATURAL SYMBOLS, (n.3 above), 23.

24. Watzlawick, THE LANGUAGE OF CHANGE (n.2/82).

25. Julian of Norwich, REVELATIONS OF DIVINE LOVE. Translated into Modern English and with an introduction by Clifton Walters (Baltimore: Penguin Books, [1966] 1976), Chp. Sixty, 169.

26. Raymond B. Blakney, ed., MEISTER ECKHART: A Modern Translation (New York: Harper Torchbooks, [1941] 1957), 288.

27. Ibid., 23.

28. Galin, "The Two Modes of Consciousness," (n.1/4), 43-44.

29. Jerre Levy, Colwyn Trevarthen, and Roger W. Sperry, "Perception of Bilateral Chimeric Figures Following Hemisphere Deconnection," Brain, (1972) 95:61-78.

30. Michael S. Gazzaniga, "Changing Hemisphere Dominance By Changing Reward Probability in Split-Brain Monkeys," Experimental Neurology, (1971) 33:412-419.

31. Galin, "The Two Modes of Consciousness" (n.1/4).

32. G. Feifer, "Rostropovitch in Midpassage," Saturday Review, March 5, 1977, 35-39. For a subsequent critique of how he has accomplished what he intended, see Tim Page, "Is Rostropovitch the Wrong Man for the Job?" Saturday Review, May 1982, 16-18.

33. Ricoeur, "Manifestation and Proclamation" (n.1/42), 35.

34. Ibid., 13.

35. In arguing against viewing evidence of sacred manifestation as merely archaic residuals, Ricoeur (ibid., 31-32) waxed eloquently about our "search of privileged places be they our birthplace, the scene of our first love, or the theater of some important historical occurrence—a battle, a revolution, the execution ground of patriots." "We return to such places," he went on, "because there a more than everyday reality erupted and because the memory attached to what took place there preserves us from being simply errant vagrants in the world.

Can the act of construction and habitation be entirely desacralized without losing all significance? Can we abolish the symbolism of the threshold, the door, and the entrance, along with every ritual of entrance and welcome? Can we completely desacralize birth—our coming into the world—and death—our passing to the place of rest? Can we strip them of every rite of passage without completely degrading (humanity) into a utensil, without ceaselessly giving (it) up to a manipulation that finds its conclusion in the liquidation of useless or worn-out people? Can we abolish all the other rites of initiation without life's 'turning points' themselves becoming simple—insignificant transitions?"

36. Gazzaniga, THE BISECTED BRAIN (n.1/1); Gazzaniga and LeDoux, THE INTEGRATED MIND (n.1/1), 142-145.

37. Grinder and Bandler, THE STRUCTURE OF MAGIC II, (n.2/80).

38. Gregory Bateson, STEPS TO AN ECOLOGY OF MIND (New York: Ballentine Books, [1972] 1978).

39. Kinsbourne, "Hemisphere Specialization," (n.2/73), 413.

40. William James. PSYCHOLOGY (New York: Henry Holt and Company, [1892] 1893), 3-4.

41. Thomas R. Blackburn, "Sensuous-Intellectual Complementarity in Science," Science, (1971) 172:1003-1007. Reprinted in Ornstein (n.1/1), 27-40. See Lawrence LeShan, THE MEDIUM, THE MYSTIC, AND THE PHYSICIST: Toward A General Theory of the Paranormal (New York: The Viking Press, 1974) and idem., ALTERNATE REALITIES: The Search for the Full Human Being (New York: M. Evans and Company, Inc., 1976) for an attempt to describe the convergence of the new view of physical reality with the older view of mystical reality.

42. Paul Tillich, SYSTEMATIC THEOLOGY. vol. 2: Christ and Existence (London: James Nisbet & Co., Ltd., 1957), 128, 137.

43. Penfield, THE MYSTERY OF THE MIND (n.1/4), 77.

44. Paul Tillich, A HISTORY OF CHRISTIAN THOUGHT. Edited by Carl E. Braaten (London: SCM Press Ltd., 1968), xi.

45. Betty Edwards, DRAWING ON THE RIGHT SIDE OF THE BRAIN (Los Angeles: J.P. Tracher, Inc., 1979), 42.

46. Norman Geschwind, "Language and the Brain," Scientific American (April 1972) 226,4:76-83. Kenneth M. Heilman, "Language and the Brain: Relationships of Localization of Language Function to the Acquisition and Loss of Various Aspects of Language." In Chall and Mirsky (n.1/1), 143-168; and John A. Wada, "Pre-language and Fundamental Asymmetry of the Infant Brain." In Dimond and Beaumont, (n.1/1), 370-379.

47. Shin'ichi Hisamatsu, ZEN AND THE FINE ARTS. Translated by Gishin Tokiwa (Tokyo, Japan: Kodansha International Ltd., 1971).

48. Stewart T. Holmes and Chimyo Horioka, ZEN ART FOR MEDITATION (Rutland, Vt.: Charles E. Tuttle Company, [1973] 1978), 109.

49. See Juliet Mitchell, PSYCHOANALYSIS AND FEMINISM: Freud, Reich, Laing, and Women (New York: Vintage Books, [1974] 1975): "It seems to be the case that contemporary anthropology supports Freud's contention that human society in many different ways equals patriarchy" (369); M. Kay Martin and Barbara Voorhies, FEMALE OF THE SPECIES (New York: Columbia University Press, 1975), concluded "that behavioral traits correlated with sex are predominantly determined by society and secondarily by biology." They examined five ecological adaptations—foraging, horticulture, agri-

culture, pastoralism, and industrialism—and demonstrated "that the relative positions of women and men are not crystallized into typical sex patterns, but in fact vary widely in response to many interacting social and biological factors." One dramatic reversal is the nineteenth century's view of women as "the architects of ancient marriage, kinship, and political relations" and the twentieth century's "emphasis on male dominance, territoriality, and aggression as cornerstones of human society. Whereas the establishment of family, moral, and religious orders were once attributed to the restraining influences of women, males are currently given credit for both the establishment and evolutionary progression of culture" (11-15). Such variations underscore the distinction between gender-related and gender-specific features of brain processing and role behavior.

50. Robert May, SEX AND FANTASY: Patterns of Male and Female Development (New York: W.W. Norton & Company, 1980).

51. Gilligan, IN a DIFFERENT VOICE (n.2/94); May, SEX AND FANTASY (see n.50 above).

52. Jo Durden-Smith "Male and Female-Why?" (n.2/93), citing Jerre Levy, 93-94.

Part II Central Images

ARCHITECTURES OF THE MIND

The divine mind creates when it conceives; when our mind conceives things, it shapes its thinking to the forms of created realities (*assimilat*). It produces concepts or intellectual visions, not the things themselves (*Demente*, 7). 'Just as the word of God creates essences, so our mind produces copies' (*To Albergati*, 22).

Nicholas of Cusa (1401?-1464)*

*Karl Jasper, ANSELM AND NICHOLAS OF CUSA (New York: A Harvest Book, 1966), 39

Chapter Four

THE LANGUAGE OF SPACE: Two Mind-Sets

In Part I I described how the brain works—its rational step-by-step process and its relational all-at-once process.

Further, I sketched two patterns of belief—proclamation with its instructional imperatives and manifestation with its immediate appearances. These central features of brain patterns and belief trajectories contributed to developing the mind as an analytic metaphor with which to understand the human significance of the brain and the theological meanings of mind. The redeeming activity of the left mind names and analyzes what is urgently right, while the creating activity of the right is immersed in an immediate context and imaginative in its discernment of the ultimately real. Finally I proposed a way of assessing how adequately these mind-sets express fully functioning reality.

Now in Part II I explore central images of how God was perceived and expressed by two different cultures. The Judeo-Christian heritage emphasizes One God, One Mind, One Reality. Yet the Christian factor generated two stories, two minds, two realities. Although the Judeo mind was unified, the Christian mind divided. From the one body of Christ came two histories: the Byzantine East and the Latin West. In their contrast and competition the one mind of God divided. It is to that split I apply the analytical metaphor. It is in those mind-sets, I suggest, that we can identify ways in which God works in and through our minds.

Before stepping into these cultural worlds we need one more element, namely, central images to gather up multiple meanings of mind. In addition to brain and belief I add architecture. Architecture provides concrete images through which and in which brain and belief combine. When people ask where and how they can know God, they are using the language of space as a way to understand the language of Spirit. In places of presence we find archetypal meanings of what matters most to our being and becoming genuinely human. Architecture presents us with outward and visible symbols of inward and spiritual significance, in essence, architectures of the mind.

The Where and How of Meaning

In the intensity of a secluded room, with an acute awareness of a roving vigilante mob, the person who made God's presence present spoke. He spoke gently of his impending death. About to be abandoned, without visible means of support, one of the group burst out, "We do not know <u>where</u> you are going, so <u>how</u> can we know the way?" (John 14:5).

Thomas' questions to Jesus express persistent questions of humanity: where is meaning and how might we find it? Some people speak the language of eternity, that is, where is God and how can we find God? Others talk in the language of the everyday, for instance, what matters and how do we realize it? However such longing is expressed, the nature of human nature includes the quest for wholeness, the Holy Grail, finding the fulness of all that we are meant to be.

In the biblical account of humanity's becoming, the first question addressed to human beings is a question which is reciprocal to the question of where God is, namely, "Adam-Eve, where are you?" (Genesis 3:9). The inquiry triggers a sense of self-consciousness. We are called upon to make explicit what is implicit in our lives. We are asked to state our location, our position, our intentions, our actions, where and how we are oriented in reality, how and what we organize as reality. Our distortions—those precarious cognitions and limited ways of knowing—are called to account.

The contrast between the "where" of humanity and the "where" of divinity makes for an eternal tension and an endless striving. How do we get from the "here" of our lives to the "there" of their meaning?

For the Hebrews, the space of their lives included wandering in the wilderness with a shadowy cloud by day and a glowing fire by night (Exodus 13:21). Eventually, the where of God and the how of finding God came to rest on the temple mount in Jerusalem. In that place, in the holy of holies, God dwelt. And to that place humanity came. The destruction of the temple and the dispersion of the people precipitated a crisis: how can we sing the Lord's song in a strange place? (Psalm 137:4). The temple is gone, only the Wailing Wall remains.

For Christians, space for the focus of their lives was dismissed—not on this mountain nor in Jerusalem but in spirit and in truth, said Jesus (John 4:21-24). Everywhere without special space. In the vision of New Jerusalem there is no temple, no special dwelling-place (Revelation 21:22). God is become All-in-All. Twelve gates open into the City. No royal entrance. No single path. Many gates, many ways. Every gate brings humanity directly into the wholeness of the Whole. New Reality is pervasive Presence with many means to Presence.

I use the metaphor of space to explore the where and how of what matters to our humanity as human beings. From the initial shock of recognition—where are you?—to the subsequent shock of abandonment—where are you going?—where we are and where God is quicken our hearts and focus our minds. We want to be with God; we want to know God.

Job's lament puts into words our longing for meaning: "O that I knew where I might find God?" (Job 23:3 KJ). The words may be traditional but the issue is universal, namely, making sense of our human experience. Spiritual meaning can never finally free itself from physical imagery. So I press the metaphor of meaning.

> What are the spaces in which we live and move and have our being?
>
> Where do we make known what matters most?
>
> How do we show forth the truth by which we live?

People express the meanings of their lives in many ways. These range from the peculiarities of individuals to patterns of historical trajectories. Underlying these social, cultural, and cosmic expressions, as I have argued, are neuropsychological processes. These are ways in which the brain works. The human mind reveals meaningfulness and also pursues meaning. This is why I describe what I am about in this analysis as neurotheological.

To explore where we are links the physical and the imaginative. Physical space manifests symbolic space, especially in architecture. What we build suggests how we get where we want to be. In this way architecture and the architecture of mind are sacramental—outward and visible symbols of inward and spiritual reality.

The Language of Space[1]

Consider this language of space in more detail. A building discloses "an attitude toward reality."[2] As such, it symbolizes a mind-set. To identify the mind-set one must interpret the way space is structured. To interpret space we need to make explicit its implicit features, its definiteness and diffuseness, its enclosures and openings.

We experience some space as definite, solid, and permanent. Long vistas draw us in specific directions. This is true whether we are simply looking or actually walking. Because the directions are clear we can anticipate the changes which lie ahead. Because we can anticipate the changes the structure itself has a rational order free of individual input. No one has to ask "what's ahead?" It is obvious to anyone who looks ahead. Each part serves a logical function in a fixed form.

A formula for such stable space might read: definite lines plus permanent patterns add up to rational certainty.

Other space we experience as moving, indefinite, ever-changing. No one feature stands out. Our attention can wander anywhere. No logical reason explains why we look and move as we do. We simply respond to an ambiguous environment, a structure capable of eliciting many responses. As with the experience of breathing, we can feel the spatial chest expanding-and-contracting, impressions drawn in and patterns flowing out, continuously. Curving lines create ever-emerging motifs, mosaics of meaning, fleeting configurations, each of which disappears with the appearance of every fresh impression. Such subtle use of space makes the architecture suggestive. That means the immediate context creates the meaningfulness of what people experience. Every impression requires the whole scene for the space to be known.

Just as I stated a formula for stable space so I submit a formula for suggestive space, namely, curving lines plus changing patterns add up to personal meaningfulness.

Paradoxically, rational space is characterized by movement. People find themselves directed in predetermined ways. Instead of wandering about they are expected to move forward. They can anticipate what lies ahead. The paths are controlled by those who created the design. Stable space represents a logical mind-set, a mind that makes everything exact.

Equally paradoxical, suggestive space is usually distinguished by symmetry. Only when human beings mark their presence does nature reveal directional signals, such as left and right or up and down. In ambiguous space, people discover themselves responding differently at different times—differently from each other and even from themselves. Because direction is unclear, the effects of balanced space are unpredictable. Patterns vary, directions emerge. What people respond to depends more upon how everything appears at that moment than upon prescribed pathways. Suggestive space reflects a relational mind-set, a mind that makes patterns in abundance.

I link this interpretation of architecture with the architecture of the mind (see Table 7).[3] Again I speak metaphorically. Physical space conveys symbolic significance. Many gates into The Way Things Are suggest many minds or, more precisely, many ways by which people become aware of what matters and organize it. Different spaces, different dwelling places.

Stable space comes from a rational process. What we sense is controlled, convergent, and clear. Fixed objectives are built in by constructing an obvious spatial focus. That focus of attention produces a sense of certainty. Every line makes "the" purpose of the place plain, a process which reflects a dominant left mind at work.

Suggestive space appears as a result of a relational process, which indicates a right mind taking the lead. We experience spontaneous and diverging and fluid impressions . . . . whole patterns . . . . full features . . . .

Table 7. **Architecture as The Language of Space**

Experienced as:	definite solid permanent	moving/breathing shifting expanding/contracting
Therefore:	long vistas specific directions anticipate changes rational with logical function	impressions several directions subtle and unpredictable relational with interacting parts
Formula:	definite lines +permanent patterns =rational certainty	curving lines +changing patterns =personal meaningfulness
Summary:	stable and definite controlled and convergent focused and objective directed movement	suggestive and varied open and divergent impressionistic and subjective different movements
Reflective of:	rational processing	relational processing

---

immediate appearances. What we perceive is both personal and changeable. Others only know what we see as we share what we see. And what we see varies—with the light, the time, our mood, our viewing place. Patterns of attention are unique. Because so much depends upon what we make of what we find little is obvious. Much must be inferred or intuited.

Archetypal Architecture

Two architectural forms represent these basic mind-sets: the dome and the spire.[4] I refer specifically to the hovering dome of St. Sophia, the Church of Holy Wisdom in Istanbul, and the thrusting spires of the Cathedral at Chartres. These physical images give material expression to spiritual reality. They represent where God is and how we get to God. Beyond their historical significance [5] each offers a glimpse of universal meaning. Thus, we can speak of dome-like reality and spire-like reality. These architectural spaces are archetypal patterns of what matters most in human experience.

In St. Sophia space quickens and expands. The one dome protects the earth. Inside, shining planes and luminous surfaces generate rhythmic vistas which, in turn, lessen any imperative to move directly toward the alter. An imaginative eye discerns unity in the flickering lights. As a result divine presence permeates spacious space.

St. Sophia expresses the Byzantine vision of God. For them everything belonged together. The locus of the holy was "tantalisingly always ambiguous."[6] God could be manifested in a physician in Alexandria as likely as in a Saint Anthony in the desert or a farmer in an Egyptian village. Because the Church and the world were one, harmony was assumed. Whether in the natural order, the communal order, or the cosmic order the really Real disclosed itself in varied ways.

In contrast, at Chartres one experiences space as complex and exalted. The two spires point the way. Even though the height of the arches and the length of the nave compete for attention, the narrow length steers people to the far front. The inquiring eye follows where it is directed. As a consequence Divine purpose makes itself known in the sacrifice at the altar.

Instead of experiencing mystical presence, the Latin West inquired about the location of God. It divided everything rationally. The locus of the holy was "fixed with increasing precision."[7] God appeared in a set structure with a clear hierarchy. Because The Church battled The World for humanity's undivided obedience, tension between the two was unavoidable. God's judgment called for the rejection of the world, the flesh, and the devil. The Right Order of Reality could only be known in sacramental presence.

Dome-like space presents the holy as paradoxical and therefore unpredictable. God can be present anywhere, at any time, to anyone. Transcendent meaning infuses the material indiscriminately. Whatever appears to be true is in truth what is true.

Spire-like space represents the holy as rational and therefore predictable. God can be found only in a specific place, at a special time, by a select few. A conscious mastery of what matters builds an objective reality. Since appearances may deceive, an established authority defines and decides what is definite.

While the dome and the spire each expresses the integrity of Byzantine and Medieval cultures, respectively, as metaphors of meaning they open up images of what matters. The expansiveness of a dome-like mind and the intensiveness of a spire-like mind are related to what we are learning about how the human brain works. Of course the richness of human life and the complexity of brain activity make simple connections between mind and brain misleading. Nevertheless, I find that neuropsychological data inform these images and the realities they reflect. People do perceive and process reality in right mind and left mind ways. As dome and spire provide central images, so right mind and left mind add refinements in exploring the activity of God.

The double brain contributes to divided minds, in theology and society. The issue now is to interpret how the ways the mind works show themselves in these two structures. For in St. Sophia and at Chartres we see how Christians have perceived the mind of God at work in the world.

One Mind—Two Mind Sets

Both the Byzantine and Latin churches arose from the New Testament community as the New Israel. Yet that common source gave birth to a mind-set conflicted in its preferences and deficient in its functioning. Influenced by Hebrew and Greek forces, the Western mind struggled with complexity. No simple pattern nor single preference dominated. Tension characterized the perceived mind of God. Not surprisingly, One Mind appeared to be of two minds.

The Christian part of the Judaeo-Christian tradition split. Judaeo-Christian actually means Judaeo-Graeco/Roman. Graeco refers to the Greek-Byzantine story/history/mind; Roman identifies the Latin-Germanic story/history/mind. The Greeks came to be known for their "cunning," the Romans for their "boldness."[8] Each claimed to be Christian.

That affirmation of commonality must not be lost. Though Greek and Roman are distinguishable, they are inseparable. Each belongs to the one mind of God. They partook of a homogeneous Mediterranean world. It was an urban world, [9] fed by Palestinian imagination and informed by North African intellect. Carthage, Rome, Alexandria, Antioch, and Constantinople all moved to similar rhythms. The chasm which "separated the Mediterranean itself from the alien societies which flanked it" "dwarfed" any division between Greek East and Latin West.[10] Both arose from the Christianized Roman Empire with its orientation to classical Hellenism. In short, what they shared overshadowed how they differed.

Yet differ they did. To say that Greek and Roman are inseparable obscures the schisms which ripped them apart. The following five events give evidence of their splitting the mind of God:

-330: Constantine minimizes the old Rome by establishing the New Rome in Constantinople . . .

-717-741: in the East Emperor Leo the III of Syria rejects Latin by reinstating Greek as the official language of government; in the West Pope Gregory II resists Leo's attempt to enforce Iconoclasm . . . [11]

-800: the coronation of Charlemagne by Pope Leo III denies the Byzantine claim to imperial succession . . .

-1054: the representatives of both the Eastern patriarchy and the Western papacy excommunicate each other . . .

-1204: the Latin army sacks Constantinople during the Fourth Crusade . . .

By late twelfth century the Greeks regarded the German rulers as sinister, while the Franks viewed the Greeks as treacherous. Each felt superior to the other. Between 1050-1204 bitterness escalated. Though Nicetas Choniates' words sound exaggerated they were not atypical: "Between us and the Latins is set the widest gulf. We are poles apart. We have not a thought in common. They are stiff-necked with a proud affectation of an upright carriage, and love to sneer at the smoothness and modesty of our manners. But we look upon their arrogance and boasting and pride as the snot which keeps their noses in the air; and we tread them down with the might of Christ, who giveth unto us the power to trample upon the adder and the scorpion."[12] Such abrasiveness reflects more differences in their perceptions of God than in any basic antagonism between the Graeco and Roman societies in themselves.[13]

The minds of the Byzantine East and the Latin West struggled with each other to express the true mind of God. In the following chapters I examine these differences in more detail. Hopefully in understanding dome-like and spire-like minds, the places in which people dwell, we can understand the architecture of our own minds, the places in which we dwell. Hopefully we can dwell together in peace. Hopefully we can find what matters most in and to our humanity.

NOTES

1. For my understanding of architecture I have used the following works:

   Sigfried Giedion, THE ETERNAL PRESENCE: The Beginnings of Architecture. A contribution to Consistency and Change (New York: Pantheon Books, Bollingen Series, Vol. 35, 1964).

   Idem., SPACE, TIME, AND ARCHITECTURE: The Growth of a New Tradition. 5th ed., rev. (Cambridge, Mass.: Harvard University Press, 1967).

   R. Krautheimer, EARLY CHRISTIAN AND BYZANTINE ARCHITECTURE (Baltimore: Penguin Books, [1965] 1967).

   Liels Luning Prak, THE LANGUAGE OF ARCHITECTURE: A contribution to architectural theory (The Netherlands: Moutin & Co., 1968).

   Heinrich Wölfflin, PRINCIPLES OF ART HISTORY: The Problem of the Development of Style in Later Art. Translated by M.D.Hottinger (New York: Dover Publications, Inc., [1932] 1950).

   Bruno Zevi, ARCHITECTURE AS SPACE: How to Look at Architecture. Translated by Milton Gendel and edited by Joseph A. Barry (New York: Horizon Press, 1957).

2. Prak, THE LANGUAGE OF ARCHITECTURE (n.1 above), 23.

3. Architecture has been linked with social circumstances as a combination of Freudian unconscious and Marxian economics. To interpret architecture as "a symbolic language with a definite iconographical meaning" is recent. For instance, Prak in THE LANGUAGE OF ARCHITECTURE (n.1 above, v-vi) wrote: "The gradual worsening conditions in the

declining Roman Empire may have been conducive to the spread of Christianity and have promoted an 'introverted' architecture. The insecurity of the Age of the Great Migrations may have led to the concept of the Romanesque church as a 'sacred fortress,' a bulwark against evil, and have caused an outspoken timidity in construction. Conversely, when conditions improved in the Later Middle Ages, construction became gradually more daring, and churches light and more festive, more 'opportunistic'."

4. Architecturally speaking, Christianity combined two orientations: a human scale and interior space. The human scale derived from Greek temples, since the proportion between building and people was manageable. Only deity used inside space. The closed space inhibited, or reflected the lack of, reflective introspection. Activity occurred in the space around the temple. Interior space only developed with the grand scale of the Romans. The thick walls and biaxial grandiosity of their buildings made for "an absolute autonomy with respect to neighboring spaces" (Zevi, ARCHITECTURE AS SPACE [n.1 above], 81). Inside, the structure oriented people toward a raised dias. The massive building, with its specific direction, affirmed authority while it diminished the individual. Once Christians began gathering outside their homes in public places their buildings reflected these influences. They borrowed, or inherited, the Roman basilian structure with its interior space and directed focus, combining it with the Greek gathering as a communal event. The path to the altar organized their belief in gathering to commune with Christ and one another.

5. Unless specifically cited, the following sources contributed to the discussion:

   Peter Brown, "Eastern and Western Christendom in Late Antiquity: a parting of the ways." In Baker, THE ORTHODOX CHURCHES AND THE WEST (n.5), 1-24.

Idem., "The Rise and Function of the Holy Man," Journal of Roman Studies, 1971, 61:80-101.

Derek Baker, ed., THE ORTHODOX CHURCHES AND THE WEST (Published for the Ecclesiastical History Society Oxford: Basil Blackwell, 1976).

George Every, MISUNDERSTANDINGS BETWEEN EAST AND WEST (Richmond, Va.: John Knox Press, [1965] 1966).

William Fleming, ARTS & IDEAS. New and Brief Edition (New York: Holt, Rinehart and Winston, Inc., 1974).

Deno J. Geanakoplos, BYZANTINE EAST AND LATIN WEST: Two Worlds of Christendom in Middle Ages and Renaissance (Oxford: Basil Blackwell, 1966).

Idem., BYZANTIUM AND RENAISSANCE (Hamden, Conn.: Shoe String Press, 1973).

Idem., INTERACTION OF THE 'SIBLING' BYZANTINE AND WESTERN CULTURES (New Haven: Yale University Press, 1976).

Hans Jonas, PHILOSOPHICAL ESSAYS: from ancient creed to technological man (Englewood Cliffs, NJ: Prentice-Hall, 1974).

Harry J. Magoulias, BYZANTINE CHRISTIANITY: Emperor, Church, and the West (Chicago: Rand McNally & Company, 1970).

Martin Marty, A SHORT HISTORY OF CHRISTIANITY (New York: Meridian Books, 1959).

Janet L. Nelson, "Symbols in Context." In Baker, THE ORTHODOX CHURCHES AND THE WEST (n.5), 97-119.

6. Brown, "Eastern and Western Christendom in Late Antiquity" (n.5 above), 11-16. "The holy escaped social definition or, rather its absence of social definition became intelligible—because it was thought of principally as a power that 'manifested' itself in a manner that was as vivid as it was discontinuous with normal human expectations . . ." (Ibid., 14).

7. Ibid.

8. Geanakoplos, INTERACTION OF THE 'SIBLING' BYZANTINE AND WESTERN CULTURES (n.5 above), 11.

9. The urban civilization was actually "a fragile veneer: only one (person) in ten lived in the civilized towns" (Brown, "The Rise and Function of the Holy Man [n.5 above], 84). The civilization of Late Antiquity was an intimate face-to-face community and stable society (Peter Brown, THE MAKING OF LATE ANTIQUITY [Cambridge: Harvard University Press, 1978], 3-4).

10. Brown, "Eastern and Western Christendom in Late Antiquity" (n.5 above), 2-3.

11. In 730 Emperor Leo III officially banned the veneration and the use of religious images, which he regarded as idolatry. The ban, known as Iconoclasm, lasted until 843, except for an interruption between 780-813.

12. Quoted by Anthony Bryer, "The First Encounter With the West - A.D. 1050-1204." In Philip Whitting, ed., BYZANTIUM: An Introduction (New York: Harper Torchbooks, [1972] 1973), 103-104.

13. The estrangement came because of divergences "within the churches themselves" and not because of "any overwhelming antithesis" between Greco and Roman societies (Brown, "Eastern and Western Christendom in Late Antiquity" (n.5 above), 7.

Figure 2 St. Sophia (exterior)

Chapter Five

THE DOME: Byzantine Vision[1]

Byzantium was conceived in a vision,[2] fathered by the Roman Empire, and mothered by the Christian Church.

As Eusebius, bishop of Caesarea (from ca. 263-340) declared in 335: "And thus, by the express appointment of the same God, two roots of blessing, the Roman empire, and the doctrine of Christian piety, sprang up together for the benefit of (humanity)."[3] Politics and piety fused: a political machine[4] and a religious explanation. Since the patriarch anointed the emperor, the act of coronation now expressed the will of God. The earthly kingdom mirrored the heavenly kingdom.

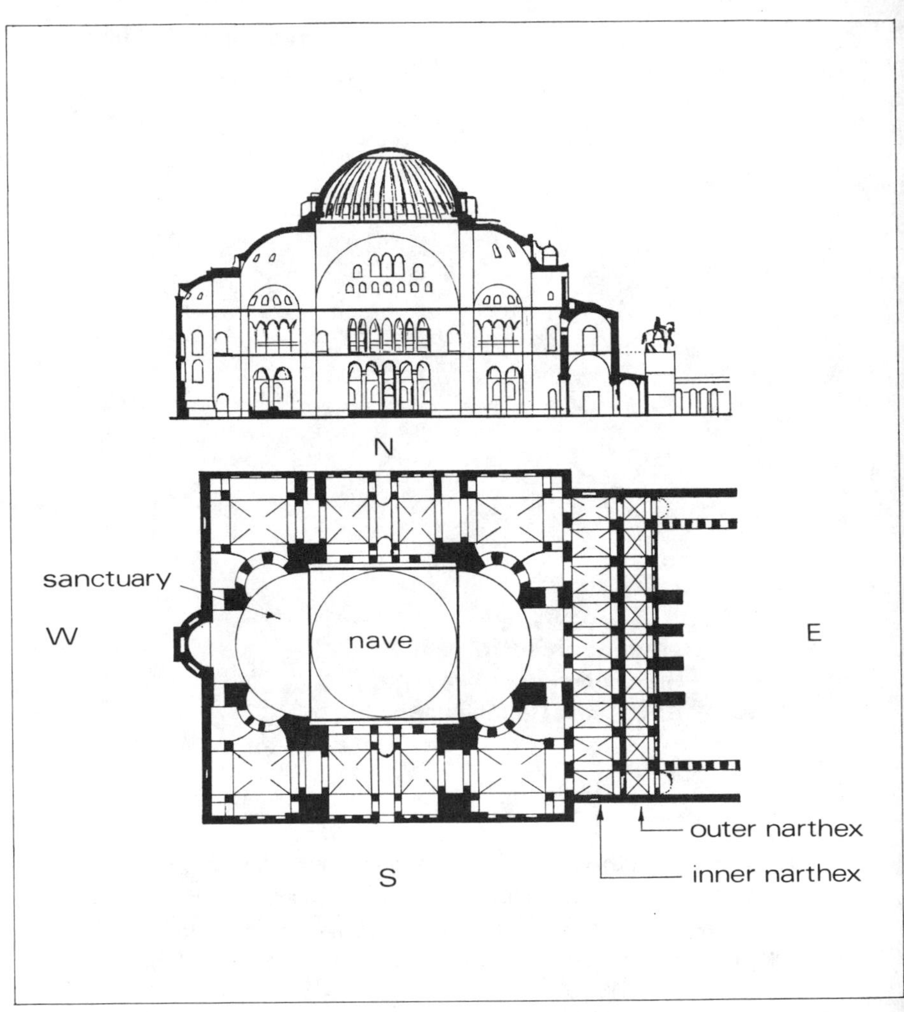

Figure 3 St. Sophia Ground Plan

On May 11, 330 Emperor Constantine inaugurated Constantinople as the New Rome. In recognition of the transformation, a statue was erected in his honor.[5] In his right hand he held a scepter, which represented authority, and in his left a globe, which symbolized the world. As head of the Holy Establishment he was to preserve the classical heritage; as head of the Church he was to defend the Faith.[6] The Christian universe meant the Roman world. Oekoumene equaled orbis romanus.

To equate the universe and world as they did took a certain kind of mind-set. John of Damascus (ca. 674-749), the greatest of the Byzantine theologians, described the way they processed reality: "Just as we listen with our bodily ears to physical words and understand spiritual things, so through corporeal vision we come to the spiritual . . . everything has a double significance, a corporeal and a spiritual."[7] In terms of the analytical metaphor, tangible forms carried more symbolic significance. A manifestation of numinous presence overshadowed historical claims (see Tables 2 and 5).

In its theology Byzantium emphasized Christ as the Second Person of the Trinity. As Justin Martyr (ca. 100-164) put it, Christ was Sophia, that is, the revealer of Divine Wisdom or, more simply, Wisdom. To the classical mind He alone constituted true philosophy. In Holy Wisdom—St. Sophia, if you will—imperial splendor merged with Christian mysticism. The Great Church displayed true Wisdom or the mind of God. The people of Byzantium built their church according to the way they perceived God at work in their world.

OUTER SPACE

In what follows I take you into the dome-like. Visually and descriptively we move into that archetypal spaciousness by means of an encounter with the Great Church of St. Sophia.[8] I translate its implicit meanings into explicit statements of what mattered to Byzantium, namely, where God dwelt and how they got to God. I connect those meanings with ways our minds work and, thereby, with how we too can know what matters to us and for us. In the dome of St. Sophia I discern the dome-like of humanity (see Figure 2).

For the people of the Byzantine world St. Sophia displayed true Wisdom. And for them True Wisdom meant the mind of God. They built their dwelling place according to the way they perceived God in the world. In entering that place we can experience that mind-set.

One Vision

From its beginnings St. Sophia has confronted people with a stark exterior and a kaleidoscopic interior. So too are we. The rough outside bears little resemblance to the exquisite inside. To the uninitiated, those not in the know, its appearance belies its reality.

From a distance the great dome hovers over the landscape like a vehicle from outer space. As we come close the dome opens upward into the sky like an umbrella (Figure 2). Whether we view it from the east end or the south-west, this massive structure carries us upward, rising as it does out of the flowing lines of half domes upon half domes upon half domes. In 562 C.E. Paul the Silentiary celebrated the completion of the building with a poem. He put the Byzantine vision of God in a way that we can see: "There overhead, looming vast in the shadowy air, arches the rounded helm of the heavenly house/ Like unto the burnished roof of Heaven."[9]

Procopius of Caesarea was the outstanding Greek historian of that period of Late Antiquity.[10] He too described the building with poetic accuracy:

> . . . a spectacle of marvelous beauty, overwhelming to those who see it . . . soaring to a height to match the sky, and, as if surging up from amongst the other buildings it stands on high and looks down upon the remainder of the city . . . dominating it . . . exulting in an indescribable beauty . . . it seems somehow to float in the air on no firm

basis . . . Yet actually it is braced with exceptional firmness . . .[11]

Except for the dome no one feature draws attention to itself. The building seems to expand-and-embrace at one and the same time. What paradoxes it maintains—bold yet simple, subtle yet sure, majestic yet austere, massive yet mysterious. Gregory of Nazianus (d. 389) described the ascetic mind which could build such a dwelling place: "Our philosophy is humble in appearance, but sublime in its hidden essence, and leads to God."[12]

Such is the dome-like mind—in style as in architecture. A unifying vision of reality. It includes everything. The splendor of St. Sophia's domes and half domes rests upon an intuited base.

The Byzantine mind embraced the whole of things, religious as well as political. Nothing separated sacred and secular. Little distinguished more important from less important. Everything mattered. The vision was simple: one citizenry obeyed one law which was based upon everyone believing one creed. All emanated from the risen triumphal Christ whom they called the Pantocrator, the Ruler of the Universe.

The vision of one dome meant the reality of one humanity. Earthly and heavenly realms mirrored each other. The Christian universe and the Graeco-Roman world shared common boundaries.

Two Concepts

Architecturally St. Sophia combines two concepts—the rectangular basilica and the central rotunda (Figure 3).

Although hidden from the outside, four huge piers support the dome. Inside, these provide the outline of a rectangle. In its classical Roman origin, rectangular space directed people toward a raised dais at the far end of a hall. The fusion of direction and dais affirmed the power of authority and diminished the freedom of individuals. And so, Sophia's rectangular base conveys the suggestion that people move from the western entrances toward the eastern sanctuary.

Despite the square base, however, the dome dominates the inside as much as it does the outside. The continuous lines of that inner expansiveness envelop people more than directing them. Patterns yield to one another, in Procopius' words, as "in a choral dance." As he pointed out, "Both its breadth and its length have been so carefully proportioned (i.e., 234' by 253'), that it may . . . be said to be exceeding long and at the same time unusually broad." Such blanketing by Holy Wisdom plays down specific authority and fosters personal responses.

A sense of centralized space with its radiating spaciousness characterizes dome-like reality. In symbolic language the rectangle or square represents the earth with its four corners, while the circle signifies the wholeness of heaven. Together square and circle reveal the whole of earth and heaven. So in approaching the hovering dome people felt they were moving into the very presence of Holy Presence. Regardless of where one stood one glimpsed the fullness of the whole.

The dome opens up the numinous presence of intuited truth. Here is Wisdom. Here is God. From such architecture I infer a relational mind at work.

Many Entrances

Although the one vision synthesized two concepts of space, its expansive space dominated directed space. Understandably, therefore, no one way stood out as the only way. People entered into Wisdom in many ways.

From the Western end two sets of five doors each opens onto three sets of three doors each. As many as one hundred and ten attendants served as doorkeepers,[13] facilitating people moving into the midst of the mystery. These entrances reflect the open quality of human nature. Life is process, an ascending to God and a communing with God. The divine-human relationship, for the Byzantine mind-set and for the dome-like mind, is both a given and a task, "an immediate experience and an expectation."[14] People are encouraged to enter in, to be part of the Reality which the building models.

As we glance through the doorways leading from the outer narthex on into the nave, the structure intensifies the transition from the ordinary world into another realm. The modest entrances limit what we see. Still they direct us where to move. Through the openings we glimpse quickening space and expanding surfaces. Each of the two lobbies or porticos stretches the width of the building. Thus, neither can be a passageway to and from anywhere. Rather they serve as successive thresholds, like the swell of the ocean, carrying us on into radiant openness.

The fact that the inner narthex is twice as deep and twice as high as the outer one only heightens our sense of something marvelous unfolding before us. Even the cross-vaulting and ceiling pull us forward, carrying us on waves of mounting expectation. The vision which hovers so massively over the landscape opens before us with unanticipated lightness. Our imagination floods into the spaciousness before us.

INNER SPACE

These many entrances, opening into the successive narthexes, create a sense of our being bourne by the quickening rhythm of breakers cresting onto a shore line. From the threshold of the nave the space ahead loses its shape and seems to expand beyond any natural limit. We are about to step into the very realm of the transcendent itself.

Wondrous Light

Just above the central door we can see a mosaic of Christ. Even in the realm of the undifferentiated some distinctions are found. The inscription reads: "Peace be unto you. I am the light of the world." For Byzantium, light as the first-created element transformed darkness into life. And for the dome-like, words expressive of light predominate—insight, illumination, enlightenment, manifestation. Just ahead of us through the doorway we can see light playing continuously as it filters down from above.

We try to find the source of this light. Yet we see no windows through which the sun shines. Instead light appears to radiate from within the space itself. Once over the threshold we find ourselves bathed in light. The Light of the world shines everywhere.

If we could have attended the major festivals of Byzantine Christianity, we would have experienced even more wondrous light. The festivals lasted through the night. Lamps glowed and candles flickered, continuously licking the luminous space on every side. Toward dawn, to draw on a phrase of Procopius, the first slivers of daylight would smile through the dome,[15] bathing the interior even more brightly than it had been bathed with the shimmering of many lamps.

> Every stone catches the light with a loveliness that touches the heart. . . One might imagine that (one) had come upon a meadow with its flowers in full bloom. For (one) would surely marvel at the purple of some, the green tint of others, and at those on which the crimson glows and those from which the white flashes, and again at those which Nature, like some painter, varies with the most contrasting colours.[16]

Light floods the dwelling-place with illumination. Light bears us up into the very light of life itself. For the dome-like mind all of life radiates with the light of the world.

Open Space

Amidst the many entrances back in the narthex we had experienced height and width held together. But once inside the nave we feel space simply flowing outward and soaring upward. Immense though the cavern may be, we feel drawn into the holiness of the whole.

Its breadth diffuses its height even as its height enfolds is breadth. Overhead the dome radiates outward in a way that lightens everything equally.

We can imagine what Procopius must have sensed when he spoke of the infinite detail of the structure inviting an infinite wonder in the soul.

> All the details, fitted together with incredible skill in mid-air and floating off from each other and resting only on the parts next to them, produce a single and most extraordinary harmony . . . and yet (they) do not permit the spectator to linger much over the study of any one of them, but each detail attracts the eye and draws it on irresistibly to itself.[17]

Each detail, extraordinary in and of itself, invites our attention. Yet no detail is so extraordinary as to be distinguishable by itself alone. Our eyes roam from one detail to another and on to another and another. Every piece is exquisite in itself and equally part of an exquisite whole.

In examining the structure more closely we discover that the weight, the function, and the differences among the columns, the capitals, the beams, the piers, and the arches are softened in a way that creates a rarified atmosphere (Figure 4). Edges dissolve and boundaries blur. Walls and stories and planes and vaults and half domes and windows and decorations and domes flow into one another. Spaciousness fills every space as every space spreads out as a harmonious presence.

The open space suggests the ever-present presentness of the holy. In St. Sophia, as in Byzantium, the holy "manifested" itself indiscriminately. Epiphanies or God-appearances came suddenly, unexpectedly, repeatedly. In dome-like reality the holy escapes confinement, whether in the midst of the flowing lines of the dome-dwelling or in doctrinal statements of the Church Fathers. The tantalizing ambiguity of "reality" discloses a harmony of church and world, of sacred and secular, of special

Figure 4 St. Sophia (interior)

places and all places. God is accessible to anyone, anywhere, at anytime.

Open space makes for open roles. Anyone can play big parts in the divine drama. Just as no line sharply defines the parts of the building so no boundary sharply divided person from person or group from group. In Byzantium any child born in that society was "qualified" to be anointed emperor.[18] The throne stood open "regardless of rank, fortune and ancestry."[19]

For instance, Leo I had sold meat, Justin I had tended swine, and Leo III had done odd jobs. In spacious places no one can monopolize power and authority. These are accessible to all.

The lack of hierarchy, sharp boundaries, and social stratification, designate it as we will, means the playing down of specialization. Every role bears the meaning of the whole. Each part of the building or society can be taken as the structure of Holy Wisdom, in itself, without diminishing the harmony.

For instance, two stoa-like colonnades on each side of the nave actually make the effect of the width greater even though they are distinct in themselves. They do not rise to the height of the nave yet they are vaulted and decorated like the nave. In fact, because they stretch the length of the building they replicate the basilican-rotunda of the whole.

Furthermore, the stoa expressed the non-stratified nature of Byzantine society. One stoa was assigned to men worshippers, the other to women worshippers. Nothing distinguishes the stoae from each other. As Procopius pointed out, "their very equality serves to beautify the church, and their similarity to adorn it."[20] Like the colonnades, the separation of the sexes did not result in exclusive male domination. While patriarchy was overt, shared responsibility was not uncommon. Some women played prominent roles, even to reigning from the throne.[21] Others administered their own private fortunes, gave audiences, held banquets, and conferred gifts—all in parallel fashion to their emperor husbands.

Logos-Sophia had come into the world through a woman and continued in the world through His people.[22]

The openness of the dome suggests an openness in the social order. The whole shows itself in the parts. Even as Byzantium believed it lived out the Kingdom of God in the world, so the dome-like affirms every part in every place.

Living Drama

St. Sophia stood as "a single vast icon"[24] in which the drama of life was staged. Neither its massive exterior nor its transitional narthexes provided clues to what waited inside. Only in the nave, from inside the belief-structure itself, could people behold "the harmonious sequences of the parts."[25] Spaciousness combined with light to infuse majesty with mystery. Only by entering in did people perceive the whole.

The Liturgy expressed the central feature of the Byzantine mind-set. It stabilized society even as it guided Orthodoxy. By using the vernacular[26] it kept tradition alive. The will of God and the will of the State were voiced in the words of the people.[27]

The drama was at once simple and grand.[28] Each day it re-presented Christ's suffering on earth. The appearance of the Bishop symbolized the coming of the Christ. With the presence of Christ people would turn from unbelief to faith, from vice to virtue, from worldly distraction to divine knowledge. Everyone took part in that divine disclosure.

The first acts of the Liturgy instructed those who sought to learn more about the faith by singing, reading Scripture, and preaching. Just as the building was dazzling, so too was the preaching. Norman Baynes described its rhetoric as "a radiant mosaic of purple patches," with "no true climax," "a wealth of imagery and elaboration," much "too decorative and too little discipline," a monotonous yet "intensely human" style.[29] Words flowed the way space flowed. The First Entrance was an invitation to those outside to enter into the life of the dome-like mind of God.

Then came a break in the service. The catechumens left. Only the faithful remained. Just as the exterior of the building gave onlookers few clues to its interior, so those outside the Faith could hardly anticipate or know the glory waiting for them inside. The division came at the boundary of the structure of belief and building. Although the mysteries of bread and wine were concealed from the catechumens, the mysteries were accessible to the faithful.

In the Liturgy of the Faithful, otherwise known as The Entrance of the Mysteries, bread and wine were carried to the altar as offering. The faithful greeted one another with the Kiss of Peace, demonstrating by that act the "harmony of hearts and minds which . . . is to be expected in the coming kingdom of God."[30] While only the priest distributed communion, the boundary between priest and laity was less legalistic than in the Latin West. Believers participated in the mysteries as fully as was possible this side of heaven itself.[31]

For Byzantium, knowledge of God was innate, arrived at neither by deductive reason nor inductive logic. It was direct, immediate, and natural. God's reality simply was The Way Things Truly Are. The key was participation. In the words of Gregory of Nyssa (ca. 331-395): "God made human nature a participator of every good. Hence there is within us the idea of every virtue and all wisdom . . ."[32] Humanity partook of the divine substance.

A RELATIONAL MIND

The one dome of St. Sophia disclosed a synthesizing mind. Its bleak exterior contrasts with its dazzling interior. The many entrances encouraged people to enter. Once through the narthexes the inside made everything "open to view." Nothing remained hidden. All flowed together creating one magnificent mosaic. People knew God by taking part in the living drama that raised them up into the light of God.

The crucial feature of Byzantine vision was the responsive eye of faith. Physical forms carried spiritual meaning. What architecture expressed kinesthetically the mosaic expressed visually. The Byzantine mind perceived the appearances of things as the appearances—the manifestations—the epiphanies—of the Divine Light in and through the world.

Consider but one example, the mosaic of Christ as the Light of the World, which we observed over the central door of the inner narthex. I return to it now as a way of emphasizing the prominence, if not the dominance, of the visual system in the relational processing of the Byzantine world. The central door is known as the Imperial Door because the mosaic portrays an emperor prostrating himself before the triumphant Christ. Above him on the left Mary stretches out her hands to carry his prayers to Christ as the Celestial Overlord, the Logos-Sophia, or Eternal Wisdom.

This interpretation is one among many. In fact the ambiguity of Byzantine iconography fosters alternative explanations. For instance an altar may be the tomb of Christ as well as the cradle of Christ. "And why not?" asked Byzantinist Cyril Mango. "Everything in Christian doctrine is interconnected."[33]

Even more than in architecture, the mosaics represent the inner eye of Byzantine vision. Two dimensional images and flat surfaces invite us to add our own meanings to that which the artists portray. A transcendent realm replaces the ordinary world. The material world manifests the mystery of another reality.

No controversy racked Byzantium more than the issue of images or icons. The iconophiles argued that images affirmed what was "manifested" in the material world, namely, that the spiritual could be seen and Christ's humanity was complete. For those who responded to the visual representation of the divine, St. Theodore the Studite stated the formula: "Christ is not Christ if he cannot be represented."[34] Christ had lived as a human being, the iconophiles argued, so Christ could be portrayed as a human being.

I say more about the iconoclast controversy in the next chapter but here I emphasize the power of Byzantine imagination. Icons focused on the face and especially the eyes. Whether the figures are Christ himself or holy ones, generally they looked out on the faithful, searching their hearts and inviting their devotion. These icons are visible shadows of invisible beings. They witness to the presence of Christ and his saints.

John of Damascus insisted that those who opposed images did so from an inadequate understanding of Christ. Books as well as icons were images. Both portrayed the divine Son in earthly form. In words which expressed the dominant view of the culture, John identified the inner eye of imagination as central to the mind-set:

> When we set up an image of Christ in any place, we appeal to the senses; and indeed we sanctify the sense of sight, which is the highest among the perceptive senses, just as by sacred speech we sanctify the sense of hearing. An image is, after all, a reminder; it is to the illiterate what a book is to the literate, and what the word is to the hearing, the image is to the sight.[35]

Initially I noted that Byzantium was conceived in a vision, an all-at-once experience. No surprise, then, that John made the point even more precise when he wrote that "our (human) soul has the mind as a sort of eye which sees and has the faculty of knowing. . ."[36] The mind of Byzantium reflected an imagination open to constant manifestations of the whole, anywhere and everywhere.

Let me translate the implicit meanings of St. Sophia's wondrous light, open space, and living drama into explicit features that permit us to correlate Byzantine vision and the dome-like mind with the way the brain works (see page 153, Table 8).

(1) Because its architecture, art, and theology were oriented to reality as a mosaic creation, I identify its features as primarily relational (see Tables 3, 4, and 5). That means the environment elicited its responses, resulting in a broad attentional pattern characterized by tangible and symbolic associations. God manifested God through natural and concrete symbolism. Humanity participated in the divine life as in a changing yet harmonious scene.

2) Because its authority structure, role responsibilities, and language pattern were organized in personal, contextual, and immediately involved ways, I identify its input as impressionistic and its output as expressionistic (see Table 5). Reality was anchored subjectively. People attended to patterns in ways that allowed diversity and unity at one and the same time. The whole could be experienced in its parts. The ambiguity of blurred boundaries made it possible for the divine to appear anywhere and therefore everywhere. No part and no person were cut off or shut out from meaningful presence.

3) The configuration of light, space, and drama suggests that seeing and sensing were its major and auxiliary representation systems, respectively. People viewed reality from their own unique positions—naturally, spontaneously, imaginatively (see Table 7). Impressions came rapidly. An imaginative mind expressed one theme in many ways, and that theme was the disclosure of the transcendent in and through the material world.

Byzantium perceived God's mind primarily as a relational creating one. The one Dome, enfolding and unfolding simultaneously, generated many mosaics, many appearances, many manifestations of one Light. The spaciousness of the dome-like responds to and trusts the appearances of the ultimately real.

In the next chapter I assess how adequately the imaginative mind, with its visual-kinesthetic preference, worked.

NOTES

1. Unless specifically cited, I have drawn upon the following material for my interpretation:

   Norman H. Baynes, THE BYZANTINE EMPIRE (London: Oxford University Press, [1925] 1962).

   Idem., BYZANTINE STUDIES AND OTHER ESSAYS (London: University of London, The Athlone Press, 1955).

   Peter Brown, THE CULT OF THE SAINTS: its rise and function in Latin Christianity (Chicago: The University of Chicago Press, 1980).

   Idem., THE WORLD OF LATE ANTIQUITY: From Marcus Aurelius to Muhammad (London: Thames and Hudson, [1971] 1974).

   Constantine Cavarnos, BYZANTINE THOUGHT AND ART: A Collection of Essays (Belmont, Mass.: Institute for Byzantine and Modern Greek Studies, [1968] 1974).

   René Guerdan, BYZANTIUM: Its Triumphs and Tragedy. Translated by D.L.B. Hartley. With a preface by Charles Diehl (New York: Capricorn Books, [1957] 1962).

   Saint John of Damascus, WRITINGS. Translated by Frederic H. Chase, Jr. (New York: Fathers of the Church, Inc., 1958).

   Cyril Mango, BYZANTIUM: The Empire of New Rome (New York: Charles Scribners' Sons, 1980).

   John Meyendorff, BYZANTINE THEOLOGY: Historical Trends and Doctrinal Themes (New York: Fordham University Press, [1974] 1976).

Idem., CHRIST IN EASTERN CHRISTIAN THOUGHT (St. Vladimir's Seminary Press, 1975).

Georgije Ostrogorsky, HISTORY OF THE BYZANTINE STATE. Translated by Joan Hussey (Oxford: Basil Blackwell, 1956).

Jaroslav Pelikan, THE CHRISTIAN TRADITION: A History of the Development of Doctrine. Vol. 1 THE EMERGENCE OF THE CATHOLIC TRADITION (100-600); Vol. 2 THE SPIRIT OF EASTERN CHRISTENDOM (600-1700) (Chicago: The University of Chicago Press, 1971, 1974).

David Talbot Rice, ART OF THE BYZANTINE ERA (London: Thames and Hudson, 1963).

Steven Runciman, BYZANTINE CIVILIZATION (London: Edward Arnold & Co., 1933).

Steven Runciman, BYZANTINE STYLE AND CIVILIZATION (Baltimore: Penguin Books, Inc., 1975).

Philip Sherrard, BYZANTIUM (New York: Time-Life Books, 1966).

Paul Tillich, A HISTORY OF CHRISTIAN THOUGHT (n.1/44).

Timothy Ware, THE ORTHODOX CHURCH (Baltimore: Penguin Books, [1963] 1964).

Philip Whitting, BYZANTIUM (n.4/12).

The period of the Byzantine East lasted from the founding of Constantinople as the New Rome in 324 C.E. to its fall to the Ottoman Turks in 1453. Its Early Period, which extended into the middle of the seventh century, marked its greatest achievements: geographical expansion, political power, cultural expressions in literature and art, an integration of Christianity with the Graeco-Roman heritage, and the setting up of structure in the thought and life of Christianity. Its Middle Period began with "the catastrophic break" in the seventh century when it was overwhelmed by Persian invasion, Arab expansion, the end of "the urban civilization of Antiquity," urban violence, food shortages, and bubonic plague. Its Late Period stretched from either the occupation of Asia Minor by the Turks in the 1070s or the capture of Constantinople by the Crusaders in 1204 (Mango, BYZANTIUM [n.1], 1, Ch. 3 "The Disappearance and Revival of Cities").

2. In 312, when Constantine approached Rome at the Milvian bridge, he stood on the threshold of a decisive battle with his rival Emperor Maxentius. Some accounts say he had a vision, others a dream, in either case he is reported to have had a revelation. Eusebius ("The Life of the Blessed Emperor Constantine," Book I, chps. xxviii-xxxi. In A SELECT LIBRARY OF NICENE AND POST-NICENE FATHERS. Second Series, vol. 1, 490-491) adapted the story as told by Lactantius that Constantine saw a luminous cross or Chi(X) and Rho(P), which are the first letters of the name of Christ in Greek. As a result he inscribed a new sign on his banner, later declaring he had had a vision of the cross on which was inscribed a Greek inscription which in Latin read: in hoc signo vinces, "In this sign conquer!"

3. Eusebius, quoted by Magoulias, BYZANTINE CHRISTIANITY (n.4/5), 1.

4. "The history of Rome is the history of the Roman army, and in nothing is Byzantium more truly the heir of Rome than in her military policy" (Baynes, THE BYZANTINE EMPIRE [n.1 above], 132).

5. Actually the statue had served as a statue of Apollo. The heads were changed but the body remained the same. Such examples of change-and-continuity characterized Late Antiquity. For instance, a fourth century sculpture yard near Rome produced statues "impeccably dressed in the old Roman toga (with a socket for detachable por-

trait heads!)" (Brown, THE WORLD OF LATE ANTIQUITY [n.1 above], 21).

6. As defenders of the Faith, the Roman (Byzantine) emperors, not Western popes nor Eastern patriarchs, convened the first seven ecumenical councils, which struggled to clarify and define Christianity's doctrinal content. See Henry R. Percival, ed., THE SEVEN ECUMENICAL COUNCILS of the undivided church. Edited with notes. Nicene and Post-Nicene Fathers. Second Series. Vol. XIV (Grand Rapids: Wm. B. Eerdmans Publishing Company, 1956).

7. John of Damascus, quoted by Magoulias, BYZANTINE CHRISTIANITY (n.4/5), 48.

8. Unless specifically cited I have drawn upon the following material related to St. Sophia:

   Heinz Kähler, HAGIA SOPHIA. With a chapter on the mosaics by Cyril Mango. Translated by Ellyn Childs (New York: Praeger Publishers, 1967).

   Thomas F. Mathews, THE EARLY CHURCHES OF CONSTANTINOPLE: Architecture and Liturgy (University Park: The Pennsylvania State University Press, 1971).

   Procopius, BUILDINGS, Volume VIII. Translated by H.B. Dewing. The Loeb Classical Library (Cambridge, Mass.: Harvard University Press, [1940] 1961).

9. Paul the Silentiary, quoted by Kähler, HAGIA SOPHIA (n.8 above), 11.

10. Procopius wrote in the style of the great classical historian Thucydides. His books, known as the <u>Wars</u>, provided a general history of the Persian, Vandal, and Gothic Wars (527-553). The first seven volumes criticized Justinian's policies indirectly. The eighth, ON BUILDINGS, praised Justinian's building program as worthy of the imperial goal of one,

empire, one law, one church, and of the emperor's humanity. In a shorter work, SECRET HISTORY (translated by Richard Atwater. Foreword by Arthur E.R. Boak [Ann Arbor: The University of Michigan Press, 1961]), he viciously attacked the Emperor, the Empress Theodora, and the court: e.g., Chp. XI "How the Defender of the Faith Ruined his Subjects" or Chp. XII "Proving that Justinian and Theodora Were Actually Fiends in Human Form." See Mango, BYZANTIUM (n.1 above), 244, for a critique of Procopius' work.

11. Procopius, BUILDINGS, I (n.8 above), i, 21, 34; VII, 13, 17-19. Emperor Julian the Apostate (361-363) rendered a contrary judgment. While referring to the old Hagia Sophia, the mocking remarks would apply even more to the new building: "To be sure, the Christians have a magnificent church. On my return from Persia, I will turn the central space into a hay mow and the aisles into horse stalls. Then I will see upon what they set their faith" (quoted by Kähler, HAGIA SOPHIA [n.8 above], 12).

12. Gregory of Nazianus, quoted by Cavarnos, BYZANTINE THOUGHT AND ART (n.1 above), 20.

13. Mathews, THE EARLY CHURCHES OF CONSTANTINOPLE (n.8 above), 152.

14. Meyendorff, BYZANTINE THEOLOGY (n.1 above), 1-2.

15. Procopius, BUILDINGS, VIII (n.8 above), 21.

16. Ibid., 27.

17. Ibid., 21. "The interior vistas curve in strange ways; the columns are of different sizes and proportions; the upper order has consciously been made not to line up with the lower" (Mango, BYZANTIUM [n.1 above], 262). The old Hagia Sophia, begun in 326 and consecrated in 360, was probably first known as "the Great Church," the first cathedral of the new capital. Only later did it

come to be known as "Hagia Sophia in honor of Christ, the Wisdom of God." Destroyed by fire in 532, Emperor Justinian I rebuilt it by 537 and revised it between 558 and 563. Though in a class by itself—in size and prominence and engineering—"it set the example for other churches to follow" (Mathews, THE EARLY CHURCHES OF CONSTANTINOPLE [n.8], 77). "(T)he building has come down to us almost intact. The visitor need only remember that the original dome was lower than the present one by some twenty feet so that the curvature of the ceiling formed a more continuous canopy and produced a more daring effect; and that the interior illumination was stronger than today's since the side-walls (tympana) of the nave appear to have been pierced by huge windows. (One) should also make allowance for the vast expanse of gold mosaic (now preserved only in fragments) and the splendour of the furnishings, all riveted with sheets of silver—the chancel screen, the ciborium over the altar table, the curving seats for the clergy in the apse, the monumental pulpit in the middle of the nave" (Mango, BYZANTIUM [n.1 above]), 262.

18. Nelson, "Symbols in Context" (n.4/5), 115.

19. Guerdan, BYZANTIUM (n.1 above), 31.

20. Procopius, BUILDINGS VIII, (n.8 above), 25-27.

21. Women rulers included Irene (790-802), Zoe (1042), and Theodora (1042, 1055-1056). Moreover, empresses exercised considerable influence and displayed remarkable independence, the Empress Sophia (565--578) perhaps being the most powerful of all. She was paired with her husband Justin II in power and status, in fact, was "the dominant partner." For forty years she exercised a dominant influence in politics, including directing "the choice first of a caesar and then of the next emperor" on two occasions (Averil Cameron, "The Empress Sophia," Byzantion 45 [1975], 5-21). The Empress Theodora kept Justinian from fleeing in the midst of the Nika riots of 532. Her own behavior ranged from ruthless

autocrat to compassionate helper. Leo IV's (775-780) widow Irene (790, 797-802) tried to maintain the government for her young son. Zoe (1028-1050) exercised power under a variety of circumstances, while Irene, wife of John II Comenus (1118-1143), not only helped maintain the authority of the throne but founded the famous monastery of St. Savior Pantocrator. Mothers passed on to their children society's values in the face of distant and awesome fathers. Artemidorus reported one woman dreamt of having a beard on one side of her face, expressive of managing her husband's estates while he was away. See Guerdan, BYZANTIUM (n.1 above), 32-38, for examples of the prominent presence of empresses. On the whole, however, it appears that women played secondary roles. See Rosemary Ruether, "Mothers of the Church: Ascetic Women in the Late Patristic Age." In Rosemary Ruether and Eleanor McLaughlin, eds., WOMEN OF SPIRIT: Female Leadership in the Jewish and Christian Traditions (New York: Simon and Schuster, 1979), 71-98. Anti-feminism was basic in Byzantine thinking (Mango, BYZANTIUM [n.1 above], 225-226).

22. The audacity of women can be sensed from an encounter related to a royal marriage (Guerdan, BYZANTIUM [n.1 above], 33). Empress Euphrozyme had assembled the most noted beauties of the Empire for her stepson Theophilus. Their presence so excited the young prince that he could not decide among them. Eventually, he approached a radiant candidate, wanting to pay her a compliment. In his embarrassment the compliment came out sounding like an accusation: "It was your sex, you know, which brought unhappiness upon us." She snapped back immediately, "But salvation, in the person of Jesus Christ, came to the world through a woman."

23. See Mathews (THE EARLY CHURCHES OF CONSTANTINOPLE [n.8 above]), who examined the early Byzantine churches of Constantinople archeologically to identify characteristics of church planning and the ceremonial-liturgical services for which

they were built. A description of the preliminaries and proceedings of worship can be found in the Ceremonial Book by Emperor Constantine VII Porphrogenetos in the tenth century (see Kähler, HAGIA SOPHIA [n.8 above], 63-66). Also see Casimir Kucharek, THE BYZANTINE-SLAV LITURGY OF ST. JOHN CHRYSOSTOM: Its Origin and Evolution (Canada: Alleluia Press, 1971), and Ware, THE ORTHODOX CHURCH (n.1 above). By medieval times the liturgy had become more complex and restricted.

24. Runciman, BYZANTINE STYLE AND CIVILIZATION (n.1 above), 97-99.

25. Ibid., 59.

26. Latin was the language of the military. The use of the vernacular varied. In areas like Bulgaria the Liturgy was translated into Slavic. In some provinces, however, even though the local language differed from Greek the Liturgy remained in Greek.

27. Nelson, "Symbols in Context" (n.4/5), 111-112.

28. Mathews, THE CHURCHES OF CONSTANTINOPLE (n.8 above), 178.

29. Baynes, THE BYZANTINE EMPIRE (n.1 above), 166--169. See Mango, BYZANTIUM (n.1 above), 233-234, for a characterization of the literature of the educated Byzantines as full of clichés, rhetoric, and verbiage.

30. Mathews, THE CHURCHES OF CONSTANTINOPLE (n.8 above), 162.

31. Maximus' words (d. 662), cited by Mathews, ibid., 125.

32. P.G., Vol. 44, Col. 184, quoted by Cavarnos, BYZANTINE THOUGHT AND ART (n.1 above), 35.

33. Cyril Mango, in Kähler, HAGIA SOPHIA (n.8 above), 54. The mosaic was painted in the ninth century.

34. St. Theodore the Studite, quoted by Magoulias, BYZANTINE CHRISTIANITY (n.4/5), 50.

35. John of Damascus, quoted by Marty, A SHORT HISTORY OF CHRISTIANITY (n.4/5), 50, Chp. 7, n. 4. John went on to say: ". . . The hill, Calvary, the tomb, the stone, the very source of the Resurrection—all are material; the ink and the pages of the Gospels, the table from which we take of our salvation and all its furniture, the very body and blood of the Lord—all are material. You must either forbid all respect to these things, or you must allow with it respect to the images consecrated to the name of Christ and to his friends, the saints, as being overshadowed by the grace of the Holy Spirit."

36. John of Damascus, WRITINGS (n.1 above), Philosophical chapters, I, 7.

Chapter Six

TOO MUCH VISION, NOT ENOUGH SIGHT

The hovering dome of Holy Wisdom, like an extraterrestrial umbrella, protected humanity from the barren external world by gathering it within a strikingly wondrous space.

The building stood as a mighty icon—an image—of the belief that God manifested divinity in predominately a right mind, visual-kinesthetic, way of working. God became human in Christ as the Second Person of the Trinity in order that humanity could show forth its divinity through participation in living liturgy. The vision of the invisible realm glimmered throughout the material world.

One light
from one source
symbolically present
in any and every place
drew humanity into its radiant sphere.

Now that I have identified the way in which the people of Byzantium reflected their perception of God at work in the world I go on to evaluate that perception: how adequately did this Byzantine mind disclose the mind of God? We look first at the adequacy of its all-at-once processing and then at its seeing-and-sensing representational systems. Table 8 identifies the central features and summarizes the assessment of its dome-like mind.

ENCLOSED SPACE — INCOMPLETE STYLE

The great dome quickened space; it also enclosed it. I find in that encapsulating of reality a key to its limitation.

Within the boundaries of the building, of the culture and its belief, diversity enriched unity. For the people of Byzantium the "otherness" of the meaningful manifested itself everywhere in the natural and symbolic power of divine presence. All had been revealed. Nothing remained to be realized.

The left mind, with its capacity for observation and analysis (Table 3), was given free sway within the confines of the living Liturgy, but beyond that boundary it was granted no independent status. The imaginative heart, with its ever-renewing power, dominated the rational process. The Word, as proclaimed with intentionality and explanation, suffered from neglect.

Simple Vision

Reliance upon right mind relational process resulted in an incomplete style. Its simple vision over-

Table 8. **Byzantine Vision: Identification and Assessment**

Identifying Features

Oriented to:	a mosaic creation - the world elicits responses - broad attentional pattern - natural/concrete symbolism - participation in a changing scene
Organized in:	personal/contextual ways - subjective anchor - unity-in-diversity - ambiguity - anything/everything
Utilized:	impressionistic input expressionist output
Re-presentational Systems	relational processing - uniqueness (i.e., natural, spontaneous, imaginative) (visual) - shifting patterns with many meanings (sensory) - single theme of light (auditory)

Assessing the Vision

Brain process:	incomplete (enclosed space) - overlook negative (simple vision) - rationality secondary (undeveloped ideas) - disruptive personalization (inadequate procedures for transitions in governance)
Re-presentational Systems:	restricted (inner light) - empirical minimized (incomplete input) - everything ultimate (illusory reality) - optimistic polishing of experience (nearsighted)
Summary:	
strengths:	diversity enriched unity pervasive presence
limitations:	incomplete intentionality undeveloped explanatory rationality subordination of step-at-a-time procedures
counter-balances:	spiritual and sensual mystical and rational

looked the negative and the limited within itself. Consequently Byzantium lacked discernment in both thinking and acting. It took its style from that of Late Antiquity in which pagan sentiment maintained an "easy-going unity of heaven and earth."[1] Unlike Latin Christianity's rejection of the world and its temptations, Byzantine Christianity continued that "gentle communion" between heaven and earth which made for strong solidarity within society.

They perceived the mind of God as affirming The Way Things Are. In such an unqualified bias toward the creative activity of God the "mosaic" of Byzantium was taken as reality. Nothing was allowed to complicate its vision. No one was tolerated who questioned its light. Even though they believed humanity could not comprehend the mind of God, they acted as though they did in fact know the mind of God.

Because the relational mind took in everything it connected everything: heaven-and-earth, empire-and-kingdom, patriarch-and-emperor, "the two halves of God"[2] as they perceived it. What they saw with their inner eye was greater than what they saw with their outer eye. While the image presented but a pale shadow of the original, it was, nevertheless, a manifestation of the Truly Real. People could glimpse the divine even though they could not define the divine.

The overlay and infusion of the earthly with the heavenly, however, could not be sustained. It generated increasing deficiency. For instance, Justinian's effort to restore the glory of the empire failed. His excessive demands strained resources to the breaking point. He simply demanded too much of the empire on behalf of the kingdom. The inclusive mind-set—with its "grandiloquent opportunism"[3]—could not encompass enough. Neither could it be selectively discriminating.

Simple intuition overrode the caution which the analytical process contributes. Their immediate experience carried the passion of absolute certainty. Thus we find that ideas remained undeveloped. Procedures seldom became regularized. In terms of doctrine, disputes raged over the meaning of divine presence; in terms of politics, chaos characterized the means of governing the kingdom on earth. In the language of neuropsychology, the all-at-once process struggled with the meaning and means of truth without the specifics of a step-at-a-time approach. In terms of the central symbol, there was too much dome.

Undeveloped Ideas

In the area of doctrine the relational style essentially co-opted the rational process, reducing its contribution to that of secondary input. Reason could clarify what God was not, but reason could make no statements about what God was. In the words of Gregory of Nyssa, God could only be known as "the Unknowable and Incomprehensible."[4] Such simple vision contributed to ideas remaining undeveloped.

Orthodoxy preserved a living tradition, but "living" referred to the eternal presentation of fully disclosed truth. Since the whole had been manifested in Christ, reason could only elaborate what that meant. Nothing more remained to be known. What had been revealed to the Fathers of the Church was the truth-once-for-all manifested to humanity, in humanity. Any inquiry beyond that was irrelevant.

Thus the Fathers used the rational approach of classical philosophy for the sole purpose of apologetics.[5] They tried to clarify the limits within which Christian reason could move without specifying the particulars of that enclosure. For them philosophy served as the handmaiden of Faith. Reason had no independent status.

Understandably, then, their prose lacked "exactness" as did the interior of St. Sophia. Words carried wide meanings. Metaphor, paradox, wonder, and words flowed in ways that submerged the formal use of language to the logic of felt-meaning. All was "yes" in the light of the Light of Logos.

John of Damascus was known as the Aquinas of the East. Yet he never attempted systematic theology[6] nor does his work display careful internal distinctions. Consider, as an example, his opening discussion of "An Exact Exposition of The Orthodox Faith:"

> Now, we both know and confess that God is without beginning and without end, everlasting and eternal, uncreated, unchangeable, unalterable, simple, uncompounded, incorporeal, invisible, impalpable, uncircumscribed, unlimited, incomprehensible, uncontained, unfathomable, good, just, the maker of all created things, all-powerful, all-ruling, all-seeing, the provider, the sovereign, and the judge of all. . .[7]

Such rhetoric pervades the writings of John and the Orthodox theologians. No assumptions were questioned—not in theology, not in politics, not in technology, not in aesthetics. With so few calls on the analytic "the brain atrophies," as one interpreter put it; "in Byzantium the whole of intellectual life was stagnant."[8]

Except for isolated instances such as the Chalcedonian definition of Christ as fully divine and fully human, statements by the Church Councils were invariably negative. The councils identified when the trajectory of belief was off-track and remained silent otherwise. They condemned distortions more than stating doctrine.

Yet no council avoided controversy. In fact, they were called precisely because of controversy. The matter of who was in and who was out, of who was right and who was wrong, of what was true and what was false, is a boundary issue. The councils sought to define the boundary. Traditionally this has been called a matter of heresy. The word derives from the Greek "hubris," which meant the sin of transgressing proper limits. Like the dome of Sophia, Holy Wisdom was definite at the boundary line which separated the outside from the inside but within that boundary all sharp distinctions blurred.

With the Council of Nicea in 325 and its rejection of the Arian Christ,[9] that is, Christ was neither perfect God nor perfect human, heresy became an issue of treason and not simply a matter of mistaken belief. Since the State replicated the Kingdom, to profess another faith constituted an act of treason. Thus, for example, the Jews were hardly tolerated because of their beliefs whereas prisoners of war were viewed less as conquered enemies and more as potential converts to the cause of Byzantine Orthodoxy. The policy of "grudging toleration" gradually changed into "one of forced conversion and persecution."[10]

Although heresy now meant treason, correct belief eluded definition. Nicea did not resolve the Arian-Athanasian conflict. The Orthodox insistence on the boundary limits of the Person of Jesus Christ (neither dividing the persons of God nor confounding their substance) only contributed to continuing controversy. In the next century, although they started with Nicean orthodoxy, the Nestorians insisted on the Human element in Christ while Monophysites fought for the divine element. Some forces argued for "one will" in the divine and others for "two wills." Similarly, some insisted that the formula should read that the Spirit proceeded "from the Son" and others claimed it came "through the Son." At best conciliar declarations tried to determine what was <u>not</u> the truth and failed in focusing upon what <u>was</u> the truth.

Ideas of belief remained flowing expressions of felt-meaning. They seldom developed into formalized conceptions of experience. In fact a key to abstruse points of doctrine lay more in people's loyalty to their own regional solidarity—its own church, its own bishop, its own neighborhood holy men—than in objectively developed ideas.[11] Right mind participation excluded left mind observation.

Inadequate Procedures

Concepts remained inadequately articulated experience. So, too, procedures of governing failed to develop into standard procedures. The circular quality of the Byzantine mind showed itself in its pragmatic orientation in politics. What mattered was what worked, which is a right brain process (see Table 5). As I have noted, some have called it the "cunning" of the Greeks. It is more commonly known as Byzantine diplomacy. Nothing is straight forward and up front. Reflecting the idea and wording of Clement of Alexandria, Constantine Cavarnos could speak of Byzantium as "a Christian eclecticism."[12]

Perhaps the most blatant evidence of the deficiency of the Byzantine vision appeared in the chaos of its political structure. Leadership depended more on personal charisma than on rational considerations. Changes seldom came peacefully. Personal pragmatism made for volatile imperial government. Almost every transition precipitated a crisis. The facts are astonishing (see Table 9): "Of 109 sovereigns, 65 were assassinated, 12 died in convent or prison, 3 died of hunger, 18 were castrated or had their eyes put out, their noses or hands cut off, and the rest were poisoned, suffocated, strangled, stabbed, thrown down from the top of a column or ignominiously hunted down. In 1,058 years there were 65 revolutions of palace, street or barracks and 65 dethronements."[13] Politically, Byzantine style was "an absolute monarchy tempered by assassination." Guerdan called it "The Empire of Coups D'Etat."[14]

The simple vision, undeveloped ideas, and inadequate procedures, which went with Byzantium's enclosed space, made for a vigorous rejection of what it did not include and an uncritical affirmation of all that it did include. We have learned that right brain damage results in an exaggerated mood pattern which denies negative features and ignores limitations. The ordinary inhibition of an undifferentiated elation is lifted with cerebral damage or deficiency. In juxtaposing the brain and belief I discern something of that right brain elation in the Byzantine and dome-like mind. Its optimism lacked discrimination in what it thought and how it acted. The

Table 9. **Unlucky Emperors***

Basilicus	477	Starved in prison
Zeno	491	Buried alive
Maurice	602	Decapitated
Phocas	610	Dismembered
Heracleonas	641	Mutilated
Constantine III	641	Poisoned
Constans II	668	Bludgeoned in his bath
Leontius	705	Decapitated
Tiberius III	705	Decapitated
Justinian II	711	Decapitated
Philippucus	713	Blinded
Constantine VI	797	Blinded
Leo V	820	Stabbed, decapitated
Michael III	867	Stabbed
Constantine VII	959	Poisoned
Romanus II	963	Poisoned
Nicephorus II	969	Stabbed, decapitated
John I	976	Poisoned
Romanus III	1034	Poisoned, drowned
Michael V	1042	Blinded
Romanus IV	1071	Poisoned, blinded
Alexius II	1183	Strangled, decapitated
Andronicus I	1185	Mutilated and tortured
Isaac II	1193	Blinded
Alexius IV	1204	Strangled
Alexius V	1204	Blinded, maimed
John IV	1261	Blinded
Andronicus IV	1374	Blinded
John VII	1374	Blinded

*Philip Sherrard, BYZANTIUM (New York: Time-Life Books, 1966), 76.

encompassing space of St. Sophia revealed the enclosed space of the society.

Magnificent as the Byzantine relational style was I have assessed that dome-like mind as inadequate in itself. While it revealed disturbance, the disturbance appeared to come from a one-sided repetition of an all-at--once pattern (see Table 6). There was simply too much dome. Life was more integrated than polarized, more stabilized than dialectical. This is why I assess it as more incomplete than disturbed. There seems to have been more repetition of the relational than opposition to the rational.

More can and needs to be said about that limitation, especially in terms of the representational systems.

INNER LIGHT — LIMITED SYSTEM

St. Sophia symbolized the transition from the earthly to the heavenly sphere by its subtle shift from the square piers on the ground to the circular dome above. Where the square stops and the circle begins is blurred, thereby blurring the perception of sensory and non-sensory time-and-space. Despite its impressive appearance the building is plain on the outside. Like Christian teaching itself, the truly real lay within. What people could imagine meant more than what they could observe.

I regard the imaginative and intuitive process as central to Byzantine sensitivity. That sensitivity gave rise to its mystical orientation, generating what John Meyendorff termed "a theology of participation."[15] For them the true nature of human was not "autonomous" but rather a disclosure of the "image" of God. To know God therefore meant to "participate" in "becoming God." In becoming that which they were created to be, people participated in a unifying experience of an encompassing oneness.

Two implications are associated with this emphasis upon continuous communion with God. First, the intellect, which primarily refers to formal language, could not express the fullness of truth. Second, in relation to God, love, not knowledge, was primary.

Paradoxically, in encompassing everything Byzantium failed to take in enough. Its all-at-once style saw only an impressionistic mosaic of reality. Its expansive optimism spiritualized everything from gold to light. By relying exclusively upon the inner eye it failed to notice the ordinary world. A preference for the imaginative deprived the culture of needed input. The illusory reality ended in nearsighted blindness.

Input Deprivation

The global-synthetic strategy not only underutilized the logical-analytic strategy but did so in a way that was itself inadequate. I discern an absolute reliance on inner vision. Fuller maps of reality, which depend upon a configuration of seeing, hearing, and sensing in both their sequential and holistic forms, remained undeveloped. People simply failed to see anything as ordinary. For them the everyday, reflective of the old order of fallen reality, did not exist. They perceived everything under the conviction of the New Dispensation.[16] Everything shimmered with divinity. God infused each person and thing in the fullness of being all in all. Symbolic imagination dominated the re-presentation of reality. Or, to be more precise, explicit images rather than symbols conveyed Truth and Grace directly.

Every activity was theological. For instance, when Gregory of Nyssa visited Constantinople around 370, he described the atmosphere in a way that is as startling to us as it was annoying to him: "If you desire a man to change a piece of silver, he informs you wherein the Son differs from the Father; if you ask the price of a loaf, you are told by way of reply that the Son is inferior to the Father; and if you inquire whether the bath is ready, the answer is that the Son was made out of nothing."[17] Inner vision pre-empted everything else.

More specifically, empirical data were minimized. I note that fact in their rejection of Aristotle's conviction that the purpose of art meant pleasing the senses.

Thus they viewed representational art as reflecting only shadow images of original essences, a continuation of the Platonic tradition. Symbolic theology transformed the physical world, what we mean by the ordinary world of time-and-space, into a spiritual realm. The psychic or spiritual significance of things replaced natural philosophy which viewed them on their own terms.

Two dimensional scenes replaced three dimensional views. In the icons and mosaics we see madonnas with the legs of boys, saints proportioned like pyramids, and imaginary creatures adorning the Throne.[18] The formal figures stare out from their sacred poses in ways expressive of their importance. No one questioned these immutable types, for the individual and the particular were secondary. In short, the inner significance dominates every scene. The naturalism of the classical tradition was not lost but incorporated into the distinctly Byzantine style of abstraction. David Talbot Rice defined the style using the modern term of "expressionism."[19]

The goal of such sensory distortion was spiritual purification, <u>katharsis</u> as they called it. All that was not God was to be stripped away. To see ordinary sights, hear ordinary sounds, sense ordinary sensations, and smell ordinary scents only opened the way to being possessed by demons. In the words of Gregory the Sinaite (1255-1346), "They alone are rational according to nature, who have achieved purity, namely, the Saints."[20] And by purity he meant stripping away ordinary sensory input. Only the spiritual realm was the really real.

This abstract imagination suggests very selective input, even in its right mind processing. Although immersed in the Graeco context, the imaginative mind-set transformed everything into symbolic significance.

Illusory Reality

The minimizing of sensory data created an illusory world. Imperialistic faith took in too little and ignored too much. It ignored historical developments, life remaining basically the same across ten centuries. Each revival only reasserted the tradition. While no period was the same—and variations were sharp—the culture tended "to express itself in inherited moulds,"[21] whether theological or artistic.

Theology consisted of an endless recital of the tradition. Conciliar formulae invariably read, "Following the holy fathers . . ."[22] Reality had been disclosed once-for-all, which meant that the past mattered more than the present or future. Nothing new remained to be known.

Byzantine hagiography also illustrates the exclusive use of inherited molds in a liturgical manner.[23] Classical literary style showed no trace of emerging patterns. Because history meant divine destiny, no one attempted critical analysis of people or events. Imaginative narration avoided systematic concerns as well as questions of the accuracy of what had been handed on.

Perhaps the most acute expression of its illusory view came because the State replicated the Kingdom. In breaking the law a person committed a sacrilege. Thus crimes against the State were punished severely. The offense was not so much a violation of social laws as a denial of divine ordinances. For instance,[24] a baker who sold his goods above the legal price was hurled into his own oven. A dishonest police official was burned alive in the great forum, and a merchant caught using false measuring weights had his hands cut off. The issue was not heresy, which I have mentioned above, but sacrilege.[25]

Nothing in society could be viewed casually. Everything carried the burden of being of ultimate significance. The inner eye paid no attention to the observing eye.

Near-Sighted Blindness

Near-sighted blindness followed from an exclusive reliance upon a limited representational visual system. Autonomous distinctions failed to develop. Optimism polished everything. The inner eye set empirical input aside in favor of symbolic imagination.

Divine knowledge had to be seen and not simply heard. St. Symeon the New Theologian (ca.949-1022) declared that "the only way for someone to know God is through the vision of the light, the light of knowledge, which is sent out from that light." Only thus are "the eyes of the heart cleaned, that is, the mind and the intelligence [which I identify as left mind], and they see . . . God."[26]

The imaginative mind failed to re-present anything other than its own imagination. The dome-like dwarfed all else.

By the fourth century Christians had taken over the representational arts of the pagans. The Cappadocian Fathers[27] argued the usefulness of such realistic picturing for education as well as contemplation.[28] Those who could not read the Bible could at least see the story painted on the walls. But what was "portrayed" and what was "seen" constituted the focus of the dilemma. Which counted most: symbolic representation or symbolic imagination?

Beginning with Leo III (717-741) and ending with Theophilus (829-842), the iconoclasts, who rejected the power of imagery, repressed the iconophiles, who affirmed the validity of expressionism. The image-breakers viewed the efforts of the image-worshippers as blasphemous. The mysteries of the Spirit could not be re-presented in the medium of matter. To their minds the expressive destroyed the symbolic. They were reacting against an emphasis on icons which began as early as the second half of the sixth century.

> To make images is to reduce (the divine spirit) to the material plane. To worship them is to fall back into paganism, to reduce the saints to something resembling the ancient gods.[29]

The iconoclasts feared idolatry. To them the eye could see too much.

In contrast those who worshipped images claimed that the rejection of matter meant a denial of the incarnation. Matter was the medium of the spirit.

> If you do not worship images, you do not worship the Son of God, who is Himself the living image of the invisible God.[30]

Pictures of Christ and His Saints aided devotion without falling into idolatry. Or at least so they argued. By 843 the iconophiles prevailed.[31] Images reappeared with the belief that icons manifested invisible reality.[32]

Byzantium confused the transparency of images with the power of the divine itself. While the divine was "effective <u>through</u> the pictures," according to precise theological formulation, it was "never identical <u>with</u> them."[33] Because it rejected other re-presentational systems the intended veneration of right mind imagination turned into superstition.

In triumphing the iconophiles established the near-sightedness of sensory limitation. The divine and human natures of Christ were affirmed in theory but denied in emphasis. Only the divine nature was portrayed in the mosaics. The eternal Logos had taken over the personal center of a person. In that divine possession personal characteristics of His humanity were abolished. Thus in the icons Christ appears in a gold-enveloped setting. His humanity is missing. All that remains is the universal Ruler, the Pantocrator. The historical Jesus, crucified, dead, and buried, has disappeared. That imaginative abstraction process of Byzantium eliminated temporal reality. The human Jesus disappeared; only the divine Christ remained.

The inner eye had shut out the observing eye, overwhelming the analytical with abstract imagination. The cumulative effect of a view of God which translated an imaginative mind into dome-enclosed space and the representational system of inner sight meant the loss of the human as well as the natural. The limitation contributed to the brilliance of the culture but guaranteed its downfall. If the iconoclastic view had prevailed, the near-sightedness would have been greater. The iconophiles achieved an incomplete victory. Although they affirmed the material realm, divinity absorbed humanity. Not without justification Cyril Mango spoke of Byzantine "myopia."[34] Only the dome-like is seen.

COUNTERBALANCES

Despite deficiency in the way a brain works, the mind is resourceful. It compensates in amazing ways. One side cannot be ignored permanently nor can all the representational systems be shut down. Hope lies in people becoming aware of deficiencies and utilizing the whole range of input and output. I find such persistence of the neglected processes within the Byzantine perception of God.

The Spiritual and The Sensual

Sensory input was not lacking in Byzantium. In fact the concrete world played a prominent part in its right mind orientation. Although symbolic immediacy was its primary pattern, it never deserted the material realm. Concrete images were seen as manifesting The Truly Real.

For example Byzantium coated churches, domes, icons, in fact, its very civilization in "a cloud of gold."[35] Why did it do so? Because the Book of Revelation (21:15) stated that Jerusalem was measured by gold. Believing itself to be the actual New Jerusalem, Byzantium naturally covered itself in gold.

The society had a genius for the sensual as well as the contemplative.[36] It could put on violent pagan spectacles under the guise of spiritual festivity. It could amass splendid treasures in order to dazzle beholders. Its rejection of natural space and time did not cut it off from the material realm as a manifestation of the holy.

By the twelfth century its artistic style had become more personal, more intimate, and more linear. Symbolic interpretation grew less and human illustration emerged. The Christ Child now pressed his face affectionately against the Mother. A sense of intimacy was modifying its spiritual austerity. Even though symbolic imagination persisted, people softened that abstractionism as they became more aware of natural spontaneity.[37]

The Mystical and The Rational

The Byzantine insistence upon the relational mind never resulted in the rejection of rational process. In preserving classical rationality two kinds of reason were identified, each distinct in itself.[38] The highest form was pure prayer, an intuitive reason or inner attentiveness to pure being (nous). The other form referred to discursive or analytical reasoning (dianoia). Thus mystical reason and rational reason were associated.

St. Symeon the New Theologian made the point that the mystical provided the source for the rational: "Within all of human nature (God) placed a loving power so that the rational nature of (humanity) might be helped by the natural power of love."[39] In essence the divine drama portrayed humanity's eyes longing to see that which it loved.

Perhaps the most majestic expression of this style is found in the last great Byzantine mystic Kikolaos Kabasilas (died 1471). In making piety solely an issue of inner intention he avoided the otherworldly asceticism which had so dominated the East. He wrote:

> The law of the Spirit, which is love of God, is a law of friendship and gratitude. To follow this law one need not expend effort or expense or shed perspiration . . . Nor is it necessary to leave your work or go to out-of-the-way places . . . Because there is no place where God is absent, it is not possible for God not to

be with us . . . He will come to us even if we are evil, because God is good.[40]

Kabasilas invited Christians to discover their basic nature through which God communicated with each person. Secular learning was not deceitful nor was reason disparaged. Religious mysticism and worldly wisdom were reconcilable.

Such wholeness, however, played only a minor role in the Byzantine mind-set. The inner eye dominated the observing eye. Only the ethereal light of a vast enclosed space mattered. For ten centuries the right mind of God manifested its presence in every material form. The dome-like mind has difficulty reflecting upon itself.

We know from research on the brain that the effects of euphoria are long-lasting. Everything becomes "polished" with optimism, a quality I have associated with the gold-plating quality of Byzantium. It managed to minimize the negative and the tragic in ways similar to those who suffer from right hemisphere damage.[41] Even when the Empire was limited to Constantinople toward the end of the fourteenth century, it maintained the myth of the "emperor's ultimate authority."[42] Myopia makes people blind to the realities around and within.

With the fall of Constantinople to the Turks in 1453 the splendor that was Byzantium ended. Light went out and life ended. Yet with its exclusive preference for right brain process the external state of Byzantium became the universal state of Orthodoxy. A spiritual empire replaced the physical empire, which only confirms identifying its dome-like mind as imaginative. Although the physical-political reality no longer existed, the "true" reality of Byzantium, its spiritual reality, continued in The Orthodox Church of Eastern Christianity.[43]

Now that we have identified and assessed the dome-like mind of Graeco-Byzantine Christianity I turn to a consideration of the other major part of the Christian tradition, namely, the spire-like mind of Latin-

-Germanic Christianity. After identifying and assessing its perception of God I add a further note on the contrast between vision and inquiry.

NOTES

1. Peter Brown, THE MAKING OF LATE ANTIQUITY (n.4/9), 99. Even so, for Byzantium "demons were a reality." The whole of life was seen as a real but unequal battleground "between the battalions of good and evil," with fate being "decided by the bureaucracy of angels and demons" (Mango, BYZANTIUM [n.5/1], 159). Pessimism was not absent from Byzantine consciousness. Even in the midst of the military successes of the latter part of the tenth century, an eschatological sense of the end was present (Mango, BYZANTIUM [n.5/1], 211-212).

2. Cited by Guerdan, BYZANTIUM (n.5/1), 20.

3. Brown, THE WORLD OF LATE ANTIQUITY (n.5/1), 134.

4. Gregory of Nyssa, In Cant., or. VI; ed. W. Jaeger (Leiden Brill, 1960), 6:182; PG 44:893B, quoted by Meyendorff, BYZANTINE THEOLOGY (n.5/1), 12.

5. Unlike the Latin Tertullian, (ca.160-230) the Greek Fathers thought Athens had a partnership with Jerusalem. See Mango, BYZANTIUM (n.5/1), Chp. 6 "Education."

6. Meyendorff, BYZANTINE THEOLOGY (n.5/1), 4. See Meyendorff, CHRIST IN EASTERN CHRISTIAN THOUGHT (n.5/1), Chp. 8 "An Effort at Systematization." Maximus the Confessor (ca.580-662) is known as "the real father of Byzantine theology" but his "organic system . . . falls far short of appearing as a system in his own writings" (Meyendorff, CHRIST IN EASTERN CHRISTIAN THOUGHT [n.5/1], 131-132; idem., BYZANTINE THEOLOGY [5/1], 37-39).

7. John of Damascus, WRITINGS (n.5/1), "An Exact Exposition of The Orthodox Faith," I, 20 (167).

8. Guerdan, BYZANTIUM (n.5/1), 69. While the point is basically accurate, note must be made of "a dramatic upsurge in scholarship" in the ninth century and of "a lively intellectual climate" in the eleventh century (Mango, BYZANTIUM [n.5/1], 140--142).

9. Arius was a devout and learned churchman of Alexandria who insisted that Christ was a substance like that of God (homoiousios), i.e., Christ as Son was less than God as Father. Arius also insisted that Christ was not fully human because he did not have a human soul. Athanasius, while neither a speculative nor systematic thinker, grasped an essential issue, namely, that Christ was of the same substance as God (homoousios), i.e., Christ as Son was of the same substance as God and so fully equal with God. Athanasius also insisted that Christ was a real human being with a human soul. Largely at the urging of Constantine the following Nicean Creed was adopted:

> We believe in one God, Father Almighty, maker of all things visible and invisible; and in one Lord Jesus Christ, the Son of God, begotten from the Father, only begotten; that is, from the substance of the Father, God from God, light from light, true God from true God, begotten not made of one substance with the Father; and through whom all things were made both in heaven and the things on earth; who for us men and our salvation came down and was made flesh and became man and suffered and rose the third day and ascended into heaven and will come to judge the quick and the dead.

Arius and his followers were banished, only to return to stir up trouble. Athanasius was in constant danger. In 381 the Council of Constantinople reaffirmed the Nicean formula and settled the issue. See Tillich, A HISTORY OF CHRISTIAN THOUGHT (n.1/44), 68-76, for an excellent discussion of the

Trinitarian controversy. See Magoulias, BYZANTINE CHRISTIANITY (n.4/5), 20ff and Dennis E. Groh, "Grace and Backsliding in the Nicean Age: A Footnote on Triumphant Orthodoxy," explor: A Journal of Theology, Fall 1981, 76-84, for excellent discussions of Arianism. See Meyendorff, CHRIST IN EASTERN CHRISTIAN THOUGHT (n.5/1), Chp. 1, 13-28, for a discussion of "Christology in the Fifth Century" and Chp. 2, 29-46, for a comparison of "Chalcedonians and Monophysites."

10. Mango, BYZANTIUM (n.5/1), 92. An imperial enactment in 380 was later placed at the beginning of Justinian's Code (Cod. Theo., xvi. 1,2; Cod. Jus., i, 1.1, quoted by Mango, BYZANTIUM [n.5/1], 88): "It is Our will that all the peoples who are ruled by the administration of Our Clemency shall practice that religion which the divine Peter and apostle transmitted to the Romans . . . We shall believe in the single Deity of the Father, the Son and the Holy Spirit under the guise of equal majesty and of the Holy Trinity. We command that those persons who follow this law shall embrace the name of Catholic Christians. The rest, however, whom we ajudge demented and insane (dementes vesanosque), shall sustain the infamy attached to heretical dogmas. Their meeting places shall not receive the name of churches, and they shall be smitten first by divine vengeance and secondly by the retribution of Our own initiative which we shall dispense in accordance with the divine judgment." As Justinian himself wrote (Jus. Nov., xxxvii, praef., quoted by Mango, BYZANTIUM [n.5/1], 88): "If we strive by all means to enforce the civil laws, whose power God in His goodness has entrusted to Us for the security of Our subjects, how much more keenly should We endeavour to enforce the holy canons and the divine laws which have been framed for the salvation of our souls!" He issued an edict in 529 which specifically forbade "pagans, heretics and Jews to teach" (Mango, BYZANTIUM [n.5/1], 135).

11. Mango, BYZANTIUM (n.5/1), 30.

12. Cavarnos, BYZANTINE THOUGHT AND ART (n.5/1), 21-22, citing and quoting Clement: "The way of truth is one; but into it, as into a perennial river, streams flow from all sides." By "philosophy I do not mean the Stoic, or the Platonic, or the Epicurean, or the Aristotelian, but whatever has been well said by each of those sects which teach righteousness along with knowledge pervaded by piety. This eclectic whole I call philosophy" (Stromateis, Bk. I, Ch. 5; Ch. 7. THE WRITINGS OF CLEMENT OF ALEXANDRIA. In Ante-Nicene Christian Library. Translated, William Wilson, Edinburg, 1867).

13. Guerdan, BYZANTIUM (n.5/1), 135.

14. Ibid.

15. Meyendorff, BYZANTINE THEOLOGY (n.5/1), 3.

16. Mango, BYZANTIUM (n.5/1), 270, 264.

17. Gregory of Nyssa, Gibbon's translation, quoted by C.E. Stevens, "Constantine the Great and the Christian Capital, A.D. 324-527." In Whitting, BYZANTIUM (n.4/12), 8-9.

18. Guerdan, BYZANTIUM (n.5/1), 46.

19. Rice, ART OF THE BYZANTINE ERA (n.5/1), 35; Mango, BYZANTIUM (n.5/1), 263.

20. Gregory the Sinaite, in Philokalia, Athens, 1893, Vol. 2, 243, quoted by Cavarnos, BYZANTINE THOUGHT AND ART (n.5/1), 38.

21. Baynes, THE BYZANTINE EMPIRE (n.5/1), 243.

22. The decree of the Council of Chalcedon provides a prime example of the once-for-all understanding: "This wise and salutary formula of divine grace (provided by Nicaea) sufficed for the perfect knowledge and confirmation of religion; for it teaches

the perfect doctrine concerning Father, Son, and Holy Spirit, and sets forth the Incarnation of the Lord to those who faithfully receive it. But, inasmuch as persons undertaking to nullify the preaching of the truth have through their individual heresies given rise to empty babblings . . . this present holy, great, and ecumenical council, desiring to exclude every device against the Truth, and teaching that which is unchanged from the beginning, has at the very onset decreed that the faith of the 318 fathers (of Nicaea) shall be preserved inviolate" (Chalcedon, Definitio fidei, Conciliorum oecumenicorum decreta [Bologna: Instituto per le Scienze Religiose, 1973], quoted in Meyendorff, BYZANTINE THEOLOGY [n.5/1], 10-11).

23. Personal conversation with Susan Ashbrook Harvey, May 1983.

24. Guerdan, BYZANTIUM (n.5/1), 39.

25. See ibid. for a description of the mutilation and torture of Emperor Andronicus I (1185), for supposedly usurping the throne.

26. St. Symeon the New Theologian, quoted by Magoulias, BYZANTINE CHRISTIANITY (n.4/5), 79, 80.

27. Basil the Great (ca.330-379), and the Gregories of Nazianus (ca.329-390) and Nyssa (ca.332-398).

28. Mango, BYZANTIUM (n.5/1), 132-133; Magoulias, BYZANTINE CHRISTIANITY (n.4/5), 42-43.

29. The Iconoclast argument reconstructed by Guerdan, BYZANTIUM (n.5/1), 51.

30. The Iconophile argument reconstructed by Baynes, THE BYZANTINE EMPIRE (n.5/1), 91. Also see the Iconophile argument reconstructed by Guerdan, BYZANTIUM (n.5/1), 51.

31. Hebraic and Arabic influences were the strongest sources of the Iconoclast concern about the worship of images. "The victory of Orthodoxy (in the Iconoclastic Crisis) meant, for example, that religious faith could be expressed, not only in propositions, in books or in personal experience, but also through (humanity's) power over matter, through aesthetic experience, and through gestures and bodily attitudes before holy images. All this implied a . . . religious consciousness (which) involved the whole (person), without despising any function of the soul or of the body, and without leaving any of them to the realm of the secular" (Meyendorff, BYZANTINE THEOLOGY [n.5/1], 52). See Meyendorff, CHRIST IN EASTERN CHRISTIAN THOUGHT (n.5/1), Chp. 9 "Vision of the Invisible: The Iconoclastic Crisis," 173-192.

32. Kinesthetic exaggeration also accompanied the visual. By the sixth century people would prostrate themselves (prokynesis) before the images. A whole range of sensory responses grew in popularity: lighting candles, burning incense, kissing the image, carrying the icon in procession. At times the symbolic bordered on the magical. A passage from a homily when Constantinople was under siege in 626 refers to the prominent display of icons to aid in the defense of the city: "The Patriarch caused sacred images of the Virgin holding in her arms her Son, our Lord, to be painted on all the gates of the city that faced west. They were like the sun of righteousness scattering darkness with its rays, since it was from the west that the progeny of darkness (the Avars) had come. In so doing the Patriarch was, as it were, crying out in spiritual language to the throng of barbarians and to the demons that led them: 'It is against these, O alien nations and demonic tribes, that your war is directed. Your pride and insolence will be crushed by the command of a woman, the Mother of God, whose Son sank the Pharaoh and his whole army in the Red Sea and reduced all demons to impotence'" (L. Sternbach, Analecta Avarica [Cracow, 1900], 8, a homily probably by Theodore Syncellus, quoted by

Cyril Mango, "Heraclius, the Threats from the East and Iconoclasm: A.D. 610-843." In Whitting, BYZANTIUM [n.4/12], 46).

33. Tillich, A HISTORY OF CHRISTIAN THOUGHT (n.1/44), 96, 89-90. Italics added.

34. Mango, BYZANTIUM (n.5/1), 216, 220.

35. Guerdan, BYZANTIUM (n.5/1), 45-46.

36. Mango, BYZANTIUM (n.5/1), 63-65. See Guerdan, "The Hippodrome - an Ersatz Forum" and "The Empire of Miracles and Palmistry," BYZANTIUM (n.5/1), 53-73, as illustrative.

37. In the last phase, especially in medieval Serbia, "gentleness" graced the major works. What distinguishes the work "above anything else is its vividness, its new humanism, and its new feeling for gaiety and decoration. The figures are more personal, more individual, the scenes are brighter, and fuller, and there is a new concern with detail, which is in itself wholly delightful" (Rice, ART OF THE BYZANTINE ERA [n.5/1], 220).

38. Cavarnos, BYZANTIUM (n.5/1), 51.

39. St. Symeon the New Theologian, quoted in Magoulias, BYZANTIUM [n.4/5], 78.

40. Kabasilas, quoted in Magoulias, BYZANTIUM (n.4/5), 84.

41. See n.11, Chp. 2.

42. Mango, BYZANTIUM (n.5/1), 220.

43. The continuity of the earthly heaven came to rest in Moscow as the Third Rome. In his famous letter to Tsar Basil III in 1510 the monk Philotheus of Pskov made the transition explicit: "I wish to add a few words on the present Orthodox Empire of our ruler: he is on earth the sole Emperor (Tsar) of the

Christians, the leader of the Apostolic Church which stands no longer in Rome or in Constantinople, but in the blessed city of Moscow. She alone shines in the whole world brighter than the sun . . . All Christian Empires are fallen and in their stead stands alone the Empire of our ruler in accordance with the Prophetical books. Two Romes have fallen, but the third stands and a fourth there will not be" (Quoted in Baynes and Moss, BYZANTIUM: An Introduction, 385. In Ware, THE ORTHODOX CHURCH [n.5/1], 113).

Figure 5 Chartres Cathedral (exterior)

Chapter Seven

THE SPIRE: Medieval Inquiry[1]

In the two previous chapters I explored the dome-like mind of Byzantium.

I turn now to the spire-like mind of Medieval culture. I remind you I am juxtaposing three disciplines: theology, which articulates the ways people have perceived God working; neuropsychology, which deals with the way the brain functions; and architecture, which expresses a culture's perception of reality. In this chapter I identify the spire-like mind of God by analyzing the Cathedral at

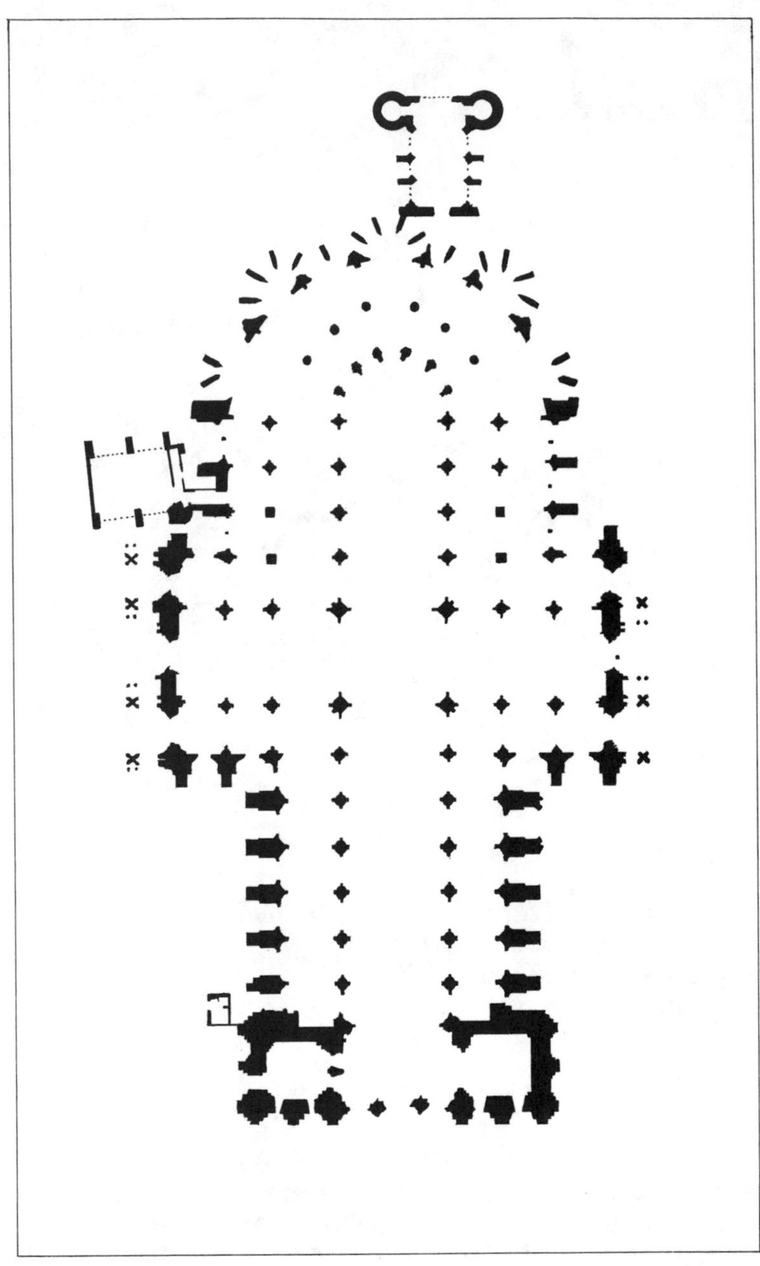

Figure 6 Chartres Cathedral Ground Plan

Chartres. In the following chapter I assess how adequately the spire-like mind perceived God.

The anxiety of finitude haunted the Middle Ages,[2] driving people in search of certainty. Augustine (354-430)[3] personified the perplexity. Conceived by a pagan father and a Christian mother, he struggled with a divided psyche. Three themes emerged from his confrontation with finitude:

1. sensuality versus spirituality or the issue of sin;

2. the ambiguity of the Church versus the ambiguity of the State or the issue of authority;

3. doubt about the appearance of reality versus certainty about the source of the unconditional or the issue of truth.

Each of these—sin, authority, and truth—expressed a facet of the one issue: how could the transcendent, he asked, be immanent in the face of finitude? Throughout succeeding centuries this persisted as the dominant theme of the Medieval period.

Six hundred years after Augustine, Anselm (1033-1109), bishop of Canterbury, uttered a central aphorism: "I do not seek to understand in order to believe, but I believe in order to understand."[4] I believe in order to understand. Inquiry rested upon belief. One participated in what one inquired after. While retaining the concepts, Peter Abelard (1079-1142) shifted the emphasis: "Nothing is believed unless it first be understood."[5] I understand in order to believe. Belief rested upon inquiry.[6] One inquired into what one believed.

Just as Abelard's approach has been called "methodical doubt," so Anselm's approach can be called "methodical faith." Anselm gave more credence to "necessary" reason than his words convey.[8] Abelard drew back from an indiscriminate use of understanding in a way his words obscure.[9] Nevertheless, for each thinker, the phrase "in order to" connects both belief and understanding with a "methodical mind" (Tables 2, 3, and 5).

Against the unreliability of appearances, Augustine had found the place of certainty within the doubting person per se: "Everyone who is aware that (one) doubts knows the truth and is certain of it . . . and should not doubt that (one) has the truth within (oneself)."[10] Paradoxically, "the immediacy of the truth in every human being"[11] led people to doubt immediacy in the experience of what today we call awkward self-consciousness. Doubt about appearances also established the primacy of the observer over what was observed. I understand that primacy to be left brain dominance (Table 3). As the methodical mind tried to identify and organize proper order, explanation took the lead over experience.[12]

In the appearances of things passing, humanity inquired about permanent order. The methodical mind stood between belief and understanding, between conceptualization and experiencing.

Earlier I identified correlates between architectural space and the way the mind works. Left mind architecture presents step-by-step sequences. Straight lines pass through stable space giving the impression of progression. And that is what we discern in the Medieval cathedral.[13] Nowhere is the methodical mind with its methodical method more elegant than in the Cathedral at Chartres.[14] Here in "the Gothic Image"[15] we find the invisible made visible. Whereas in St. Sophia space is the foreground and structure the background of perceptual organization, here structure is the foreground and space the background, just the reverse.

Reactions to the architecture, then and now, continue to be analytic.[16] In the very structure of the cathedral itself Christian doctrine, formal logic, and rational inquiry merged. In what follows I take you through that spire-like mind. Visually and descriptively we move into archetypal intensity. I translate its structure into explicit statements of what mattered to them, namely, where God dwelt and how they got to God. I connect those meanings with ways our minds work and, thereby, with how we too can know what matters to us and for us. In the spires of Chartres I discern the spire-like of humanity. My analysis starts with the outside, pauses at the entrance, and finishes at the altar with the Liturgy.

OUTER STRUCTURE

Seen from distance the cathedral's[17] spires and transepts seem, in the words of Emile Mâle, "like a mighty ship about to sail on a long voyage."[18] Indeed, to the Medieval mind it was the ark of the world, offering refuge from the flood of sin, ignorance, and death. The spire-like mind organized finitude's chaos with the precise order of the hierarchical relationship of churchly and earthly authority.

One Rationale

For most Medieval inquiry, the symbolic statement took precedence over factual reference.[19] Sin had torn the fabric of creation and required the visible manifestation of God's redemptive work in order to be repaired. This sacramental vision provided the rationale for the inquiring mind.

Hugh of St. Victor (1096-1141) wrote the first systematic treatise outlining the symbolic method. In it he argued as follows:[20]

1. To understand humanity the world must be understood.

2. Humanity's body, i.e., its material nature, existed for its spiritual nature.

3. Therefore, matter carried spiritual significance.

In Chartres the visible edifice disclosed—manifestatio—that invisible order. The spires show us the spire-like mind at work.

William Durandus translated the objective order of the rationale into architectural design. In his work of 1286, *Rationale of the Diving Offices*, he explained the theological meaning of *everything* in the building. The ground plan corresponded to the human figure and to abstract proportions: "The arrangement of a material church resembleth that of the human body: the chancel, or place where the altar is representeth the head: the transepts, the hands and arms, and the remainder (nave)—towards the West—the rest of the body. The sacrifice of the altar denoteth the vows of the heart."[21]

The western entrance to the cathedral marked the region of the setting sun, that is, the region of Death and Judgment. The duller light of the northern side expressed Old Testament anticipation of divine knowledge, while the sun of the South shone with New Testament warmth and brightness. Each direction pointed the seeker to the eastern sunrise, to the birth of Christ as the Light of the World.

According to Augustine, God thought in the precise manner of mathematical ratios with music as the clue.[22] The perfect ratio was 1:1 because symmetry, equality, and unity made for a one-to-one correspondence between the parts. Similarly the octave (1:2), the fifth (2:3), and the fourth (3:4), as expressions of the principle of numbers, kept the cosmos from returning to chaos.

Just as mathematical ratios determined musical values, so proportions determined visual values.[23] One could be led from the world of appearances to contemplate the divine order by means of the symbolic method which enabled people to know the truth underneath the literal statement.[24] Whereas the East depended upon icon and imagination to *lift people into the Light of God*, the West pursued idea and inquiry to *bring people to the Knowledge of God*. Whether in mathematics, geometry, music, or architecture, perfect ratios disclosed the divine order. Harmony and proportion anchored the invisible rationale in the rational process. Appropriately, therefore, Mâle could characterize the mathematical harmony of Chartres as "frozen music."[25]

Two Powers

In looking at the building we can feel clear order harmonizing sharp contrasts. Flying buttresses hold together the thrust and counterthrust of the upward and outward directions. The two towers soar into the sky, conveying a balanced aspiration as the straight lines carry our eyes heavenward—two limbs outstretched in supplication.

The towers provided a clue to the Medieval mind and its perception of God. While Durandus asserted that "(t)he towers are the preachers and prelates of the Church," serving as "her bulwark and defense" and signifying "the life or the mind of a prelate which aspireth heavenwards,"[26] the sharper meaning came with their political significance. Most cathedral plans projected two spires crowning a pair of towers. Because it possessed a complete set Chartres was a rarity. But whether the two towers were seen or only projected, to symbolic-minded interpreters two towers proclaimed the supremacy of spiritual power over temporal power.[27] By the fourteenth century urban citizens were declaring their freedom from church control by building churches with one tower only. One tower stood for political liberation and local autonomy; two towers meant submission to Roman dominance. The spire-like mind struggles for supremacy.

Architecturally, then, the complex system of opposing forces disclosed logical relationships everywhere. Opposing forces re-presented the ambiguity of finitude: time versus eternity, matter versus spirit, expanding curiosity versus centered faith. Two towers, two powers: one eternal, spiritual, and true; the other temporal, material, and limited.

Despite their similarity the towers differ.[28] As with the human brain, close inspection reveals basic contrasts. Each contributes to the whole yet each contributes differently.

The southern tower shows a decorative base with a simple spire. The northern spire stretches 27 feet higher with its base simpler and its upper areas more intricate. Like the right mind (Table 3), the South tower looms as more complex (i.e., impressionistic) in what it takes in and simpler (i.e., pragmatic) in what it shows forth. It rests solidly upon the ground. Like the left mind, the North tower appears simpler in what it takes in (i.e., detached) and more complex (i.e., refined) in what it puts out. It develops in the air. Each is the reciprocal of the other.

Though the towers are similar in form and function, they differed in status. Medieval rationale set the priority: the spiritual stretched higher than the temporal. Authority "descended" from God-to-pope-to-priest-to laity.[29] Two towers meant different powers. To the imperial power, however, the higher power was not free to meddle with earthly affairs. And that difference in perception fueled the fire of disturbance.

Gregory the Great (540-604, Pope 590-604) laid the foundation of a spire-like mentality. Christendom, he declared, was organized hierarchically as was the universe. Each power, whether spiritual or temporal, and each person, whether religious or lay, had a proper place in The Divine Scheme: "Universal society could subsist by no other principle than that of a great system of order preserving its diversity of operations."[30]

The issue of two powers focused on who controlled the locus of the holy. When Charlemagne knelt before Pope Leo III to be crowned emperor of the Holy Roman Empire in 800, the question was answered,[31] or so those in Hildebrand's (Pope Gregory VII, 1073-1085) time interpreted the event. In contrast to the Byzantine coronation in which the emperor stood, the Latin order compelled the temporal power to kneel for an anointing.[32] Personal anointings defined exclusive status, making for a sharp demarcation of authority in which the clergy were greater than royalty and laity alike.[33] Access to power was restricted to a special few. The one true authority identified two powers in descending order, establishing, in the phrase of R.W. Southern, "an imperial papacy."[34]

Like the left brain dominating the right,[35] one spire reached higher than the other. Such is the spire-like intent.

Precise Order

In On The Trinity, Augustine had contemplated the mystery of the redeeming work of God.[36] By his death Christ had atoned two-fold—once for the death of the soul because of sin and the other for the death of the body. One death for two deaths. The "correspondence" or harmony of two musical notes described that reconciliation. When the ear heard the ratio 1:2, it heard the truth of redemption. Christ atoned for sin and death: two towers, one activity. Such was the second meaning of the symbolic towers.

Mathematics linked the invisible God and the visible world in precise ways. Nowhere was this Augustinian belief in number and proportion more prominent than at Chartres.[37] Theology became geometry[38] as the methodical mind transformed mystical order into trinitarian order.[39] As the Divine Architect, God used matter as the building material to bring order out of chaos.[40] The Greek word for order—cosmos—also meant ornament. Thus architecture meant "adorning" matter with order.[41]

Every part of medieval life—the building as well as the belief structure—manifested the Three-in-One: two towers, one entrance; two aisles, one nave; nave, chancel, apse; pier arch, triforium, clerestory; triple windows; all endless variations of the trinitarian motif. Three articles of faith proved the existence of God. So people could enter the cathedral through three facades—West, North, or South—each with three entrances and each entrance with three rising bands of figures surrounding a central tympanum or recessed space. The logic of the trinitarian concept fixed every form in a definite way.

Numbers combined ideas as real forces. Each number bore special meaning, interpreted by Dogma and confirmed by Scripture. Twelve, three, four and seven were the most powerful numbers.[42] Twelve represented the universal Church willed by Jesus through the twelve apostles. The four seasons stood for the four evangelists, even as the twelve months reflected the twelve apostles. Further, 12 is the product of 3 x 4.

Three represented all that was spiritual, in accordance with the trinitarian structure of reality. Four revealed all that was material, which meant earth, air, fire, and water. To multiply 3 by 4 was to infuse matter with spirit. Seven is the sum of 3 plus 4 and so represented the dual nature of humanity, its soul and body. The life cycle had seven stages, each with its associated virtues and vices. Seven petitions, sustained by the seven sacraments,[43] maintained the harmony between human and divine.[44]

The methodical mind made faith "clearer" by appeal to reason. It made reason "clearer" by resorting to imagination. It made imagination "clearer" by directing attention to the senses.[45]

Architecturally, then, Chartres shows us one rationale, two powers, and clear order. The outside anticipates the inside. The world was set. The forces were definite. The way was known. The cathedral made the invisible mind of God visible.

THREE ENTRANCES

In approaching the cathedral we are bewildered by some 2000 figures crowding the entrances. Not so for people of that time. What confuses us made immediate sense to them. Mâle described their experience:

> As one draws near her one first meets the figure of Christ, as everyone born into the world meets Him on his or her voyage through life. He is the key to the riddle of life . . . The Christian is told how the world began and how it will end

> . . . Before one's eyes are all the people whose history it is of importance humanity should know . . . Thus the world with its history becomes intelligible.
>
> Side by side with the story of this vast universe, humanity's own history is written. It learns that life must be a conflict, a struggle with nature in every month of the year, a struggle with itself at every moment . . . And to those who have fought a good fight the angels in the heavens above hold out crowns . . ."[47]

Nowhere was that message more explicit than in the entrances. Structurally they harmonize diametrically opposed principles of design: the straight lines contain the round lines; the vertical lines accord with the horizontal lines; the narrower doors accentuate the larger door; and the horizontal band of figures ties together the three portals. The sculpture specifically called weary travellers to cross the threshold into their permanent dwelling since the way was known.

Standard Symbols[48]

Explanation prevailed over experience.[49] Symbol took precedence over fact, as seen for instance in there being more symbolic representations than historical scenes.[50] By the thirteenth century concepts had replaced drama. And nowhere was the composition simpler, the meaning sharper, and the complexity clearer than at Chartres.[51] (See Table 10.)

For instance, four beasts surround Christ in glory in the central tympanum of the West facade—a man, an eagle, a lion, and an ox. They signified in turn:[52] the four evangelists—St. Matthew as a man because of the geneological table of Jesus' ancestors, St. John as eagle because it alone gazed straight into the sun's eyes, St. Mark as a lion because he spoke as one crying in the wilderness, and St. Luke as ox because of the sacrificial animal offered by Zacharias in Luke 1-2; next, the four

Table 10. **Sculpture Sequence and Content**

The West Facade: the place of sunset, death, and Judgment

the right tympanum:	Incarnation of Christ as doctrine, with Old Testament figures and the Seven Liberal Arts
the left tympanum:	the Ascension of Christ, with Old Testament figures
the central tympanum:	the Second Coming of Christ in Majesty with Old Testament figures

The North Facade: the region of duller light with Old Testament

the right tympanum:	the suffering of Job and the Judgment of Solomon, with Old Testament stories such as Esther, Samson, Gideon
the left tympanum:	the Incarnation of Christ as story, with the Visitation and Annunciation
the central tympanum:	the Death, Resurrection, and Triumph of the Virgin, with Old Testament figures such as Elisha, Abraham, Moses, David, Isaiah, and St. John the Baptist

The South Facade: the area of brightest light with New Testament

the right tympanum:	stories of St. Martin and St. Nicholas, with other saints such as Leo, Ambrose Jerome, Gregory
the left tympanum:	the Story of Stephen, with other saints such as Theodore, Vincent, George
the central tympanum:	the Last Judgment, with apostles

symbols of Christ—as man in His Incarnation, as eagle in His ascension, as lion in His Resurrection, and as ox in His Death; and then, the four virtues necessary for salvation—reason in the man, contemplation in the eagle, courage in the lion, and renunciation in the ox.

The symbolism was standard.[53] Numbers ordered the relationships. Symmetry determined the contrasts. Nothing was left to chance.

Divine History

The sculpturing of doctrine was as precise as the sculpturing of symbols.

In the central tympanum of the West facade, Christ faces forward, greeting the approaching wanderer as the fearful Judge.[54] People lived in a state of agitated expectancy as hell loomed on every side. Located as it was in the West, the facade witnessed to sunset, Death, and Judgment. Here was the final act of The Divine Drama.

In the tympanum the wanderer saw The Doctrine of the Word Made Flesh: from His Incarnation on the right, His Ascension on the left, to His Second Coming in the center. Underneath, Old Testament figures signified "the pillars of humanity,"[55] even as they served as the pillars of the entrance itself. The North and South entrances completed the history of redemption, setting out the earlier stages and declaring the end of the pilgrimage, respectively.

Mary was as central to salvation as Christ Himself.[57] And Chartres believed itself the chief haven of the Virgin.[58] It named its cathedral after her, Notre Dame, Our Lady.[59] It dedicated its sculpture and stained glass to her. Scenes of The Annunciation and The Visitation reinforced her role in salvation. In truth she was its source.[60] To honor Her as the Mother of God was to glorify Christ as the Savior of the world. She was <u>the throne</u> upon which the King of Glory rested.

Although the Virgin was glorified, what mattered was the masculine. The feminine split in two: the capricious Eve versus the loving Virgin, the source of sin which tempted reason versus the source of salvation which carried reason. Only reason—objective, symmetrical, lawful—created order. Only reason—methodical, systematic, intentional—sustained order. The freedom of order came with the masculine quality of reason,[61] in short, the redeeming mind of God (Table 2).

The rationale of Divine History reflected the rationality of Divine Order.

Divine Order

In the thirteenth century, during the height of the Middle Ages, Vincent of Beauvais (ca. 1190-1264) compiled a comprehensive explanation of the Divine Order in his work on The Great Mirror of Knowledge[62] and Thomas Aquinas (ca. 1225-1274) synthesized the whole of Christian doctrine with the whole of Aristotle's logical empiricism. The cathedral stood as the "visible counterpart" of those intellectual edifices.[63] Each laid out the final perception of the Divine Order.[64]

The worlds of matter, mind, and love—the three orders of significance—were reflected in the four mirrors of knowledge.

* The Mirror of Nature reflected each creature as a thought or symbol of God.

* The Mirror of Instruction reflected labor and learning as the means of perfection.

* The Mirror of Morals reflected the clash between the twelve virtues and twelve vices, whether one followed the Active or the Contemplative life.

* The Mirror of History reflected the three ages of humanity: the age of symbols, with humanity waiting for the Law; the age of realities with the Law Incarnate in the Gospels; and

the age of the saints, with humanity conforming to the Law which brings history to a close.

At the three facades of the cathedral, people saw the three epochs (symbols, realities, and saints) and the three realities (Law, Gospel, and Consummation).

The three entrances made the mind of God explicit. The order of creation was known. History was a three-act drama of Redemption from sin. Spire-like thinking has an explanation for everything on earth and in heaven.

INNER STRUCTURE

Once through the entrance and inside the building we are dazzled by its majesty.[65] The 130 feet of receding nave pull our eyes away from the 122 feet of soaring vault. Unlike the impressionistic mosaic of St. Sophia's One Dome, the Two Towers articulate the trajectories—upward and forward. The gigantic clerestory, the monumental windows, and the vertical piers each play a breath-taking crescendo of exalted space with clear direction.

As our eyes adjust to the splendor, the parts appear more distinguishable. Under the rainbow of vaults we see three horizontal levels: an immense arcade, the triforium passage, and the clerestory windows. The columns simultaneously separate the bays and accentuate the verticals. Distinct yet round surfaces ripple forward, drawing us to the altar. We sense confidence, harmony, and peace.

Glass and Luminosity

As with the sculpture, so with the stained glass: function and form combine. The walls enclose the space, frame the glass, and direct us forward. The synergy of window-and-light, of arch-and-vault-and-pier, creates an illusion of infinite space filled with intelligible light.

Figure 7 Chartres Cathedral (interior)

Hugh of St. Victor commented about the symbolic meaning of the windows: " . . . by the windows the five senses of the body are signified: which ought to be narrow without, lest they should take in vanities, but should be wide within to receive spiritual good."[66]

Consistent with the symbolic method Durandus added: "The glass windows . . . are Holy Scriptures, which expel the wind and the rain, that is all things hurtful, but transmit the light of the true Sun, that is, God, into the hearts of the faithful. These (windows) are wider within than without, because the mystical sense is the more ample, and precedeth the literal meaning."[67]

The transparent walls make the inside accessible to the outside. The effect is to etherealize space. The Light of God transformed the life of the world. As the sun rose in the East, so Christ was the Light of the World. As it set in the West, so the faithful passed from this world to the next. As in the Virgin Conception, so light penetrated glass without breaking its form.

By giving light both form and content, the glass manifested the visible idea of the invisible presence. The mind of God showed itself in The Word of God. The intense light emphasized specific space.

Space and Dialectics

Once we see the towers we know the plan. Inside space re-presents outside structure. We can see where to go. We know what to expect. People met God at the altar and nowhere else. There were no surprises in this place.

In the nave we can feel space marching forward. Gone is the diffused spaciousness of St. Sophia. Straight lines accent every feature: upward to the vaulted ceiling, onward through the receding nave. Simple boundaries separate nave from aisles. The nave is more than twice as high as it is wide and taut by virtue of its being twice the size of the sides. Thus we are led irresistibly toward the altar. The forward direction controls opposition between height and depth.

Such an intensified atmosphere defined the holy.[68] What had originated in experience now ended with explanation. Twelfth century speculations[69] culminated in thirteenth century synthesis. The locus of the holy was fixed—at the altar. Method had mastered mystery—spatially and symbolically.

The Yes-and-No of the scholastic parallelled the thrust-and-counterthrust of the architecture: <u>I believe in order to understand/I understand in order to believe.</u> The rational balance of asymmetrical forces determined the direction and resolved the oppositions. The methodical mind perfected this dialectical perception.

Until the eleventh century, experience and explanation had commingled.[70] The brain functioned as one mind, though left mind rationality was the preferred strategy. The autonomy of reason informed the authority of tradition. So reason collected, harmonized, and commented on the diverse authorities of Scripture, the Councils, and the Fathers. But as explanations accumulated interpretations became more necessary.

Reason took over when it asserted its right to examine everything which belonged to faith. Whereas the authorities had informed piety, now the intellect analyzed it. The infinite reaches of reason at last challenged the finite limits of authority itself.

Anselm applied the dialectical method to every dogma of faith—to God, the Trinity, the Incarnation, the Virgin Mary, original sin.[71] To forget faith was presumptuous but to reject reason was negligence. Faith stood between blind belief and a direct vision of God. In his words: "I understand the <u>intellectus</u>, which we receive in this life, to be a kind of mean between faith and vision."[72] In the language of the working brain I describe this as a right mind response with a left mind explanation.

Tillich correctly called this pattern "dialectical monotheism," that is, "a monotheism in which movement is seen in God himself."[73] Because God was living God,

God disclosed a "yes" and a "no" in himself. The idea of the Trinity expressed dialectical thinking. God's ways of being God came through "a living separation and reunion of his life with himself."[74]

This dialectical mind made mystery understandable. The Greek word "dialectics" meant "to discriminate" and "to converse."[75] Dialectics pursued truth with a question-and-answer method of "discriminating through cooperative discussion."

In his famous Sic et Non ("Yes and No" or "Pro and Con"), Abelard carried the method further.[76] Beneath the discrepancies among the Fathers, the Councils, and the Scriptures he wanted to demonstrate a unity. To him the steps were clear:[77]

1. Questions were asked.

2. Answers were advanced.

3. Contradictions were pressed.

4. Finally decisions were made.

Once the intellect resolved the discrepancies the faith was believable.[78]

We see a transition from left mind dominance to complete domination in the iconography of Chartres. Christ's public life is restricted to such theologically saturated episodes as the Baptism, the Marriage Feast at Cana, the Temptation, the Transfiguration, and the Entrance into Jerusalem. Missing are picturesque events of the human Jesus. The method had translated the mysteries into clear, consistent, dogmatic statements.

In other words the thrust-and-counterthrust of questions-and-answers led to a preconceived synthesis.[79] The rational solution harmonized the opposites of spirit and matter: theologically in doctrine, politically in papal supremacy, and architecturally in the gothic cathedral. Few people questioned whether the method corresponded to reality. The method was The Reality:

Three-into-One concentrated and controlled space. The dialectics of experience solidified into an explanation of the description.

Two spires stretched upward: the South side was strong, simple, and towering, whether it represented the rule of the state or the rule of the rational; the North side was slimmer, more intricate, more lofty, whether it disclosed papal dominance or definitive faith. Two aisles, a vaulted ceiling, an elongated nave. The inquirer left the world of conflict to meet God at the altar.

What Chartres was to architecture, Aquinas was to theology. They shared a "sweep and proportion, balance and harmony"[80] which thoroughly rationalized reality. As the Pope sought to unify the Church and the Empire under one head, so Aquinas aspired to unify faith and reason into One Mind of God.[81]

Both in content and style his Summa theologica reflects geometric precision. Like the stones of Chartres the syllogisms fit tightly into place. He divided knowledge according to the three theological virtues, and the four cardinal virtues. Each step of the summation started with a question. The question suggested an affirmation. The affirmation was critiqued by philosophical objections. The philosophical objections were countered with biblical assertions. Finally, the oppositions of questions, affirmations, philosophical objections, and biblical assertions were resolved by reason.

A typical passage displays the gothic splendor of scholasticism's dialectical method. Aquinas asked whether God could be known in this life by natural reason. After declaring that (1) natural reason knows "both good and bad," and (2) grace relates only to knowledge of God's existence, he filled in the details:[82]

> Our natural knowledge begins with sense. Hence our natural knowledge can go as far as it can be led by sensible things.

Note that he has correctly identified the left mind's dependence upon what it observes as the primary, if not the sole, source of what it knows. What it knows means what it explains.

> But our intellect cannot be led by sense so far as to see the essence of God; because sensible creatures are effects of God, their cause.

Note again that he has identified the left mind's inability to grasp the configuration of parts—the gestalt—and its dependence for that global integrated-synthesis upon right mind process.

> Hence, from the knowledge of sensible things the whole power of God cannot be known; nor therefore can His essence be seen. But because they are His effects and depend on their cause, we can be led from them so far as to know of God whether he exists, and to know of Him what must necessarily belong to Him, as the first cause of all things; exceeding all things caused by Him.

The mediated and indirect knowledge of the unconditional—what I identify as left mind explanation of what it observes—was called the cosmological argument for the existence of God. In contrast to John of Damascus' incomprehensible God, Aquinas "proved," that is, explained, the existence of God in five ways:[83]

1. Since motion demanded a mover, logic led to an unmoved mover.

2. Since every effect was both caused by a previous effect and the cause of a subsequent effect, logic led to an efficient first cause.[84]

3. Since every thing was dependent upon something else for its existence, logic led to an ultimate necessity.

4. Since degrees of perfection existed in every thing, logic led to absolute perfection.

5. Since purposes ("ends") appeared in the way the world was governed, logic led to a final purpose.

Like the cathedral, the Thomistic edifice rested upon the material and the sensory. Like the higher spire, the structure stretched into rarified space. The steps were clear: first, sensory data; second, abstract concepts; third, universal principles; fourth, fixed laws; and finally, precise dogmatic statements. The step-by-step process moved from the visible realm of motion, causes, contingency, imperfections, and purposes to the invisible realm of the permanent. The limitation of the sensory brought people to the point where spirit transformed matter, namely, in the Eucharist.

Liturgy and Pilgrimage

Medieval people accepted Augustine's view that life was a pilgrimage, a journey to the celestial city.[85] Humanity wandered through this valley of corruption in search of the incorruptible dwelling place of God. The disorder of humanity contrasted with the rational order of nature.

Set in the floor of the nave we can see a labyrinthian maze which symbolized the journey to Jerusalem.[86] With its central rosette it mirrors the huge circular rose window above it on the West facade.[87] Only one path brought people to the center.

Like every aspect of the Medieval mind-set, pilgrimage to the Holy Land or other sacred places represented the infusion of matter with spirit. People journeyed to the place where eternal order ordered earthly disorder. So political pilgrimages—the crusades—mirrored personal pilgrimages. They arose out of the vision of recovering the special space of the Holy Land from the infidel Muslim Turks.

A song from the Second Crusade (1147) expressed the longing and the ideals of power:

> God has brought before you his suit against the Turks and Saracens, who have done him great despite. They have seized his fiefs, where God was first served and recognized as Lord.
>
> God has ordained a tournament between Heaven and Hell, and sends to all his friends who wish to defend him, that they fail him not.[88]

With the haunting cloud of judgment and the clear direction of action, people swept across the Latin West into the Byzantine East. Once, twice, three times they entered the lists to liberate the Light.[89]

The goal of pilgrimage—whether political or personal—was to come to the place where the invisible penetrated the visible. What had appeared in Palestine continued in the Mass. In contrast to the elaborate liturgy of Orthodoxy, Catholic liturgy was more straightforward. Instead of being lifted up into the Light of One Dome, the faithful were directed by the Two Towers to the one place where God came down to meet humanity, at the altar. The drama was simplified. One knew what was happening. Everything worked to arouse the mind to contemplate the invisible God in the crucified Christ.

Privately and publicly, people responded to The Word Made Flesh as individuals.[90] Conscious intention replaced the more natural responsiveness of Byzantine Liturgy.

DECLARING A RATIONAL MIND

Chartres' asymmetrical towers present an analytic mind-set. The dialectics of thrust-and-counterthrust, of height-and-depth, parallelled the dialectics of spirit-and-matter, of faith-and-reason, of papacy and empire. The two towers and one altar concentrated the luminous light so that people could make their own pilgrimages to the place where The Word came down—whether in the Holy Land or the sacred shrines. But God met humanity preemptively in the Eucharist at the altar.

I emphasize this crucial feature of Medieval inquiry, namely, the observing eye of dialectical reason. The physical only "mediated" the spiritual indirectly. One had to inquire after the Divine order: I believe in order to understand/I understand in order to believe. Method characterized both the belief and the understanding. With Augustine the methodical mind had displayed an intuitive rationality, a reflecting upon primary experience. With the synthesis of Aquinas it had simplified data into an objective systematic analysis of a pre--determined structure.

"Nothing exists in the intellect unless first in the senses," Thomas asserted.[91] Theology derived from the application of concepts, which, in turn, had been abstracted from sensory input. But sensory reality only actualized nonsensory reality. As he put it: "All things must pre-exist in the Word of God before they exist in their own nature. That which is in a things is in it according to the mode of that thing and not according to its own: the house exists in the architect intelligibly and immaterially; and so must be understood things pre-existing in the Word according to the mode of the Word."[92]

By making existence the actualization of essence, Thomas reconciled the Hellenistic discrepancy between being and becoming, between non-being and actual being. What was conceivable demonstrated what was sensed. God became flesh-and-blood in the crucified Christ.

The cathedral's architecture made the invisible Trinity visible in trinitarian form. In the midst of the disorder of this world, it called people to submit themselves to the true order of creation, the hierarchy of being in which the spiritual power towered over the earthly powers of royalty and laity.

Initially, I implied that the inquiry precipitated by finitude emerged from uncertainty in Augustine's psyche, generated by the opposition between his Christian mother and his pagan father. How to reconcile the contrast became the task for subsequent interpretations. Eventually, the scholastic method provided a step-by-step approach that claimed to resolve the conflict between spirit and matter.

Let me translate the implicit meanings of Chartres' penetrating light, dialectical space, and liturgical pilgrimage into explicit features in order to correlate the Medieval mind-set with the way the mind works (Table 11).

(1) Because its architecture, art, and theology were shaped by a conceptual reality structured by rational proportions, I identify its features as primarily left mind (Tables 3 & 5). That means, individuals were instructed to initiate a focused inquiry about the permanent order of reality. By God manifesting God through mathematically determined elements, people could be directed specifically to the fixed meeting place with God.

(2) Because its authority structure, role responsibilities, and language pattern were structured according to objective, abstract, and formal procedures, I identify its input as exact and its output as analytic (Table 5). Reality existed apart from individuals, objectively and realistically. People abstracted and generalized in a way which created a convergent and standard view of the world. Ambiguity was rejected by setting clear boundaries. The divine could be known in only one place and in only one way. Every part and every person had a specific and exclusive place in the scheme of creation.

(3) The configuration of intense light, space, and sacrifice suggests an analytic mind-set. People

Table 11. **Medieval Inquiry: Identification and Assessment**

Identifying Features:	
Oriented to:	a mapped world - individuals initiate responses - narrow attentional focus - specific/realistic/rational signs/symbols
Organized in:	impersonal/conceptual terms - objective anchor - diversity-in-unity - little ambiguity - things in sequence of standard order
Utilized:	temporal input deliberate output
Re-presentational Systems:	rational processing - universal (deliberate, controlled, fixed) (visual) - basic patterns with repeatable meanings (sensory) - single theme of inquiry (temporal)
Assessing the Inquiry	
Brain process:	disturbed (intense space) - fixed formulae freeze contrasts (rival powers) - methodical dissection (conflicting inquiries) - willing the rational order (onesided will)
Re-presentational Systems:	conflicting (inner structure height/depth) - orders (intuitive vs. intellectual) - obediences (free devotion vs. unquestioned autocracy) - pieties (interior desires vs. philosophical inquiry)
Summary: strengths:	unity contained diversity penetrating rationality
limitations:	too dominant intentionality overdeveloped explanatory rationality subordination of all-at-once process

> observed reality with the special vigilance of a specific explanation (Table 3). The parts/steps/places/roles were separate and fixed. Because reality was stable, symbolic meanings were few and repetitive, that is, the ratio was 1:2, the proclamation of Christ's death for the double death of humanity's soul and body.

The people of the Medieval period perceived God's activity as primarily the redeeming process of a rational left mind. Even more than its conceptual input, it displayed an analytic output (Table 5). The Two Towers, differentiated and asymmetrical in their structures, revealed one map, one truth, one way to the Source of Life. The spire-like mind identifies what is urgently right in reality.

NOTES

1. Unless specifically cited, I have drawn upon the following works for my interpretation:

   H. Daniel-Rops, HISTORY OF THE CHURCH OF CHRIST: 3 (1050-1350). CATHEDRAL AND CRUSADE. Translated by John Warrington (New York: E.P. Dutton & Co., Inc., [1957] 1961).

   Carolly Erickson, THE MEDIEVAL VISION: Essays in History and Perception (New York: Oxford University Press, 1976).

   Joan Evans, LIFE IN MEDIEVAL FRANCE (London: Phaidon Press, [1925] 1957).

   Eugene R. Fairweather, A SCHOLASTIC MISCELLANY: Anselm to Ockham. Edited and translated for the Library of Christian Classics, Volume X (The Westminster Press) (New York: The Macmillan Company, 1970).

   Etienne Gilson, HISTORY OF CHRISTIAN PHILOSOPHY IN THE MIDDLE AGES (New York: Random House, 1955).

   Etienne Gilson, REASON AND REVELATION IN THE MIDDLE AGES (New York: Charles Scribner's Sons, 1938).

   Gordon Leff, MEDIEVAL THOUGHT: St. Augustine to Ockham (Baltimore: Penguin Books, 1958).

   Colin Morris, THE DISCOVERY OF THE INDIVIDUAL 1050-1200 (New York: Harper Torchbooks, [1972] 1973).

   Jaroslav Pelikan, THE CHRISTIAN TRADITION: A HISTORY OF THE DEVELOPMENT OF DOCTRINE. Vol. 3 THE GROWTH OF MEDIEVAL THEOLOGY (600-1300) (Chicago: The University of Chicago Press, 1978).

Jeffrey Burton Russell, A HISTORY OF MEDIEVAL CHRISTIANITY: Prophecy and Order (New York: Thomas Y. Crowell Company, 1968).

R.W. Southern, THE MAKING OF THE MIDDLE AGES (New Haven: Yale University Press, [1953] 1980).

Idem., WESTERN SOCIETY AND THE CHURCHES IN THE MIDDLE AGES (Baltimore: Penguin Books, [1970] 1979).

Walter Ullmann, THE GROWTH OF PAPAL GOVERNMENT IN THE MIDDLE AGES: A Study in the idealogical relation of clerical to lay power (London: Methuen & Co. LTD, [1955] 1965).

Idem., THE INDIVIDUAL AND SOCIETY IN THE MIDDLE AGES (Baltimore: The John Hopkins Press, 1966).

Idem., PRINCIPLES OF GOVERNMENT AND POLITICS IN THE MIDDLE AGES (New York: Barnes & Noble Inc., [1961] 1966).

2. The papal librarian Giovanni Andrea first used the term "Middle Ages" in 1469 when he distinguished "the ancients of the Middle Ages from the moderns of our time" (quoted by Daniel-Rops, HISTORY OF THE CHURCH OF CHRIST [n.1 above], 51). See also Fairweather, A SCHOLASTIC MISCELLANY (n.1 above), 21, note 20. The period of the Latin West parallelled that of the Byzantine East. It began during the early fifth century with the collapse of the Roman Empire (through over-expansion and barbarization) and the achievement of Augustine as the aftermath of Rome (400-1000). It blossomed between ca. 1050-ca. 1270 in a one hundred mile radius around Paris, with such achievements as those of Anselm, Abelard, and Aquinas in The Triumph of Scholasticism (1000-1300). It broke apart between ca. 1270 and ca. 1330, ending finally with the fall of Constantinople in 1453 and the

Triumph of Skepticism over Authority. The changes in thought and society "gave rise to a diversity of problems which prevented any uniform state of development" (Leff, MEDIEVAL THOUGHT [n.1 above], 17). The series of independent and unstable kingdoms, cut off from the culture in the East, were divided between the areas north and south of the Alps. With the loss of Imperial Authority, Franks and Romans had little in common.

3. Cf. Augustine's The Confessions, The City of God, and On the Trinity, especially BASIC WRITINGS OF SAINT AUGUSTINE. Edited, with an introduction and notes by Whitney J. Oates. Volumes One and Two (New York: Random House Publishers, 1948). See Tillich, A HISTORY OF CHRISTIAN THOUGHT (n.1/44), 103-133, for an excellent discussion of Augustine.

4. Anselm, Proslogion, I (Fairweather, A SCHOLASTIC MISCELLANY [n.1 above], 73), reflected Augustine's statement: "Understanding is the reward of faith. Therefore seek not to understand that thou mayest believe, but believe that thou mayest understand" ("On the Gospel of St. John," XXIX, 6, quoted by Gilson, REASON AND REVELATION IN THE MIDDLE AGES [n.1 above], 19). Anselm was more rationalistic than usually perceived by virtue of his emphasis on necessary reason in demonstrating faith.

5. Pierre Abailard, HISTORIA CALAMITATUM. The Story of Abelard's Adversities. A Translation with Notes by J.T. Muckle, With a preface by Etienne Gilson (Toronto: The Pontifical Institute of Medieval Studies, 1954), 39.

6. "By doubting we come to enquiry; by enquiring we perceive the truth." Abelard, quoted by Leff, MEDIEVAL THOUGHT (n.1 above), 111. Abelard is less rationalistic than on first reading. His statements are "an affirmation that faith is not merely 'talking,' but 'understanding' . . . neither the repe-

tition of unintelligible formulas, nor the immediate knowledge of an object through sense-perception, nor full comprehension of God" (Richard E. Weingart, THE LOGIC OF DIVINE LOVE: A Critical Analysis of the Soteriology of Peter Abelard [Oxford: At the Clarendon Press, 1970], 6). Despite the priority of revelation in his rational loyalties and the similarity of his approach to that of Anselm, "he manifests an intransigent confidence in his own reason which is lacking in Anselm and his dialectical skill is not balanced by profound metaphysical insights like (Anselm) . . . a failure to appreciate the 'ontological' dimension of human experience. Over against this, however, . . . set the genuine faith and piety expressed in (his) liturgical poetry" (Fairweather, A SCHOLASTIC MISCELLANY [n.1 above], 224-225).

7. Cited by Leff, MEDIEVAL THOUGHT (n.1 above), 111.

8. Anselm resisted subordinating reason to faith. He placed it between faith and vision. See Fairweather, A SCHOLASTIC MISCELLANY (n.1 above), 49, note 8.

9. Abelard pulled back from an indiscriminate use of the dialectic: "Insofar as reason is hidden let us be content with authority." "What greater affront can believers receive than to have God Himself examined and for small intellects to be able to understand Him and language to discuss Him" (quoted by Leff, MEDIEVAL THOUGHT [n.1 above], 112).

10. Augustine in DE TRINITATE, X, 10, quoted by Leff, MEDIEVAL THOUGHT (n.1 above), 39. In Enarr. in Ps. 130, 12, quoted by Morris, THE DISCOVERY OF THE INDIVIDUAL (n.1 above), 66, he expressed the loss which precipitated the search for certainty: ". . . while (the soul) is still in the body, it is said to her, 'Where is your God?' But her God is within and spiritually beyond . . . the soul cannot succeed in finding him, except by passing through herself."

11. Tillich, A HISTORY OF CHRISTIAN THOUGHT (n.1/44), 104.

12. Augustine described order as "an arrangement assigning their proper place to equal and unequal things," quoted by Russell, A HISTORY OF MEDIEVAL CHRISTIANITY (n.1 above), 40, emphasis added.

13. Most prominent in conceiving of the Gothic structure was Abbot Suger of St. Denis (1081-1151) in the second quarter of the twelfth century. Gothic devices included: pointed arches, flying buttresses, the triforium gallery, and spacious arches, which maximized window space. The design made for lofty vaults and a sense of rarified space. I have consulted the following works as background on Gothic Architecture:

    Von Reinhard Bentmann and Heinrich Lickes, CHURCHES OF THE MIDDLE AGES. Translated by Anthony Lloyd (London: Cassell, [1970, 1978] 1979).

    Jean Bony, FRENCH CATHEDRALS. Photographs by Martin Hürlimann; descriptive notes by Peter Meyer (New York: A Studio Book, The Viking Press, 1961).

    Flavio Conti, THE GRAND TOUR SPLENDOR OF THE GODS. Translated by Patrick Creagh (New York: HBJ Press, Inc., [1977] 1978).

    Georges Duby, THE EUROPE OF THE CATHEDRALS: 1140—1280. Translated from the French by Stuart Gilbert (Geneva: Skira, 1966).

    Louis Grodecki, GOTHIC ARCHITECTURE. In collaboration with Anne Prache and Roland Recht. Translated from the French by I. Mark Paris (New York: Harry N. Abrams, Inc., [1976] 1977).

    Emile Mâle, THE GOTHIC IMAGE: Religious Art in France of the Thirteenth Century. Translated by

Dora Nussey (New York: Icon Editions, Harper & Row, Publishers, [1913, 1958] 1972).

Josef Grünenfelder, CATHEDRALS OF EUROPE. Photographs by Michael Wolgensinger. Translated by David Lawrence Grumbs (New York: Thomas Y. Crowell Company, [1973] 1976).

Erwin Panofsky, GOTHIC ARCHITECTURE AND SCHOLASTICISM (New York: Meridian Books, 1957).

Helen Huss Parkhurst, CATHEDRAL: A Gothic Pilgrimage (Boston: Houghton Mifflin Company, 1936).

Auguste Rodin, CATHEDRALS OF FRANCE. Translated by Elisabeth Chase Geissbuhler. With a preface by Herbert Read (Boston: Beacon Press, [1914] 1965).

Win Swann, THE GOTHIC CATHEDRAL. With an historical introduction by Christopher Brooke (London: Elek, 1969).

Otto von Simson, THE GOTHIC CATHEDRAL: Origins of Gothic Architecture and the Medieval Concept of Order (Princeton: Princeton University Press, Bollingen Series XLVIII, [1956] 1974).

14. The following works deal exclusively with the Cathedral at Chartres:

Robert Branner, ed., CHARTRES CATHEDRAL: Illustrations, Introductory Essay, Documents, Analysis, Criticism (New York: W.W. Norton & Company, 1969).

Adolf Katzenellenbogen, THE SCULPTURAL PROGRAMS OF CHARTRES CATHEDRAL: Christ * Mary * Ecclesia (New York: W.W. Norton & Company, Inc., [1959] 1964).

Raymond Klibansky, THE SCHOOL OF CHARTRES. In Twelfth Century Europe and the Foundation of

Modern Society. Edited by Marshall Clagett, Gaines Post, and Robert Reynolds (Madison, Wis.: University of Wisconsin Press, 1961), 3-14.

Mâle, THE GOTHIC IMAGE (n.13 above), 390-391, concluded his monumental study by stating that the cathedral of Chartres lacked no essential element in Medieval thought. Other French cathedrals developed only aspects of the thought, i.e., Amiens and the prophetic messianic idea, Notre Dame at Paris and the centrality of the Virgin, Laon and learning, Rheims and French rationalism, Bourges and the virtues of the saints. Chartres alone was "a whole unqualified in Europe."

15. The term "Gothic" refers to Medieval artistic style. High Gothic expression culminated in the twenty-six year period around the beginning of the thirteenth century with the construction of cathedrals at Chartres (1194), at Rheims (1211), and at Amiens (1220). All this occurred in the Ile-de-France, a triangle of areas which joined these towns with the southern tip which included Paris and St. Denis. The French "passion for the universal" combined with its wide range of ideas and finely ordered scheme of thought "to make the cathedral an image of the world, a summary of history, a mirror of the moral life" (Mâle, THE GOTHIC IMAGE [n.13 above], 399).

16. E.g., Michael Cohalan, "Tension in the Cathedral: Gothic beauty: Was it form or function?" Science 81, December, 1981, 32-41.

17. The name "cathedral" came from the building which housed the bishop's chair, i.e., his *cathedra* or throne seat.

18. Mâle, THE GOTHIC IMAGE (n.13 above), 396.

19. While Augustine used the principle of symbolic interpretation, he insisted on the factual basis of allegory. "Do not destroy the historic foundation of Scripture, without it you will build in the air," he

declared. "Abraham really lived and he really had a son by Sarah his wife . . . " (Sermo, ii, quoted by Mâle, THE GOTHIC IMAGE [n.13 above], 135-136). By the thirteenth century, theologians taught ex cathedra that Scripture was both fact and symbol. Symbol, however, took precedence over fact, as seen, for instance, in symbolic statements being more common in the iconography than historical scenes (Mâle, THE GOTHIC IMAGE [n.13 above], 173).

20. Hugh of St. Victor, cited by Gilson, HISTORY OF CHRISTIAN PHILOSOPHY (n.1 above), 170-171; Pelikan, THE GROWTH OF MEDIEVAL THEOLOGY (n.1 above), 207-209, 263; Tillich, A HISTORY OF CHRISTIAN THOUGHT (n.1/44), 175; von Simson, THE GOTHIC CATHEDRAL (n.13 above), 36.

21. William Durandus (1220-1296), THE SYMBOLISM OF CHURCHES AND CHURCH ORNAMENTS. A translation of the first book of the Rationale Divinorum Officiorum. Introductory essay and notes by John Mason Neale and Benjamin Webb. Third Edition (London: Gibbings & Company, 1906), I, I, 14; I, I, 8; Appendix B. For instance: "The faithful predestined to eternal life are the stones in the structure of this wall which shall continually be built up unto the world's end. And one stone is added to another . . . Those stones which are of larger size, polished, or squared, and placed on the outside and at the angles of the building, are men of holier life than others . . ." (I, I, 9). Or again: "The cement, without which there can be no stability of the walls, is made of lime, sand, and water. The lime is fervent charity, which joineth to itself sand, that is, undertakings for the temporal welfare of our brethren . . . Now the lime and the sand are bound together in the wall by an admixture of water. But water is an emblem of the Spirit. And as without cement the stones cannot cohere, so neither can men be built up in the heavenly Jerusalem without charity . . . All the stones are polished and squared—that is, holy and pure, and are built by

the hands of the Great Workman into an abiding place in the Church . . ." (I, I, 10).

22. Music was the science of measuring accurately, "since in all things well made measure must be observed" (Augustine, "On Music." The Fathers of the Church: WRITINGS OF SAINT AUGUSTINE. Volume 2. Translated with Introduction by Robert Catesby Taliaferno [New York: CIMA Publishing Co., Inc., 1947], I, 2, 2). Written between 387 and 391, and among his earliest works, in it he examined the hierarchy of numbers as constituting the soul, the universe, and the angels. "The Divine Wisdom is reflected in the numbers impressed on all things" (Augustine, _De libero arbitrio_, lib. II, chp. xvi, quoted by Mâle, THE GOTHIC IMAGE [n.13 above], 10).

23. Cf. Boethius (480?-?524) (_De music_, I, 32, PL, LXIII, 1194, quoted by von Simson, THE GOTHIC CATHEDRAL [n.13 above], 33): "the ear is affected by sounds in quite the same way as the eye is by optical impressions."

24. The Alexandrian School of Origen, Clement, and Philo had developed the allegorical method of understanding which provided the intellectual basis for Byzantine vision. The method enable them to find the "hidden treasure beneath the literal" statement, to quote Origen (G.W. Butterworth, ed., ORIGEN ON FIRST PRINCIPLES [New York: Torchbooks, Harper & Row, 1966], 275-276, 287-290, 294, 296-297, 312). An explication of the method can be illustrated from Durandus: "Anagogue is so called from _ana_, which is upwards, and _goge_, a leading: as it were an upward leading . . . Jerusalem is understood historically of that earthly city whither pilgrims journey; allegorically, of the Church Militant; tropologically, of every faithful soul; anagogically, of the celestial Jerusalem, which is our country" (THE SYMBOLISM OF THE CHURCHES AND CHURCH ORNAMENTS [n.21 above], proeme, 12).

25. Mâle, THE GOTHIC IMAGE (n.13 above), 22. Abelard also linked architecture and music. He suggested that the proportions of Solomon's temple were the "symphonic" perfection of the Heavenly Jerusalem (Theol. Christ., I, 5, cited by von Simson, THE GOTHIC CATHEDRAL [n.13 above], 37-38).

26. Durandus, THE SYMBOLISM OF THE CHURCHES AND CHURCH ORNAMENTS (n.21 above), I, I, 21.

27. Bentmann and Lickes, CHURCHES OF THE MIDDLE AGES (n.13 above), 93.

28. The southern tower dates from 1180, the northern between 1507-13.

29. Ullmann, THE INDIVIDUAL AND SOCIETY IN THE MIDDLE AGES (n.1 above), 47; idem., PRINCIPLES OF GOVERNMENT AND POLITICS IN THE MIDDLE AGES (n.1 above).

30. Gregory the Great, quoted by Russell, A HISTORY OF MEDIEVAL CHRISTIANITY (n.1 above), 40.

31. Southern, WESTERN SOCIETY AND THE CHURCHES IN THE MIDDLE AGES (n.1 above), 60-61. See "Symbolism in Coronation Ceremonies of the Ninth Century," Ullmann, PRINCIPLES OF GOVERNMENT AND POLITICS IN THE MIDDLE AGES (n.1 above), 143-166. Pope Stephen IV (816-817) crystallized the Latin form in crowning Louis the Pious, son of Charles, at Rheims 17 years later. Frankish and papal anointings were added to the previous nonliturgical rite. From 750 to 1050, however, the kings exercised sacred authority in a way that contributed to the struggle between the two powers. Consider, for instance, the advice Charlemagne received from Alcuin a few years prior to the coronation: "Our Lord Jesus Christ has set you up as the ruler of the Christian people, in power more excellent than the pope or the emperor of Constantinople, in wisdom more distinguished, in the dignity of your rule more sublime. On you alone depends the whole safety of the churches of

Christ" (quoted by Southern, WESTERN SOCIETY AND THE CHURCHES IN THE MIDDLE AGES [n.1 above], 32, from Alcuin, Ep. 174 [M.G.H. Epistolae Karolini Aevi, ii, 288]).

32. The ceremony of coronation in the East and of anointing in the West represent two types of societies and two patterns of political power. Byzantine coronations were religious acts without being essentially ecclesiastical. The absence of personal anointing in general minimized specialized and exclusive status, whether of emperor or priest. In the West the recognition of temporal power required an act of rebirth which meant the ruler knelt to receive a personal anointing at the hands of the spiritual power (Nelson, "Symbols in Context" [n.4/5]).

33. The ceremony of anointing originated in northern Europe between the seventh and tenth centuries. Olive oil, which was used for the anointings, was scarce in northern and western Europe because the olive could not be cultivated and so had to be imported. Thus, the powerful "haves" claimed "an extra share of the oil [in the acts of anointing] which was both so potent and so scarce" (ibid., 118-119). The theocratic "King, by the grace of God" stood in tension with feudal lordship. In lordship, the king entered into contractual relationships with individual tenants-in-charge, thereby making him a member of the community rather than someone above it. The feudal structure involved "counsel and consent, hence (government) by co-operation leading to teamwork" (Ullmann, THE INDIVIDUAL AND SOCIETY IN THE MIDDLE AGES [n.1 above], 66-67).

34. Southern, WESTERN SOCIETY AND THE CHURCHES IN THE MIDDLE AGES (n.1 above), 24.

35. Betty Edwards, DRAWING ON THE RIGHT SIDE OF THE BRAIN (n.3/45), 42.

36. See Augustine, ON THE TRINITY (n.3 above), especially Bk. IV, chps. III, IV, and VI.

37. Cathedral schools, as communities of secular clergy in contrast to the monasteries as communities of religious clergy, fostered medieval inquiry. The urban circumstances loosened the organization of life and thought, including the need to defend either ancient privileges or truth, which contributed to the secular clergy being more inquisitive than the religious clergy. The School of Chartres was one of two centers which carried on the Augustinian belief in number and proportion (von Simson, THE GOTHIC CATHEDRAL [n.13 above], 26-39). As a stronghold of classical learning, mathematics and musical studies made up the core of its curriculum.

John of Salisbury (1125-1180) quoted Bernard, chancellor from ca. 1119-1126, in expressing a continuity with the past and a reaching into the future: "If we see further than (the ancients), it is not in virtue of our stronger sight, but because we are lifted by them and carried to a great height. We are dwarfs carried on the shoulders of giants." Dwarfs they may have been but the remark made clear they could "see further." They carried inquiry beyond its previous limits. Bernard of Chartres' famous statement is quoted by John of Salisbury, Metalog., III, 4 (PL, 199, 900), in Fairweather, A SCHOLASTIC MISCELLANY (n.1 above), 21, and cited by Southern, THE MAKING OF THE MIDDLE AGES (n.1 above), 203.

38. Under the influence of Thierry of Chartres (?-ca. 1155), theology merged with geometry. The equality of the Three Persons of the Trinity was represented, he explained, by the equilateral triangle. The indescribable relationship between Father and Son was found in the unfolding of the square. God was unity and the Son was "unity begotten by unity," even as the multiplication of a size with itself results in its square. Thus, the Second Person of the Trinity was properly called "the first square" (cited by von Simson, THE GOTHIC CATHEDRAL [n.13 above], 27-28).

39. "The ecclesiastical hierarchy on earth is an image of the heavenly hierarchy . . . There are three times three orders of angels—making it possible to give a kind of analogy to the earthly hierarchies . . . The earthly hierarchies are: (1) The three sacraments: baptism, the Lord's Supper, confirmation; (2) The three degrees of the clergy: deacons, priests, bishops; (3) The three degrees of non-clergy: the imperfect, who are not even members of the congregation, the (laity), and the monks, who have a special function. These nine earthly hierarchies mediate the return of the soul to God . . . All reality belongs to the ecclesiastical reality, because (it) is the hierarchical reality as expressed in the different degrees of being and knowledge of God" (Tillich, A HISTORY OF CHRISTIAN THOUGHT [n.1/44], 94-95). Every hierarchy received something from above and passed it on down below.

40. von Simson, THE GOTHIC CATHEDRAL (n.13 above), 31.

41. Macrobius, Commentaries, I, 14; Hugh of St. Victor, De sacramentis Christianae fidei, PL, clxxvi, 169, cited by von Simson, THE GOTHIC CATHEDRAL (n.13 above), 29.

42. Augustine, In Psalm., vi; Hugh of St. Victor, PL, clxxv, 22; Rabanus Maurus, De Universo, xviii, 3, ix, 10; Honorus of Autun, De Imag. Mundi, II, iii, et al., cited by Mâle, THE GOTHIC IMAGE (n.13 above), 10-11, 66.

43. The seven sacraments are: baptism, the eucharist, penance, ordination, marriage, confirmation, and extreme unction.

44. Other variations of 7 included the 7 planets, the 7 days of creation, and the 7 tones of Gregorian music.

45. Panofsky, GOTHIC ARCHITECTURE AND SCHOLASTICISM (n.13 above), 38.

46. Although the three facades were conceived as an organic whole, the North and South transepts show development beyond the symbolic style found in the West facade. For instance, the iconography is more lifelike; bodies are proportioned; postures are varied; informal expressions are more flexible; plants and animals are more natural; people are more individualized. The abstract is less, the representational more. The close identity of sculpture and structure is looser. It seems that intentional process shifted from a rational mode toward a relational mode.

47. Mâle, THE GOTHIC IMAGE (n.13 above), 396-397.

48. See George Ferguson, SIGNS & SYMBOLS IN CHRISTIAN ART. With Illustrations from Paintings of the Renaissance (New York: Oxford University Press, [1954] 1977). Although drawing upon the artists of the Renaissance, it serves as a accurate and comprehensive guide to the symbolic system. These artists primarily crystallized and ordered what had been handed down by the Church.

49. Artists interpreted the world according to the theologians. As early as the Second Council of Nicaea in 787, the Church had declared (Syn. Nicaena, ii, quoted by Mâle, THE GOTHIC IMAGE [n.13 above], 392): "The composition of religious inquiry is not left to the imagination of artists, but is formed upon principles laid down by the Catholic Church and by religious tradition." By the ninth century, Walafrid Strabo (ca. 809-849) had compiled in his Glossa ordinaria precise allegorical explanations for every verse in the Bible.

50. Mâle, THE GOTHIC IMAGE (n.13 above), 173.

51. For instance, the Incarnation cycles at Chartres contrast with those of Vezelay (ca. 1125). The glorification of Christ at Vezelay is dramatic. In

the Adoration by the Magi each Magus bears a different gift embodying several meanings. In contrast, at Chartres, Virgin and Child are isolated, worshipped only by angels. Two figures symmetrically flank the central group, with only censers in their hands. Commotion has been replaced by essentials. Or again, the relationship among the three tympana of the Royal Portal are more equal in size, closer together, and convey a more unified whole than elsewhere. See Katzenellenbogen, EARLY CHRISTIAN AND BYZANTINE ARCHITECTURE (n.14 above), 7-8, 37.

52. See, especially, Rabanus Maurus, In Ezech., I, PL, cx, 514, cited by Mâle, THE GOTHIC IMAGE (n.13 above), 36-37.

53. The several meanings came in fixed form. The Parable of the Wise and Foolish Virgins, as a typical example, was always associated with the Last Judgment. The Wise Virgins stood on the right of Christ; they wore the nimbus of holiness; the door was open. The Foolish Virgins stood on His left; they had no nimbus; the door was closed. The Glossa ordinaria explained more of the symbolism: there are five virgins each because of the five forms of mystical contemplation and the five senses of the soul. The oil of the Wise Virgins is charity, which is the chief theological virtue. Opposite the Wise Virgins are the five forms of lust, which cause the soul to forget holy thoughts. These five fall asleep waiting for the Bridegroom. Their sleep depicts the many generations sleeping the sleep of death until the Second Coming (Walafrid Strabo, Matt. xxv, cited by Mâle, THE GOTHIC IMAGE [n.13 above], 198.

Illustrative of such associations Hugh of St. Victor could look at a dove and think of the Church. He reasoned: "The dove has two wings even as the Christian has two ways of life, the active and the contemplative. The blue feathers of the wings are thoughts of heaven; the uncertain shades of the body, the changing colours that recall an unquiet sea, symbolise the ocean of human passions in which the Church is sailing. Why are the dove's eyes this beautiful golden colour? Because yellow, the colour of ripe fruit, is the colour too of experience and maturity, and the yellow eyes of the dove are the looks full of wisdom which the Church casts on the future. The dove, moreover, has red feet, for the Church moves through the world with her feet in the blood of the martyrs" (Hugh of St. Victor, De Bestiis et aliis rebus, I, i, ii, vii, ix, x, quoted by Mâle, THE GOTHIC IMAGE [n.13 above], 30).

54. Bentmann and Lickes, CHURCHES OF THE MIDDLE AGES (n.13 above), 133.

55. Mâle, THE GOTHIC IMAGE (n.13 above), 152.

56. In the North transept, the region of duller light, are Malchizedek, Abraham, Moses, Samuel, and David. In them history and symbol merge. The twelve patriarchs and the twelve prophets represented historical periods and heralds of Christ at the same time. For instance, Abraham, from the era in which humanity lived under the law of circumcision, placed his hand on Isaac's head, symbolizing the Father's sacrifice of His Son Jesus Christ. John the Baptist, from the days of preparing for the appearance of the Christ, carried a lamb in his arms to remind the viewer of The Lamb of God which took away the sins of the world. From the first Adam through the patriarchs and prophets to the Second Adam, each fit into an unbroken chain of Being. The South transept, the region of brightest light, declared the end of the pilgrimage, telling of the Church as the Community of the Saints.

57. Bernard of Clairvaux (1091-1153) epitomized enchantment with the Virgin, attributing to her such metaphors as Scripture, Burning Bush, Ark of the Covenant, Star, Fleece, Bridechamber, Door, and Garden. He addressed her with the mysterious names of belief: Queen of Heaven, Queen of Earth; Mother of God, Mother of Humanity (Bernard of

Clairvaux, PL, c/xxxiv, 1017, cited by Mâle, THE GOTHIC IMAGE [n.13 above], 233).

58. Chartres possessed a "tunic of the Virgin," a piece of cloth supposedly worn by her, brought by Charlemagne from Emperor Nicephoras and his wife Irene in Constantinople to Aachen in Germany, and given to the church by his grandson, Charles the Bald. The cult site also boasted of a well and a statue of the Virgin. See Vincent Sablon, Historie de l'auguste ef vene'rable eglise de Chartres (1671), in Branner, CHARTRES CATHEDRAL (n.14 above), 107-114, 70.

59. When the fire of 1194 destroyed everything except the western towers and facade, the chroniclers reported that the destruction was a sign. The Virgin desired the building to "be restored . . .with more praise-worthy adornment . . . and this destruction might furnish an excuse for the succeeding structure next to which none in the world gleams so brilliantly" (From "The 'Philippids' of Guillaume le Breton," I, iv, in Branner, CHARTRES CATHEDRAL [n.14 above], 96-97). It is remarkable that by 1220 the main structure was finished and by 1260 the North and South porches, along with the sculpture and stained glass, were dedicated. The effort represented a tremendous outpouring of energy and resources by people of high and low status alike.

60. Anselm's prayer to Mary typified the veneration of the Virgin: " . . . Queen of angels, Mistress of the World . . . Mother of my heart's illumination . . . Nurse of my mind's salvation . . . Gate of life, Door of Salvation, Way of reconciliation, Entrance to restoration . . . Thy childbearing, Lady, redeemed a captive world . . . O Woman wonderfully matchless and matchlessly wonderful, through whom the elements are renewed, hell is remedied, demons are tramped on, (human beings) are saved, angels are replaced . . . God is the Father of the establishment of all things, and Mary is the Mother of the re-establishment of all things . . ." ("A Prayer

to Saint Mary to Obtain Love for Her and for Christ," Fairweather, A SCHOLASTIC MISCELLANY [n.1 above], 203-207).

61. Cf. note on the prominence of Byzantine women rulers (n.4/22). In the West, Empress Agnes (1056-1062) played a significant role in the intense conflict between the claims of the Empire and the claims of the Papacy. Cultural ideas spread through the migrations of women of noble birth and their company of advisers. However, according to Southern (THE MAKING OF THE MIDDLE AGES [n.1 above], 76-79, 109), it was only "the masculine quality of reason," expressed through law and submitted to freely, which provided the basis for liberty.

62. See A.L. Gabriel, THE EDUCATIONAL IDEAS OF VINCENT OF BEAUVAIS (South Bend: University of Notre Dame Press, Second edition, [1956] 1962). Mâle draws heavily upon Vincent in describing and interpreting "The Gothic Image." The Mirror of Morals was written at the beginning of the fourteenth century but attributed to him.

63. Mâle, THE GOTHIC IMAGE (n.13 above), 23.

64. In the early fifth century, Martianus Capella had created a typology of learning in which he personified the seven liberal arts (the Trivium subjects of Grammar, Rhetoric, and Dialectic with the Quadrivium subjects of Arithmetic, Geometry, Astronomy, and Music) as the bridesmaids of philosophy. Written sometime between Alaric's sack of Rome in 410 and before the fall of Carthage in 439, "The Marriage of Philology and Mercury" was the most popular textbook of the medieval curriculum. Martianus was the first to allegorize the Seven Liberal Arts and did so in a way which, in the words of Richard Johnson, provides "our best index to the course of (the tradition of Latin learning's) determination" (William Harris Stahl, MARTIANUS CAPPELLA AND THE SEVEN LIBERAL ARTS. Volume I THE QUADRIVIUM OF MARTIANUS CAPEL-

LA: Latin Traditions in the Mathematical Sciences 50 B.C.-A.D. 1250. With a Study of The Allegorical and The Verbal Disciplines by Richard Johnson with E.L. Burge [New York: Columbia University Press, 1971]). Stahl likened Martianus to the neck of an hour glass through which the classical liberal arts trickled into the Medieval world. At the very time Thierry of Chartres completed translating Aristotle's famous work on the Organon in 1142, making Chartres "the true cradle of scholasticism," the figure in the base relief of Dialectic was carved (Mâle, THE GOTHIC IMAGE [n. 13 above], 88).

65. Mâle, (ibid., 397) described the effect: " . . . this is a transfigured world . . . light shines more brightly . . . shadows have more mystery . . . Already one feels oneself in the heart of the heavenly Jerusalem . . ."

66. Hugh of St. Victor, "Mystical Mirror of the Church," in Durandus, THE SYMBOLISM OF CHURCHES AND CHURCH ARCHITECTURE (n.21 above), Supplement, 155.

67. Durandus, ibid., I, I, 24.

68. Brown, "The Rise and Function of the Holy Man" (n.4/5).

69. "Speculation" did not mean "gazing into the clouds; instead it meant analyzing the basic structures of reality" (Tillich, A HISTORY OF CHRISTIAN THOUGHT [n.5/1], 158-159).

70. Augustine had maintained the paradoxical features of experience and explanations in a dynamic harmony. For instance, in THE CITY OF GOD, he professed: " . . . the beauty of the course of this world is achieved by the opposition of contraries, arranged, as it were, by an eloquence not of words, but of things. This is quite plainly stated in the Book of Ecclesiasticus, in this way: 'Good is set against evil, and life against death: so is the sinner

against the godly. So look upon all the words of the Most High, and these are two and two, one against another'" (Augustine, THE CITY OF GOD, Bk. XVI, ch. xviii; Eccles., xxiii, 15 [Oates, BASIC WRITINGS OF SAINT AUGUSTINE (n.3 above), 159]).

71. In the Proslogium (or Address), Anselm proved the existence of God by connecting real existence with intelligent being through thought. The first title was the Augustinian formula: "Faith seeking understanding." This is the ontological argument which affirms the existence of God as the unconditional element in thought itself: "that than which nothing greater can be imagined." See Fairweather, A SCHOLASTIC MISCELLANY (n.1 above), 69-93. In the Monologium (or Soliloquy) Anselm demonstrated the existence of God as proven by reason without Scriptural authority. The original title was "Example of Meditation on the Grounds [i.e., the rationality] of Faith." There is goodness in things, which are themselves derived from (i.e., caused by) God, who is the common superior element in which they all participate. This is the cosmological argument which reasons that conditional particulars presuppose something unconditional and absolute (cited by Gilson, HISTORY OF CHRISTIAN PHILOSOPHY IN THE MIDDLE AGES [n.1 above], 128-132; Pelikan, THE GROWTH OF MEDIEVAL THEOLOGY [n.1 above], 261-262; Tillich, A HISTORY OF CHRISTIAN THOUGHT [n.5/1], 161-162; Leff, MEDIEVAL THOUGHT [n.1 above], 99-103).

72. De fide trinitatis, Praef., PL, 158, 261, quoted by Fairweather, A SCHOLASTIC MISCELLANY (n.1 above), 49; cited by Gilson, HISTORY OF CHRISTIAN PHILOSOPHY IN THE MIDDLE AGES (n.1 above), 617, n.45.

73. Tillich, A HISTORY OF CHRISTIAN THOUGHT (n.5/1), 159.

74. Ibid.

75. Ibid., 140.

76. Abelard shifted moral issues from objective criteria to subjective intention: "All acts are in themselves indifferent and only become good or evil according to the intention of their author" (PL, 178, 644a, quoted by Leff, MEDIEVAL THOUGHT [n.1 above], 113). Reality rested upon individual confidence instead of general considerations of what was good and what was evil. This reflected his failure to link his logical analysis to a general system. "His greatest contribution lay in furthering rational and dialectical argument, and in helping to develop it as an aid to faith" (Leff, MEDIEVAL THOUGHT [n.1 above], 107). Abelard's work cited by Gilson, HISTORY OF CHRISTIAN PHILOSOPHY IN THE MIDDLE AGES (n.1 above), 153-163; Pelikan, THE GROWTH OF MEDIEVAL THOUGHT (n.1 above), 223-229; Tillich, A HISTORY OF CHRISTIAN THOUGHT (n.1/44), 167-172; Leff, MEDIEVAL THOUGHT (n.1 above), 104-114.

77. Abelard's approach required three preliminary steps: (1) establishing the historical context of the texts; (2) identifying the exact meaning of the words; and (3) applying the Bible as the ultimate legal authority.

78. Abelard reads more like "an adventurous spirit" trying to make faith sensible than as an intransigent rationalist: "I do not want to be a philosopher if it means resisting St. Paul; I do not wish to be Aristotle if it must separate me from Christ." It seems that his temper sometimes carried his argument beyond the boundaries of his conscious intention (quoted by Leff, MEDIEVAL THOUGHT [n.1 above], 113-114).

79. The dialectical faith ("Yes, I believe"/"No, I need to understand") ranged widely during the eleventh and twelfth centuries. Gradually, the accumulation of exploration was consolidated. Legend conveyed that consolidation by picturing Gratian, the compiler of the Concordance of Discordant Canons (ca.

1140), Peter Comestor, the author of the Historia Scholastica (ca. 1170), and Peter Lombard, the compiler of the Four Books of Sentences of the Fathers (ca. 1150), as brothers (Southern, THE MAKING OF THE MIDDLE AGES [n.1 above], 205-206).

80. Leff, MEDIEVAL THOUGHT (n.1 above), 213.

81. Thomas Aquinas' work cited by Gilson, HISTORY OF CHRISTIAN PHILOSOPHY IN THE MIDDLE AGES (n.1 above), 361-383, 420-427, 707-717; Pelikan, THE GROWTH OF MEDIEVAL THOUGHT (n.1 above), 268-293; Tillich, A HISTORY OF CHRISTIAN THOUGHT (n.1/44), 192-198, Leff, MEDIEVAL THOUGHT (n.1 above), 211-224.

82. Aquinas, Summa, Question 12, Art. 12 (translated and edited by A.M. Fairweather, NATURE AND GRACE, The Library of Christian Classics, Vol. XI [Philadelphia: the Westminster Press, 1954]).

83. Ibid., Question 2, Art. 3. Thomas realized that analysis of logical causality was incomplete. "Sacred doctrine," he wrote, "makes use of human reason, not to prove faith but to make clear (manifestare) whatever is set forth in this doctrine" (quoted by Panofsky, GOTHIC ARCHITECTURE AND SCHOLASTICISM [n.13 above], 29, n.12). The only way he knew to move from the mediated sensory world of existence to the unmediated spiritual realm of revelation was over the bridge of intellectual intention.

84. Thomas avoided an infinite regression, i.e., causes of causes of causes, by stressing the first cause as a cause of significance rather than a cause of sequence. In other words, God was The Cause of every cause.

85. Augustine, e.g., CITY OF GOD, Bk. XIX, chp. xiv (Oates, BASIC WRITINGS OF ST. AUGUSTINE [n.3 above], 491).

86. Painton Cowen, ROSE WINDOWS (San Francisco: Chronicle Books/A Prism Edition, 1979), 98-99.

87. Ibid., 122-123. The window neatly echoes "Thierry's preoccupation with the geometric configuration of the Trinity" (136-137). Rose windows symbolized the wisdom of purification, the knowledge of illumination, and the love which comes with union.

88. J. Bedier and P. Aubry, Les Chansons de Croisade, (Paris, 1909) 8-11, in Southern, THE MAKING OF THE MIDDLE AGES (n.1 above), 55.

89. Pope Urban launched the First Crusade at the Council of Clermont in 1095 to liberate the holy places from the Moslems. "The conventional numbering of the Crusades is not particularly helpful," according to Russell (A HISTORY OF MEDIEVAL CHRISTIANITY [n.1 above], 158), "for they were not clearly separated or defined. What is significant is that from 1095 there were frequent expeditions of Western Christians (called Franks by the Easterners) to the East." The expeditions did not end with the rape of Byzantium in the Fourth Crusade of 1202-1204 but went on into the early fourteenth century (Daniel-Rops, HISTORY OF THE CHURCH OF CHRIST [n.1 above]).

90. From the eleventh into the fourteenth centuries, religious sentiment turned increasingly to individual expressions, e.g., private devotions, external acts such as genuflections and saying the rosary. Subjective observances counterbalanced objective performance. Architecture had to accommodate both the private and the public meeting places of God's coming down to humanity. A double aisled ambulatory clung like a string of pearls around the now segregated sanctuary, providing sheltered area for walking around the central apse. Its radiating chapels allowed pilgrims easy access to the altars, which housed relics of the saints and brought God to earth (von Simson, THE GOTHIC CATHEDRAL [n.13 above], 201; Russell, A HISTORY OF MEDIEVAL CHRISTIANITY [n.1 above], 98).

91. Aquinas, quoted by Leff, MEDIEVAL THOUGHT (n.1 above), 216.

92. Aquinas, *Contra Gentiles*, IV, xiii, quoted by Leff, MEDIEVAL THOUGHT (n.1 above), 221.

Chapter Eight

TOO MUCH INQUIRY, NOT ENOUGH CONTEXT

**Like giant antennae
probing hidden airwaves,
the two towers of Chartres
directed humanity to pass from
the chaotic world around them into
the ordered world of the permanent.**

The cathedral loomed as a majestic symphony—an idea—of the belief that God manifested divinity in predominantly a left mind, analytic way of working. God subjected Himself to fallen humanity in order to redeem it through the sacrifice of Christ. The conceptualization of the invisible realm ordered nature, society, and the universe in a rational mode.

Now that I have identified the way in which the people of the Medieval Period reflected their perception of God at work I go on to evaluate that perception; how adequately did this methodical mind disclose the activity of God? We look first at the adequacy of its step-by-step process and then at its rational domination of representational systems. Table 11 identifies the central features and summarizes the assessment of its spire-like mind.

INTENSE SPACE—DISTURBED PROCESS

Even as the Gothic cathedral exalted space it also intensified it. The opposition of height and depth, of spirit and matter, resisted the rational resolution. Once the methodical mind shifted from the dialectics of experience to the dialectics of explanation the analytic process turned into an end in itself.

Gothic builders strained for ever greater height. Discrepancy between the upward thrust of the ceiling and the forward counter-thrust of the nave increased. In 1284 the cathedral at Beauvais collapsed.[1] The cathedral at Wells had to be reinforced to prevent collapse.[2] The methodical method was crumbling under the weight of its own exaggerated rationality.

In effect, what reason created reason could destroy. The dialectical process resolved every question—except the question of questioning itself. In 1200 Simon of Tournai ended his lecture at Paris with an exaggerated yet not atypical claim: "O little Jesus! little Jesus! how I have strengthened and exalted Thy doctrine in this address. Yet were I Thine enemy and wished to do Thee harm, I would be just as capable of weakening and refuting it with even stronger proofs and arguments."[3]

The Gothic synthesis was elegant in expression, impressive in grandeur, but finally unstable in its Three-compressed-into-One structure of intensified resolution of opposites. Whether in the Yes-and-No of its dialectics or the point-and-counterpoint of its music (that is, note-against-note) or the restriction of Latin to the elite or the anointing of kings by popes the Gothic mind froze the contrasts. Fixed formulae replaced dynamic expressions.

Rival Powers

The asymmetrical spires of Chartres suggest our asymmetrical brain. But, unlike the functioning brain, complementary processes hardened into rival powers:

* political forces clashed

  -popes versus emperors
  -international sentiments versus national sentiments
  -clerical hierarchy versus the hierarchy of nobility

* social groups battled

  -landed aristocracy versus urban bourgeoise (as it was emerging)
  -anonymous artisans in the service of God versus individual artists in search of recognition

* church forces competed

  -clergy versus laity
  -contemplative orders versus outgoing orders

Each struggled against the other for dominance.

Consider the rival political powers. The West's struggle over investiture parallelled the East's struggle with iconoclasm. Who had final say in things spiritual—pope or emperor? More specifically, who filled ecclesiastical positions? In Byzantium the patriarchs and councils eventually reinstated sacred images in opposition to the iconoclast emperors. In Europe papal advocates overcame lay domination in the appointment of bishops.

Toward the end of the eleventh century, Gregory VII expressed the most blatant claims for papal supremacy. In various letters he declared: the pope can be judged by no one; the Roman church has never erred and never will err until the end of time; the pope alone can depose and restore bishops; the pope alone can revise his own judgments; the pope alone can depose emperors.[4]

By the end of the thirteenth century, Pope Boniface VIII (1294-1303) finalized the divine order.[5] In a papal bull entitled Unam Sanctum, "one holiness," he summed up the unequal power of the two towers: "He who denies that the secular sword is in the power of Peter does not understand the words of the Lord . . ."[6] The claim, however, was not universally acknowledged.

Both spires stretched heavenward but for most people one came closer. The higher power, designated by God through the "descending" ladder of Authority, exercised responsibility for the incorruptible order within the corrupted world. The lowest cleric in the spiritual hierarchy stood higher on the ladder than the highest lay person. The spire-like mind tries to secure its own position.

Conflicting Inquiries

As in politics so in theology. The intuitive rationality of Augustine eroded. What experience presented whole, analysis dissected into parts. The methodical mind subverted the mystical mind. Left mind reason split into the abstract mind-set versus the empirical mind-set. Right mind intuition split into the mind-set of individual piety versus the mind-set of communal pragmatism. Tolerance for variation waned. In the language of neuropsychology each mind-set competed for attentional dominance—rational or relational. Which came first: the universal or the particular? the abstract or the empirical? devotion or charity? There could be no middle ground nor mediating mind-set. All that mattered was the higher spire.

Early in the fifth century Martianus Capella had personified the Seven Liberal Arts. He depicted Dialectics as a thin, pale-faced woman, draped in black, with bright eyes and elaborately-rolled hair. She held a wax tablet and a fish hook in her right hand and in her left a serpent half hidden in her robe.[7] According to a tenth century commentator, the rolled hair represented the syllogism, the serpent signified the subtle reasoning of sophistry, and the hook denoted the insidious argument.[8]

Vigilant eyes and pale features are indicative of the fight-flight syndrome of the autonomic nervous system.[9] The pattern is one of tension, not relaxation; left mind vigilance, not right mind responsiveness (Table 3). Because the person is under attack, the system is on "alert," "aroused" in order to identify the source of the threat.

At first the eyes dilate in order to take in as much territory as possible. The face pales as blood shifts from the peripheral muscles of action to the internal organs of self-consciousness. Then the pupils narrow to sharpen the source of the threat. Perceived vulnerability intensifies left mind observation.

In its original Platonic form Dialectic presented a method of inquiry characterized by conversation.[10] The approach was distinguished from <u>eristic</u> or rhetoric which only tried to win arguments. Thus, the pure science of logic became intertwined with the practical art of persuasion. To win an argument competed with ascertaining truth. Left mind explanation no longer served or supported right mind experience.

Augustine's dialectical process had occurred in the presence of God and never solely in the presence of self. His <u>Confessions</u>, for instance, suggest a reflective method within a relational context.

Anselm tried to link the certainty of God's existence with the certainty of his own processing. Because one experienced the unconditional one sought the unconditional, so he argued. The fact that he articulated a dichotomy between belief and understanding suggests the shift away from primary experience toward secondary explanation. His biographer reported a not insignificant experience when Anselm was searching for proof of God's existence:

> . . . his thoughts took away his appetite for food and drink, and—what distressed him more—disturbed the attention which he should have paid to the morning Office. When he noticed this, and still was unable to grasp what he sought to understand, he began to think that such thoughts must be a temptation of the devil and he tried to put them from him. But the more he tried, the more his thoughts besieged him.[11]

The experience of "yes" and "no" was turning into painful self-conscious explanation.

Exaggerated left mind activity deepens one's sense of the loss of inner harmony.[12] Pessimism permeates the world-view. The anxiety of alienation comes in spasmodic episodes of fear. Ambiguity opens the flood-gates of undesirable possibilities. One demands clear structures on which to depend and conceptual skills in order to cope. Too much spire gets cut off from its base.

With Abelard a relational dialectic barely held its own in the face of rational resolution. His self-analysis was no longer confession before God, as with Augustine, but rather the awareness of the self before the self, the self-conscious ruminations of left hemisphere activity. He called his "confessions" Historia Calamitatum—History of My Misfortunes. In the midst of a candid personal narrative about his relationship with Heloise he reported:

> As chance would have it I first gave myself to discuss the foundation of our faith by (applying) analogies of reason, and composed for my pupils a theological tractate, On the Unity and Trinity of God. They had kept asking of me rational and philosophical expositions and insisting on what could be understood and not mere declarations, saying a flow of words is useless if reason does not follow them, that nothing is believed unless it first be understood and that it is ridiculous for a man to proclaim to others what neither he nor his pupils can grasp by their intelligence.[13]

A priori existence, namely, non-conceptualized data of primary experience, was neither necessary nor prominent. Only the self before the self in conscious intention constituted final authority.[14]

Bernard of Clairvaux (1090-1153)[15] tried to stem the rising tide of rationalism. In making Abelard the scapegoat he exposed his own disturbed right mind activity.[16] Dogma could not be subjected to piece-by-piece dissection. Faith was all-or-none; accepted or rejected. So he argued before the Council of Sens in 1140, which, with the subsequent approval of the pope, rejected Abelard.[17]

Abelard and Bernard contributed to the emerging clash within the Scholastic perception of God. A step-by-step empiricism, or what was known as Nominalism,[18] and an all-at-once idealism, or what was called Realism, struggled against each other.[19] R.W. Southern characterized the disputants as matadors in arenas "armed with the sharp sword of logical distinctions."[20] Such are the mind-sets of too much spire-like activity.

Actually, the Augustinian emphasis on the will[21] influenced both Bernard's mysticism and Anselm's/Abelard's rationalism. Competitive though such inquiries were, a left mind analysis united them.[22] Neither essence nor existence mattered. In the final analysis only the Will of God confronted the Will of Humanity.[23] Humanity was to hear and to heed what God demanded.

One-Sided Will

The Judaic tradition had emphasized active intention as the dominant mode of God by insisting upon the monotheistic imperative: "You shall have no gods except me" (Deuteronomy 5:7 JB). Creation was "good," in truth, "very good," but creation was separate from Creator. By strengthening divine intention, the later doctrine that God created ex-nihilo—out-of-nothing—eliminated any cosmic gradation or hierarchy. The active mind of God meant the redeeming activity of God (Table 2).

Augustine had stressed human will as the ultimate locus of redemption. However, for him the distinction between humanity as "the dust of the ground," or matter, and "the breath of life," or spirit, was an experiential paradox. By the time of Bernard and Abelard, matter and spirit had developed from polarities into distinct entities. In the words of William of St. Thierry:

> . . . when body and soul and spirit have each been ordered and disposed in their rightful place, each esteemed according to their merits and distinguished according to their qualities, a man may begin perfectly to know himself, and by progress in self-knowledge may ascend to the knowledge of God.[24]

Orders of creation now replaced the dynamic experience of paradox. This applied to belief as well as to political power, as Chartres' unequal towers symbolized. For each "thing" to be necessary meant it had to be a fixed entity, in a fixed order, with a fixed function. History itself was conceived of as a created object—contingent, particular, finite, material. God was thought to be a fixed entity—noncontingent, universal, infinity, spiritual. The issue of necessity and particularity involved God "willing" the transition from universal essence to individual existence.

Because of Humanity's fallen state God had to act to redeem it. Between The Incarnation and The Second Coming, The Holy Spirit functioned as The Third Person of The Trinity. The necessary conditions of creation combined with the contingent conditions of redemption. The truth of the trinity shifted from an experience of unity into The Doctrine of The Trinity, which called for intellectual assent. The rational intention of the Bible was linked with the rational necessity of Aristotle to construct a solely rational reality.

Albert the Great (1206-1280)[25] provided the key. He relied upon the Jewish philosopher Maimonides (1135--1204) for understanding Aristotle, and Maimonides had combined Hebraic and Hellenistic views in a way that made the active mind of God dominant. "Will" consisted of the first principle of creation and of individual existence. Reason could weigh the arguments for a created, contingent, material world as against arguments for an uncreated, necessary, eternal world.

Thus faith and reason were separated. Neither contributed to understanding the other. The effects were like splitting the the corpus callosum. The rational and relational processes no longer had direct access to what each contributed. This great divorce between revelation and natural experience prepared the way for Albert's most famous student, Thomas Aquinas.

In the "Thou shalt(s) . . . " of the Ten Commandments (Exodus 20:1-21), God voiced His intentions and demanded obedience. In other words, God willed the human will to will the will of God. The intentional mind of God intended the intentional mind of humanity to be The Dominating Mind.

In such a view active redemption opposed passive creation. The analytic approach eliminated the mysterious quality of people's experience of original sin, the trinity, the incarnation, the resurrection, and the communion of saints. These became objective facts to be observed and affirmed. Neither intuition nor intellect connected redemption and creation.

Only intention counted:

I believe in order to understand.
I understand in order to believe.

Visible matter manifested invisible spirit:

One willed to believe.
One willed to understand.

Now the existence of God could be demonstrated from the evidence of creation, or so the Scholastic synthesis contended. God's existence did not have to be assumed a priori as a universal essence. Nor did it have to be known intuitively in faith. The evidence was there—in the sensory data, open to methodical inquiry. One WILLED faith; one WILLED knowledge. Only the spire-like inspired.

I associate the principle of will with the frontal functions of the brain. Both left and right halves are the locus of The Using System, the central processing that operates apart from the raw input of the peripheral nervous system.[27] This active principle included the functions of initiating, planning, executing, and evaluating. In identifying changes in the Medieval Mind, I discern that the rational will came to dominate receptive processing. Little place remained for primary experience.

The intensified mood pattern characteristic of left brain disturbance exaggerates obsessional argumentativeness.[28] The loss of a sense of inner harmony dis-inhibits paranoid fears. Not surprisingly, then, heretics and infidels had to be identified and eliminated. We find the methodical mind obsessively discriminating what it thought and how it acted. The intensified space of the spire-like mind contributed to its disturbed style.

DIVIDED WILLS—SPLIT PATTERNS

At Chartres the passage to the locus of the holy between the tower of grace and the tower of nature sharpened the division between spirit and matter. The abstract symbolic meaning of The Trinity controlled every sensory means. Mystic and scholastic alike emphasized the directed will as the only mode of the divine-human mind.

As the image of God (Genesis 1:27) humanity disclosed and continued the intentional process (Genesis 1:28; 2:18-19a). Now "Yes" and "No" were divided realities, not unified experience. Arguments replaced dialogue. "Yes" and "No" existed outside of The Will, in other words, outside of the mind itself, as separate spheres. They could be observed, analyzed, and decided about independently of immediate experience. Neither mind let the other mind make its input.

The pattern showed itself in competition among religious orders, in the clash between approaches to obedience in relationships of authority, and in the focus of piety.

Competing Orders

Consider the developments of the religious orders. In these communities individuals could practice the will of God most fully. What is striking about these orders is their diversity. Six to eight major types, with about twenty variations, could be identified by the end of the thirteenth century. Each held together in its own unique way the things of this world and the rewards of the world to come.[29] The mind of God revealed a varied, if not a confused, mind indeed.

Behind this ambivalence about matter and spirit stood the more fully functioning mind of St. Benedict (ca. 480-547). In organizing his religious community, he had combined order and obedience, conciseness and clarity, flexibility and completeness, reason and relationship.[30] His Rule integrated step-by-step regularity with all-at-once reverence.[31]

By the late eleventh century the monastic synthesis eroded. Disorder characterized the orders. Now the things of this world loomed plentiful for some, while for others they distracted them from the rewards of the world to come.

In 1215 a Spanish priest named Dominic (1170?-1221) organized a preaching order to combat heresy.[32] The Dominicans emphasized learning and teaching by their use of the logic of the Scholastic Method. About 1210 Francis of Assisi (1181-1226)[33] founded the Order of Little Brothers. Although they developed a concern for teaching, they approached faith through right mind experience and charity.

Despite the facts that the two men were friends and each order honored the other's founder, intuitive Franciscans contended with intellectual Dominicans.[34]

Through the Dominicans and supremely in Aquinas, Aristotelian inquiry argued for rational perception by the active intellect. Because of its own division, it resorted to abstract principles, such as Three-in-One. Sensory data accumulated piece-by-piece. The systematic syllogism proceeded by distinct steps: First Cause; Final Cause; God.

Through the Franciscans and primarily in Bonaventure (1221-1274),[35] Augustinian inquiry contended for a relational perception by the active intellect. Bonaventure fluctuated between a natural knowledge of the Trinity, as in <u>The Journey of the Mind to God</u>, and a denial of the rational arrival at the mystery, as in <u>Commentary on the Sentences</u> (of Peter Lombard).[36]

What began as complementary perceptions of God ended in the estranged emphases of the Dominicans and the Franciscans. Each order competed with the other on the basis of divided wills. The spire-like mind could not order itself.

Competing Obedience

The rational arsenal included the logic of obedience. At its best it meant devotion; at its worst autocracy. Regardless, the highest power demanded the free assent of the lower powers. Thus the monastic decisions of poverty, chastity, and obedience came from the will and not from the intellect.

A freely chosen obedience found its humanistic expression in the recognition of the individual.

John of Salisbury, in his Policraticus, reversed the rational order of authority.[37] Instead of power descending from above, he suggested it proceeded up from below. The earthly power of the king "is subject to the Law of Justice." The spiritual power of the pope depended upon the effects of policies upon the welfare of the people. The people, in part, judged the politics of earthly power and the policies of spiritual power.

In this view of consent John reflected the strength of Feudalism. It served as "the most important bridge between the rarefied doctrine of the individual as an inferior [in the descending order of government] and the gradually emerging new thesis of the individual as a full member of the State, as a citizen [in the ascending order of government]."[38] No single pattern of governance typified Western Europe. Individual lords entered into individual contractual relations. Further, law came to rest upon procedures of rational evidence and principles of accountability. In cases of heresy, judgment by ordeal was banned in 1212 by Pope Innocent III, and in 1215 The Lateran Council forbade priests from administrating such ordeals.[39] Law became an instrument of liberty for high and low alike. Increasingly the rational style was tied to an actual context.

But in Aquinas unquestioned truth reinforced the thrust of reason and the counter-thrust of obedience. When uncertain he turned to the Authority of the Church: "The weightiest authority is the Church's custom. It should be constantly and punctiliously observed. Ecclesiastical writings draw their warrant from the

Church's authority. We should take our stand on the Church's traditional teaching, rather than on the pronouncements of Augustine or Jerome or any other doctor."[40] More explicitly: "No other power is competent but that of the pope."[41]

Aquinas associated doctrinal obedience with papal supremacy: "Heresy is a sin which merits not only excommunication but also death, for it is worst to corrupt the Faith which is the life of the soul than to issue counterfeit coins which minister to the secular life. Since counterfeiters are justly killed by princes as enemies to the common good, so heretics also deserve the same punishment."[42]

The delicate balance between a freely chosen and rationally evaluated obedience and a freely chosen and unquestioned submission could not be maintained. In the end the status of the individual stood against the rigidity of the structure. Each tower eliminated the other tower. The split found its most dramatic expression in Luther at the Diet of Worms: "Here I stand. I cannot do otherwise."[43]

Competing Pieties

Just as Thomas towered as the highest spire in the Medieval edifice so he disclosed the sterility of its intense rationality.

Toward the end of his life he experienced an ecstatic rapture, causing him to give up writing about God. When pressed by his servant to continue, he replied: "I cannot, Reginald, for everything that I have written appears to me . . . as so much rubbish compared with what I have seen, and what has been revealed to me!"[44] The rational mind collapsed as the experience of the relational mind asserted itself. Spaciousness overwhelmed intensity. The dome-like mind would not be denied.

Popular piety reflected Thomas' experience. In competition with scholasticism, lay religion infused scriptural history with myth and legend,[45] adding elements of naivety and tenderness. For instance one story purported that a mid-wife who attended Mary had been born without arms. As soon as she testified to the Virgin Birth, her arms grew out.[46] Beginning in the twelfth century, stories of the Miracles of the Virgin circulated. Religious imagination, directed to individual piety, appealed to people longing for healing and the repair of injustice.

One example illustrates the genre:

> A certain thief called Ebbo was devoted to the Virgin, and was in the habit of saluting her even on his marauding expeditions. He was caught and hanged, but the Virgin held him up for two days, and when his executioners tried to fix the rope more tightly, she put her hands to his throat and prevented them. Finally he was released.[47]

Such stories gained prominence by being incorporated into The Theology of Redemption.

Less imaginative and more natural, in the iconography real people replaced universal types. Mary's majesty lost its remoteness as maternal warmth appeared between mother and child.[48] The Christ-child laughed, played, and nursed at Mary's breast.[49] The individual became less an instrument of God's will and more a person who chose her or his own purposes.[50] Natural realism stood against Gothic symbolism.

Popular piety not only added legend but also attacked philosophy. In the Imitation of Christ, for instance, Thomas A'Kempis (1380-1471) began declaring: "If you knew the whole Bible by heart, and the sayings of all the philosophers, what would that profit you without the love of God and grace? Vanity of vanities, all is vanity, save to love God and to serve Him only."[51] Individuals stopped inquiring into systematic theological teaching and turned to their own inner life. Inquiry focused on the desires of the inquirer and not on the ideas of the Authority.

The methodical mind oscillated violently between explanation and experience. The towering will propelled religious orders, patterns of obedience, and different pieties into self-destructive competition. Too much spire, indeed.

THE FRACTURED MIND

In the second century Tertullian had declared Jerusalem (the Church) had nothing to do with Athens (the Academy). Because God had spoken, humanity need not think.[52] By the thirteenth century the methodical mind had synthesized faith and reason which supposedly had had nothing to do with each other.[53] Individuals inquired after their destiny in the sure place where the invisible had become visible, namely, in the Eucharist, the place where the dispersion of God converged, The Three-into-One. The Latin West was, in the words of historian R.W. Southern, "the society of rational and redeemed (humanity)."[54]

In the cathedral the powerful and the weak alike found their focus and brought their devotion. In the papacy the religious and the laity alike found their authority and brought their ambivalence. In the *Summa* the wise and the ignorant alike found their resolution and brought their dialectics.

> Two towers—two forces—One Head.
>
> But neither the rationality nor the redemption prevailed.

Popular piety clashed with scholastic precision. Heresy broke out, calling forth the suppression of heresy. Violence against the Jews matched violence against the infidels. Fanatical sentimentality collided with high spirituality. Obedience to the papacy foundered on the determination for self-determination. Each of these forces—piety and precision, sentimentality and spirituality, autocracy and autonomy—manifested a disturbed style with a conflicted pattern.

Inquiry had come to rely too heavily upon analysis, splitting the mind of God and fracturing the western mind:

- rationalism <u>versus</u> mysticism
- scholasticism <u>versus</u> empiricism
- papal authority <u>versus</u> imperial authority
- fixed fate <u>versus</u> individually chosen destiny

Because the Redeeming Mind explained everything it thereby objectified everything. Structures and functions turned into a fixed order of creation. Previously, I associated this feature with the "boldness" of the Latins, a step-by-step way of creating a world. But the harmonization of oppositions could not hold. The Analytical Mind was collapsing because of too much inquiry.

In the late twelfth century Joachim of Fiore (ca. 1132-1202) divided history into three ages: the Age of the Father, which lasted from Adam to Christ; the Age of the Son, which covered the period from King Uzziah (Isaiah 6) to 1250 A.D.; and the Age of the Holy Spirit, which stretched forward from St. Benedict in the sixth century. Since the life of the new always was conceived in and borne by the womb of the old, the ages overlapped. Joachim's vision provides a curiously relevant allegory for Medieval inquiry:[55]

> <u>The Age of the Father</u>, up into the eleventh century, marked "the stern age of creation and survival" during which the basic institutions of Europe appeared. This was the primitive period—the sociological stage of institutional establishment.

> <u>The Age of the Son</u>, from the mid-eleventh through the thirteenth centuries, constituted "the age of reason and intelligible systems." This was the period of growth—the theological

stage of the monastic ideal of renunciation in the service of God.

The Age of the Holy Spirit, coming with the fourteenth century, manifested "less emphasis on system and more on intuition, less on reason and more on will, love, and a freely moving spirit." This was the period of restless change—the spiritual stage of the autonomy of love.

Under the dialectics of history, truth now lay ahead in the new and not behind in the old. A spiritually based intellect no longer depended upon literalistic rules. The sociological period under the works of the Law had passed. The theological period under the sacramental reality of grace through faith was receding. The spiritual phase under love and contemplation, neither in Law nor works, freed humanity from external authority, whether of Church or State. Both pope and emperor had espoused a descending view of authority to which people were to be obedient without question. Now people clammored for an ascending exercise of power.[56] One tower alone rested solidly upon the ground of humanity itself—the lower one.

The Gothic Synthesis stretched high into the sky as a magnificent illusion.[57] But the price was costly. As Hans Jonas put it, we "have yet to decide whether (the combination of classical universalism and historical particularity) be a blessing or a curse."[58]

Like Joachim's third age, the fourteenth century proved "the prelude to catastrophe."[59] That "distant mirror" shows us a world "born to woe" and "plunging into chaos."[60] Such a pattern first surfaced with Augustine's confronting finitude. Subsequently, what mattered was the focused space directing people to the altar. For ten centuries the Analytical Mind proclaimed the place where the invisible was transformed into the visible.

We know from research on the brain that the effects of ecstatic "highs" and exaggerated mood swings are short-lived. Longer periods of anger, humorlessness, sadness, and depression follow. Everything becomes "tarnished" with pessimism,[61] a quality we have found in the passionate pilgrimages of Medieval inquiry. It managed to intensify a pervasive sense of things being worse than the possibilities. One-sided willfulness resulted in wild oscillations in the cultural psyche.

The synthesis shattered. Too intense light broke the locus of the holy. The spire-like mind out-thought the perceived mind of God.

NOTES

1. The cathedral at Beauvais was of huge proportions. Its vault is the highest in Gothic architecture, i.e., about 156 feet. Rebuilding was begun and suspended during the course of the next century, not to be taken up until 1500, with the south transept finally finished in 1548. Twenty-five years later the central tower collapsed (Bony, FRENCH CATHEDRALS [n.7/13], 302).

2. In the fourteenth century St. Andrew's Cathedral at Wells showed ominous signs of subsiding after the central tower was raised one story. The weight proved too much for the footing. To prevent the dangerous sway of the structure an ingenious device of spectacular inverted arches buttressed the tower. The long vista of the nave was lost but the cathedral was preserved and, because of it, a charming stone pattern was added. See Ashbrook, HUMANITAS (n.3/3), 196-197; Dimitri Kessel, SPLENDORS OF CHRISTENDOM (Switzerland: Edita Lausanne, 1964).

3. Simon of Tourni, quoted by Daniel-Rops, HISTORY OF THE CHURCH OF CHRIST (n.7/1), 316.

4. Gregorii VII Registrum, Monumenta Germaniae Historica, Epistolae Selectae, ii, ed. E. Caspar, 201-208, cited by Southern, WESTERN SOCIETY AND THE CHURCHES IN THE MIDDLE AGES (n.7/1), 102.

5. Against Edward I, King of England, and Philip IV, King of France, Boniface announced: "If the earthly power errs, it shall be judged by the spiritual power . . . but if the supreme spiritual power errs it can be judged only by God, and not by man . . . Therefore we declare, state, define, and pronounce that it is altogether necessary to salvation for every human creature to be subject to the Roman pontiff" (Pope Boniface VIII, translated by Brian Tierney in his THE CRISIS OF CHURCH AND

STATE, 1050-1300 [Englewood Cliffs: Prentice-Hall, (1964), 189], quoted by Russell, A HISTORY OF MEDIEVAL CHRISTIANITY [n.7/1], 168-169).

6. Pope Boniface VIII, quoted by Southern, WESTERN SOCIETY AND THE CHURCHES IN THE MIDDLE AGES (n.7/1), 143. In the struggle for clerical supremacy the laity gave Boniface little support. In having to recognize the king as judge of clerical taxation without papal representation, Boniface had to retreat from his exalted position. His action marked "the last stand of the papacy for the effective control of Western society" (Southern, WESTERN SOCIETY AND THE CHURCHES IN THE MIDDLE AGES [n.7/1], 40-41).

7. Martianus Capella, iv, 328. Edit. Teubner, 1866, cited in Mâle, THE GOTHIC IMAGE (n.7/13), 78.

8. Remigius of Auxerre's commentary on Capella, Corpet, Annales archéol., xvii, 89 sq., cited in Mâle, THE GOTHIC IMAGE (n.7/13), 78.

9. Nathan, THE NERVOUS SYSTEM (n.2/1), 206-209.

10. Stahl, MARTIANUS CAPELLA (n.7/64), 104f. See n.7/64.

11. Eadmer, De Vita et Conversatione Anselmi Archiepiscopi Cantuariensis, ed. M. Rule, R.S., 1884, 333, quoted by Southern, THE MAKING OF THE MIDDLE AGES (n.7/1), 190.

12. See n.2/12.

13. Under the pretext of tutoring Heloise, Abelard reported: "There was more kissing than teaching; my hands found themselves at her breasts more often than on the book." When their child was born and he thwarted the arranged marriage, her uncle and his kinsmen "wrought vengeance upon me . . . (by cutting off) the organs by which I had committed the deed which they deplored" (Muckle, HISTORIA CALAMITATUM [n.7/5], 26, 34-35, 39).

14. See Abelard, Ethics or the Book Called "Know Thyself," XII, XIII (Fairweather, A SCHOLASTIC MISCELLANY [n.7/1], 290-291, 291).

15. Ray C. Petry, ed., LATE MEDIEVAL MYSTICISM. The Library of Christian Classics, Vol. XIII (Philadelphia: The Westminster Press, 1957), 47-53ff; Tillich, A HISTORY OF CHRISTIAN THOUGHT (n.5/1), 172-175.

16. The passionate language of Bernard's love mysticism, e.g., "raptus" or ravishment or the "carnal" love of God in "the flesh of Christ" (see Sermon XX on The Song of Songs: "Of the Three Ways in Which We Love God," Petry, LATE MEDIEVAL MYSTICISM [n.15 above], 72), suggests the repression of his own sexual drive when that language is combined with his obsessional attack on Abelard.

17. Abelard could be aggravating. More than his ideas, his arrogance may have contributed to the alienation. In the attack of 1140 Bernard reflected: "Which shall I call the more intolerable in these words (of disagreement with the Fathers)—the blasphemy or the arrogance? Which the more damnable—the rashness or the impurity?" (Ep. 190, PL 182, 1062-1063, quoted by Morris, THE DISCOVERY OF THE INDIVIDUAL [n.7/1], 62.) At one point Abelard reported that the bishop of Chartres consoled him by blaming the attack as "the violence proceeding from open envy" and ought not to be taken too hard (Muckle, HISTORIA CALAMITATUM [n.7/5], 44).

18. The Nominalists, such as Peter Aureoli (d. 1322) (see Leff, MEDIEVAL THOUGHT [n.7/1], 272-276), rejected both anticipatory and experiential input, whether in thought or politics, by concentrating on the particular. In perceiving too much and abstracting too little, their mode of inquiry shrank into the formal exercise of specifying only discrete objects, which meant, in today's terminology, a reductionistic empiricism. They were called "termi-

nists" or "conceptualists" because they regarded the universals as only "terms" or "concepts." Since those arose in the mind, they had no existence in themselves (see Tillich, A HISTORY OF CHRISTIAN THOUGHT [n.1/44], 198-201). At its best, Nominalistic specificity kept an attitude of humility towards reality while affirming the individual (ibid., 142-144).

19. The Realists, such as Duns Scotus (1266-1308), rejected both empirical and experiential input, whether in thought or politics, by focusing on the universal. In abstracting too much and perceiving too little, their mode of inquiry escalated into the formal exercise of mystical Realism, which meant, in today's terminology, an abstract idealism. They started with the universal, which is how they came to be called Realists, and believed that only universal essences existed. At its best mystical Realism kept open the potentiality of reality by emphasizing the powers of being which are in humanity and which transcend the individual person (see Tillich, A HISTORY OF CHRISTIAN THOUGHT [n.1/44], 142-144).

20. Southern, THE MAKING OF THE MIDDLE AGES (n.7/1), 195.

21. Jonas, PHILOSOPHICAL ESSAYS (n.4/5), 40-41.

22. For instance, Bernard turned the Benedictine ladder of Humility into a rational sequence: first, one considered Jesus from the outside, i.e., Jesus was an object toward which one directed one's will; next, one contemplated the meaning of Jesus by loving him with the whole of oneself; finally, one was grasped by the Spirit in a rapture or excessus which carried one beyond oneself without losing one's sense of self (Tillich, A HISTORY OF CHRISTIAN THOUGHT [n.1/44], 174). Bernard emphasized the unity of the Soul and God in passages such as this: "O chaste and holy love . . . O pure and clean intention of the will, the purer in that now at last it is divested of self-will . . . To become thus is to

be deified. As a small drop of water, mingled in much wine . . . appears no longer to exist apart from it . . . so . . . human love will then ineffably be melted out . . . and poured over . . . into the will of God . . . How otherwise could God be 'all in all,' if anything of (humanity) remained in (humanity)" ("On The Love of God," Chp. Ten, Petry, LATE MEDIEVAL MYSTICISM [n.15 above], 64-65). Yet he appealed to private, individual experience. In a sermon on the Song of Songs he urged: "Turn inward to yourselves, and let each of you give heed to his own conscience about what is to be said . . . " (ibid.). Or, in another place he asserted that self--knowledge is the alpha and omega of the earthly pilgrimage: "For you, you are the first; you are also the last" (Bernard, de diligendo Deo, x, 28, PL 182, 991 AB, quoted by Morris, THE DISCOVERY OF THE INDIVIDUAL [n.7/1], 155). Cf., "the fourth degree of love . . . (is to) love (oneself) only for God's sake!" Though we are within God, "our human substance will remain: we shall still be ourselves, but in another form . . . " ("On The Love of God," Chp. Ten, Petry, LATE MEDIEVAL MYSTICISM [n.15 above], 63). Those elements in Bernard—i.e., the subjective intention, the procedural sequence, the not losing one's sense of self, and self-knowledge—are features of the analytic process.

23. See Gilson, HISTORY OF CHRISTIAN PHILOSOPHY IN THE MIDDLE AGES (n.7/1), 454-464; Tillich, A HISTORY OF CHRISTIAN THOUGHT (n.1/44), 141-142.

24. William of St. Thierry, Epistola ad Fratres de Monte Dei, ed. M.M. Davy, 1940, 153, quoted by Southern, THE MAKING OF THE MIDDLE AGES (n.7/1), 229.

25. Albert the Great dedicated his life to making "all parts of (Aristotle's works) intelligible to the Latin world" (quoted by Leff, MEDIEVAL THOUGHT [n.7/1], 207).

26. Leff, MEDIEVAL THOUGHT (n.7/1), 164-167.

27. Luria, THE WORKING BRAIN (n.1/1), 43-101.

28. See n.2/12.

29. Southern, WESTERN SOCIETY AND THE CHURCHES IN THE MIDDLE AGES (n.7/1), 216.

30. See Southern, ibid., 218-223, for an analysis of The Rule of St. Benedict.

31. "The Rule of St. Benedict." In Owen Chadwich, ed., WESTERN ASCETICISM. The Library of Christian Classics, Vol. XII (Philadelphia: The Westminster Press, 1958), 290-337.

32. Southern, WESTERN SOCIETY AND THE CHURCHES IN THE MIDDLE AGES (n.7/1), 279-280ff.

33. Petry, LATE MEDIEVAL MYSTICISM (n.15 above), 126-131; Southern, ibid., 280-284.

34. The two orders, despite their passionate instinct for their separate survival, drew extensively upon each other. "(T)he Franciscans borrowed large parts of the Dominican organization and followed the Dominicans into the universities. The Dominicans on the other hand borrowed the Franciscan attitude to poverty which gave them their urban strength. In a large sense the Dominicans provided the intellect and the Franciscans the instincts which led to universal success" (Southern, WESTERN SOCIETY AND THE CHURCHES IN THE MIDDLE AGES [n.7/1], 284).

35. Petry, LATE MEDIEVAL MYSTICISM (n.15 above), 126-131.

36. Pelikan, THE GROWTH OF MEDIEVAL THEOLOGY (n.7/1), 286-287; Gilson, HISTORY OF CHRISTIAN THEOLOGY IN THE MIDDLE AGES (n.7/1), 331-340; and Bonaventure, <u>The Journey of the Mind to God,</u>

I (Fairweather, A SCHOLASTIC MISCELLANY [n.7/1], 132-138).

37. John of Salisbury, <u>The Policraticus</u> (Fairweather, 247-260). Also see Ullmann, PRINCIPLES OF GOVERNMENT AND POLITICS IN THE MIDDLE AGES (n.7/1), 67, 92, 157-158, 160-163, 230.

38. Ullmann, THE INDIVIDUAL AND SOCIETY IN THE MIDDLE AGES (n.7/1), 104.

39. Southern, THE MAKING OF THE MIDDLE AGES (n.7/1), 97.

40. Aquinas, II <u>Quodlibets</u>, IV-7, quoted by Marty, A SHORT HISTORY OF CHRISTIANITY (n.4/5), 175.

41. Aquinas, <u>Summa</u>, I, 10, 23-2ae, quoted by Marty, A SHORT HISTORY OF CHRISTIANITY (n.4/5), 176.

42. Aquinas, <u>Summa Theologiae</u>, 2, 2, qu.xi, art. 3, quoted by Southern, WESTERN SOCIETY AND THE CHURCHES IN THE MIDDLE AGES (n.7/1), 17.

43. Roland Bainton, HERE I STAND (New York: Abingdon-Cokesbury Press, 1950).

44. Roger B. Vaughn, THE LIFE AND LABOURS OF S. THOMAS AQUIN (London: Longmans Green, Ltd., 1872), 913-919, 926.

45. Legend itself became constricted to abstract symbolism. For instance, in the Adoration of the Magi the earlier number ranged between two and six. By the fourth century the number was fixed at three. By the tenth century the magi were crowned kings. Subsequently their ages were 20, representing the enthusiasm of youth, 40, signifying the developed reason capacity of middle age, and 60, reflecting the experience of old age. In brief, all three ages of humanity paid homage to the Christ Child as King of the Universe (cited by Mâle, THE GOTHIC IMAGE [n.7/13], 213-214).

46. P. Meyer, Romania, 1885, vol. xiv, 497, cited by Mâle, THE GOTHIC IMAGE (n.7/13), 210. Cf. Jacobus de Varagine, THE GOLDEN LEGEND: Lives of the Saints. Translated by William Caxton. Selected and edited by George V. O'Neill (Cambridge: University Press, 1914). Jacobus was a Dominican who strove to hold piety and learning together. In 1305 Ludolph of Saxony compiled the most complete summary of such legends in his book Vita Christi.

47. E.F. Wilson, THE STELLA MARIS OF JOHN OF GARLAND (Medieval Academy of America, 1946), cited by Southern, THE MAKING OF THE MIDDLE AGES (n.7/1), 249.

48. Mâle, THE GOTHIC IMAGE (n.7/13), 230.

49. Southern, THE MAKING OF THE MIDDLE AGES (n.7/1), 238.

50. Ullmann, THE INDIVIDUAL AND SOCIETY IN THE MIDDLE AGES (n.7/1), 45-46.

51. Thomas A'Kempis, IMITATION OF CHRIST, I:1, 10-11.

52. Cited by Gilson, REASON AND REVELATION IN THE MIDDLE AGES (n.7/1), 6. Tertullian represented the Virtues as warrior-maidens in victorious combat over wanton Vices (Tertullian, De Spectaculis, xxix, cited by Mâle, THE GOTHIC IMAGE [n.7/13], 98).

53. Jerusalem proclaimed the intentional will of God and Athens added the rational intellect of necessity. Thus, in the Scholastic synthesis intellectual necessity and intentional will converged. The classical universalism of the Greeks and the historical particularism of the Hebrews synergized as the West held together the rational and the voluntary, the universal and the particular.

54. Southern, WESTERN SOCIETY AND THE CHURCHES IN THE MIDDLE AGES (n.7/1), 22.

55. Southern, ibid., 52. Also see Tillich, A HISTORY OF CHRISTIAN THOUGHT (n.1/44), 175-180.

56. In explaining the patterns of the Medieval period, historians are focusing on socio-economic issues of change, e.g., the rise of the cities which accentuated inquiry and dissent. In the process, the stability of rural isolation gave way to the flux of urban unrest. The sociological ramifications of the analytical metaphor of mind await further work.

57. Fairweather, A SCHOLASTIC MISCELLANY (n.7/1), 31, commented that "the medieval mind had such a strong sense both of the unity of truth and of the hierarchy of truths that it believed that the truth of faith could illuminate reason and guide it to its ultimate end . . . here, then, is the center of reference for scholastic thought. The theological problems of the nature of God, the condition of (humanity), the union of (humanity) and God, are accepted as the basic questions of human life."

58. Jonas, PHILOSOPHICAL ESSAYS (n.4/5), "Jewish and Christian Elements in Philosophy: Their Share in the Emergence of the Modern Mind," 21-44.

59. Southern, WESTERN SOCIETY AND THE CHURCH IN THE MIDDLE AGES (n.7/1), 52.

60. Barbara W. Tuchman, A DISTANT MIRROR: The Calamitous 14th Century (New York: Ballantine Books, [1978] 1979).

61. Mandell, "Toward a Philosophy of Transcendence" (n.2/12), 417.

Chapter Nine

PRECARIOUS INQUIRY VS PRECARIOUS VISION

In the five preceding chapters we have examined one thousand years of Christianity in the western world.

What had appeared in Jesus of Nazareth supposedly expressed the full mind of God. Initial responses of the Christian community to the expectation of the Lord's imminent return—"Come, Lord Jesus" (Revelation 21:20)—were both focused and fluid. In Jerusalem, in Antioch, in Rome, in the uttermost parts of the (Roman) world, Christ could come because He had come. Their experience affirmed the purposeful presence of God.

As the time of waiting stretched on—one hundred, two hundred, three hundred years—Christians came to perceive the mind of God differently. Two histories emerged, each reflecting a different understanding of God and God's way of being God. Graeco-Byzantine subtlety clashed with Roman-Germanic audacity. Tensions within both the Mediterranean East and the European West exaggerated these differences and minimized their commonality. Eventually, "alienation and estrangement made implacable enemies of (siblings) begotten of common parents."[1]

Because I have covered so much let me summarize and compare these competing perceptions of God at work in the world (Table 12).

The analytic metaphor of mind deals with issues of hemisphere dominance and representational systems. Correlated with these brain features are trajectories of belief, namely, patterns of theological emphasis about the nature of God, the nature of Christ, the nature of humanity, and the relationship between Church and Society. These focal meanings, combined with an assessment of how fully the mind is utilized, allow us to identify in the outward and visible symbols of St. Sophia's One Dome and Chartres' Two Towers the adequacy of those inward and spiritual mind-sets.

I concluded that the dome-like mind relied too much upon an abstract-mystical process. Too much vision and not enough sight. One Dome elicited imaginative participation in a vision of heavenly presence. In contrast, the spire-like mind evolved into too much of a rational-symbolic process. Too much inquiry and not enough context. Two Towers called for obedience to an explanation of Divine Doctrine. Basically, theology developed into a conflict between vision and inquiry,[2] an inner eye of imagination versus an outer eye of analysis.

Precarious Vision

The East processed in a relational, all-at-once manner. Imaginative in its central feature and visual in its representational preference, Byzantium's God was right minded. Everything glowed with divine light.

Table 12. **Precarious Vision and Precarious Inquiry: Summary Comparison**

	Byzantine Vision	Medieval Inquiry
Architectural Image:	One Dome	Two Spires
The Working Brain		
brain dominance	relational	rational
mind preference	imaginative	analytic
system preference	visual (icons)	temporal (ideas)
The Work of Theology:		
belief trajectory	manifestation of numinous presence	proclamation of historical claims
source of authority	mystical participation	rational obedience
emphases:		
God as	creating	redeeming
Christ as	triumphant	crucified
Humanity as	participating-in-grace	fallen from grace
Church/Society as	co-equal with open structure	separate spheres with ordered hierarchy
Assessment:		
dominant pattern	abstract-mystical	rational-symbolic
variant patterns	incomplete manifestation deficient proclamation	disturbed proclamation deficient manifestation

The belief trajectory of the dome-like displays the phenomenology of manifestation, an aesthetic preoccupation with the presence of the numinous. With God as Creator and Christ as triumphal Ruler, Byzantium saw humanity participating in the realization of grace. Empire-and-Kingdom were coterminus. Each included the other as the realm of the really real. As the Empire assumed responsibility for the Faith, so the (Christian) Universe embraced the (Roman) World.

Such exuberant optimism caused basilica and street to flow into each other.[3] The boundary between spirit and matter blurred as the unity of the Godhead showed itself through its dispersion. God as the One-flowing-into-three emanated from the One Dome. It spread out over all and included all. What lay outside the Christian world was stark. Inside the dome-like mind, life quickened and expanded as a single breathing organism.

For the Greeks who lived by vision, faith meant initiation into unfathomable wisdom. Their authoritarian Authority derived from mysticism. The locus of spiritual power could appear in many places—from the holy "God--bearing" men of the fourth century to the holy "God-shadowed" images of the later centuries. The structures of power were as open as they were hierarchical.[4] Participation by everyone minimized specialization by an elite.

Because Christ reigned in majesty Byzantium sought the "peace of the Church."[5] And of course the peace of the Church meant the peace of the World (Roman).

Medieval Inquiry

The West processed in a rational, step-by-step way. Analytic in its central feature and temporal in its representational pattern, the Latin God was left-minded. A clear map laid out the path to The Truth.

The belief trajectory of the spire-like is more the hermeneutics of proclamation than manifestation. For the scholastic mind God acted in the crucified Christ to redeem fallen humanity. With the fall of Rome the Church functioned to maintain cultural stability. It alone "retained a central organization and a universal character."[6] Although head of the Church, the popes found themselves coping with political developments in the Empire. Over time, the Faith assumed responsibility for the State, even as the State took on the task of extending the universe of the Church.[7] However, Church and State were separate as well distinguishable. For many people, a definite hierarchy ordered the powers of this world—clergy, royalty, and laity in that order. For others, the authority of the State parallelled that of the Church and because that also "descended" it, too, ordered the powers of the world, with nobility on top. Even so, the spire of the Papacy reached higher than the spire of the Empire.

The grim pessimism of the Medieval mind served to isolate the rhythms of the holy from the rhythms of the world.[8] The bells of both the basilica and monastery tolled for a world set apart from the world round about. God as Three-compressed-into-One declared Himself in the Two Spires which reconciled the opposition of spirit and matter. The exalted and intensified space directed everyone to the one resolution, the altar of Christ's sacrifice.

For the Latins who lived by inquiry, faith sought "an authoritarian determination of the faith once delivered."[9] Their authoritarian Authority derived from their rationalism. The locus of spiritual power was confined to a single place—the priest at the altar and the pope as supreme. Papacy and Empire were separate and stratified. Two spires stretched upward even as they directed people inward, but one spire stretched higher.

As Christ sacrificed Himself to redeem fallen humanity, so the Church Militant[10] fought to save the fallen world. And, of course, the victory of the Church meant the subjection of the State and the defeat of the World.

COMPETITION

The Graeco-Roman mind functioned like that of a split-brain patient. Each side competed with its counterpart for attentional dominance. Neither could receive the input of the other as necessary to fully functioning humanity. Both failed to perceive the full mind of God.

The split can be discerned in their early differences. For instance in the late seventh century, Theodore, a Greek-speaking monk who served as Archbishop of Canterbury, emphasized the conflicting customs of Greek and Latin churches. These included the Romans reconciling penitents within the apse (altar end) of the church, which the Greeks did not, or the Greeks excommunicating those who failed to receive communion for three successive Sundays, which the Romans did not.[11] Already the firm boundary at the edge of Empire-and-Kingdom contrasted with the fixed focus of Church-over-World at the altar. Participation in the manifestation of grace versus proclamation of the means of grace.

Eastern synthesis, which I have identified as an abstract-mystical pattern, looked to the past. Permanence lay in what had already been disclosed in Scriptures as interpreted by the Fathers. Western analysis, what I have designated as a rational-symbolic pattern, focused on change. Certainty depended on what the current Authority defined as The Truth. The Imaginative Mind contented itself with the continuity of eternity with time; the Inquiring Mind struggled with the opposition between eternity and time.

This conflict between Eastern continuity and Latin change found many expressions:

- doctrinally, the East believed the Holy Spirit proceeded eternally from one Father, while the West supposedly split the Godhead in two (Father/Son), from which the Spirit proceeded;[12]

- eucharistically, the East insisted upon leavened bread, which spread by fermentation through the whole loaf, while the West, like the Hebrews in remembrance of the Exodus, used unleavened bread, which does not spread or rise;[13]

- linguistically, the East tended to be flowery and stereotyped, while the West used plain and direct speech; [14]

- politically, the East depended upon diplomacy, while the West relied upon warfare.[15]

To the Greeks, holy images expressed living dogma. They saw the Christological definitions as icons, not concepts. Icons were whole in themselves, bearers of being, and ineffable. Participation in mystical experience took precedence over any statements about divine mystery.[16]

The vision of eternal light connected humanity directly with God. Sensory input and deductive reasoning, both left brain processes, were secondary. Their active imagination neglected and, in effect, excluded the temporal capacity of step-by-step analysis. Little wonder, then, that its art conveys an other-worldly asceticism[17] through subdued colors and passively presented personages. All could be discerned because all was eternally present.

In contrast, the Latins believed conceptual clarity could specify The Truth objectively. For them decisions made by the Authority, that is, the <u>magisterium</u> of the Pope and the bishops, could be taken as definite lines in The Map of Reality itself. They could explain what they observed because of the rational structure they assumed.[18]

The explanation of eternal truth required humanity to inquire about what could be understood only indirectly. Deductive rationality and sensory data each contributed to Truth, even though each was separated from the other. Active knowing relied upon the logical process of the left brain. People had to hear about what was Right because they could not know it directly. Understandably, then, its art built upon an idealistic naturalism[19] in which color was plentiful and human beings appeared active. The Truth had to be pursued because it had yet to be realized.

Both minds assumed reality beyond the ordinary sensory realm. Transcendent truth took priority, whether that transcendence was manifested everywhere and anywhere or proclaimed somewhere specifically. Yet how contrasting and competitive the cortical processing became.

In the East, the trinitarian One-flowed-into-three lacked a tension between faith and reason.[20] The iconic style incorporated differences in such a way that everything was "like"—similar to—everything else: essence and existence, faith and reason, God and nature. Intelligibility meant that nature was in the image and likeness of God. What was rational was what was necessary. Because of that abstract vision of the whole nothing worthwhile remained to be explored. What "was" constituted what "was to be."

I have determined, thereby, that the dome-like mind of Byzantium was incomplete. It presented a double message: reason was primary yet faith was what mattered. Left mind inquiry was acknowledged but right mind abstractionism dominated. One Dome protected the Universe!

Two ironies appear in this encapsulation of ambiguity. On the one hand, the unchanging character of necessary reason contributed to its synthesizing capacity. On the other, its intuition lacked the clarification of a critical process. Their loyalty to the Fathers crippled their ability to love God with all their mind. In effect, Byzantium "lacked the courage to let the spirit of truth lead her into all truth, that she might be free indeed."[21] The Imaginative Mind needed input from both the concrete and the rational-analytic.

In the West, Augustine laid the foundation for separating God-and-world. In distinguishing the heavenly City of God from the earthly realm of the State he provided a formulation which later interpreters hardened into a formal dichotomy. He emphasized the partial identification of the two realities and, more importantly, the partial nonidentification of God and nature.[22] Islamic and Jewish influences, in combination with classical rational philosophy, further divided the empirical and the spiritual. Everything had to be dissected dialectically into either spirit or matter. In such an unfinished universe they had to identify and reconcile both the heavenly and the earthly. The trinitarian Three-focused-into-One meant a fundamental break between faith and reason.[23] Mind and nature were divorced. What "was" was not what "was to be."

I contend, therefore, that the spire-like mind of the Latin West was more disturbed than incomplete. It too presented a double message: faith was primary[24] but reason mattered more.[25] While right mind wholeness was assumed, left mind analysis dominated. The Spire directed fallen humanity to the only sure place of reconciliation!

The elimination of ambiguity also produced two ironies. On the one hand, faith in the act of creation contributed to belief in the active will as well as to the importance of each particular. In short, reality was eternally divided or split between the creator and each individual part of creation. On the other hand, its rationality lacked contact with immediate experience, which comes with right half processing. Whether in the Augustinian solution of the primacy of faith or in the Thomistic dissolution with the triumph of the primacy of reason,[26] the West segregated reason and experience. The Analytic Mind needed input from relational experience.

Despite these differences I return to the fact that Graeco-Roman were offspring of common parents. The ambiguity of step-by-step explanation was parallelled by a similar ambiguity of all-at-once experience. Samuel Laeuchli has compared the analogous structural tensions within the conceptualization of the West and the visualization of the East.[27] His analysis supports their basic similarity.

The Nicaean Creed, representative of left mind process, struggled to hold together explanation and experience. It proclaims One God, but immediately it speaks about three entitities, mixing personal nouns (Son, Father, Maker, Man) with abstract notions (visible, essence, light). It defines as it celebrates. Laeuchli outlined the resulting pattern as follows:

we believe

we celebrate we fight

we define

Through the Patristic Period, and even more throughout the Medieval Period, the dilemma between believing and defining intensified. Rational explanation eliminated relational experience. Despite its experiential base the Creed functioned as "a partisan" and "divisive" statement of reality.[28]

Laeuchli used the mosaics on the floor of the Cathedral of Aquileia to identify Constantinian Christianity. Whereas the Creed fostered "ideas," mosaics expressed "images." But the mosaics present both explicit Christian symbolism and nonChristian natural decoration. Both images and inscriptions, designs and stories, events and scenery, exist side-by-side. Sometimes they tell a story, such as Jonah and the Whale; other times they convey a kind of hidden message or code, such as a ram looking at a basket with twelve eggs or loaves of bread or stones. They combine the simple and the sophisticated. The pattern is as follows:

the mosaics are symbolic

the mosaics tell a story the mosaics hide a story

the mosaics are decorative

The dilemma between expressing one meaning and suggesting many meanings persisted through the centuries. Despite their explanatory symbolism the mosaics included more contextual components than an exclusive Christian content.[29] In order to be understood the ambiguity requires a context.

The proclamation trajectory of the West combined right mind poetry with left mind definitions. Initial celebration led to distinctions between belief and definition, with the consequence of a redeeming mind-set finally set <u>against</u> the world. Similarly, the manifestation trajectory of the East maintained naturalistic expressions as part of its symbolic rationale. The right mind immediacy of mosaic stones split into symbolic and decorative features, with the consequence of a creating mind-set actually <u>hiding</u> the manifestations of meaning. Together both trajectories made up the Judeo-Christian/Hellenistic convergence. I suggest that not only the distinctions of the Latins but the disguises of the Greeks present a pattern that is primarily left mind rationality.

THE SPLIT MIND OF GOD

Recall that the frontal lobes, especially the left, function as the locus of initiative. When the lobes are intact, people plan, carry out, and evaluate preconceived ideas. When these lobes are damaged, people are unable to plan, execute, or evaluate ideas. They are victims of outer stimuli and inner impulses, all competing for attentional response.

Furthermore, with Broca's area damaged, that is the left frontal lobe, people cannot speak even though they comprehend what is going on. In a reciprocal way, with impairment of Wernecke's area, which means the left temporal area, people talk easily but make no sense.

These features suggest that the frontal areas constitute neurological correlates of will. Similarly the back areas, particularly the association-integrative cortex of the left half, are the anatomical substrata of intellect. Together, will and intellect explain and comprehend what the person observes.

From such a correlation of the brain and cognition I now propose how the Greeks and the Latins derived from the rational-empirical orientation of the Hebrews yet differed so radically in the way they elaborated that preference.

The active _will_ of the Latins reflects a subjective intentionality. With their autonomous particularity they pursued precise concepts with an obsessive disregard of context. Finally, the active will found articulation through the Papal drive for absolute authority.

The active _intellect_ of the East suggests an objective intouchness. A relational patterning failed to critique its assumption that _orbis romanus_ equalled _oekoumene_. Even though its emperors were fallible, it never questioned its Imperial faith.

The commonality of Graeco-Roman rationality finally cannot obscure the split between their perceptions of God. The tension between inquiry and imagination characterizes God's divided mind. The intense space and penetrating light of the Cathedral of Chartres overwhelmed the impressionistic luminosity of St. Sophia. The spire-like mind subjugated the dome-like mind. God was met at the altar; humanity was not lifted up into divinity. The left mind of God, as explained in the West, demanded recognition from the right mind of God, as seen in the East.

In 1112 words written by Pope Paschal II (1099-1118) to Emperor Alexius I Comnenus (1081-1118) about the latter's proposals for negotiating an East-West reconciliation conveyed the irreconcilability of the two minds: "The first step toward unity is that our brother the patriarch of Constantinople should recognize the primacy and dignity of the apostolic see . . . and correct his former obstinacy. The causes of diversity of faith and custom between Greeks and Latins cannot be removed unless the members are first united to the head. For how can questions be discussed between dissenting and antagonistic bodies when one refuses to obey or agree with the other."[30] The Spire insisted on towering over the Dome.

Such a onesided arrogance deepened the division. By the thirteenth century even the Dominicans in Constantinople described the demands of papal legates as rapacious.[31] The clash between pro-Latin and anti-Latin factions escalated.

Eastern historian Pachymeres (1242-1310) described the fallout from the Council of Lyons in 1274 in a way that had been said before and would be said again: "The church schism had reached such a point that it separates the dwellers of one house: father is opposed to son, mother to daughter, sister-in-law to mother-in-law."[32] Every heretical controversy split families apart. The hostility continued right up until the fall of Constantinople itself in 1453.

Anti-Latins grew more suspicious of the hated West. In exchange for military assistance against the encroaching Turks, the West demanded submission to papal authority. To preserve its body, the East felt it had to sell its soul. Eventually, the unity of politics and piety collapsed. The will-to-resist no longer prevailed against the desire-to-submit.

At the Council of Florence (1438-39) the Greek delegates subscribed to the doctrinal demands of the Latins: The Holy Spirit had "His essence and substantial being equally from the Father and the Son," "the word Filoque had been lawfully and reasonably added to the Creed," the pope was "the true vicar of Christ with full power given him by our Lord Jesus Christ in St. Peter to nourish, rule, and govern the universal Church."[33] By affirming all that the Romans had defended the effect was to deny all that the Greeks had asserted.

The final gesture of the West's onesided willfulness came after Mahomet II breached the walls of Constantinople in 1453, thereby ending Imperial faith.[34] While the Eastern Emperor perished, the Patriarch escaped to Rome. The aggressive left mind no longer had to compete with the less assertive right mind for attentional dominance in processing reality. With a blindness as massive as that of the Byzantine mind, Pope Pius II (1458-1464) offered Mahomet worldly power in exchange for heavenly obedience. "Be baptized and no prince in the world will be your equal in glory and power. We will call you Emperor of the Greeks and of the Orient, and what you now possess by force and injury, you will hold by right. All Christians will venerate you, and make you the judge of their disputes . . . The see of Rome will love you like any Christian king, and so much the more as your position will be greater than theirs."[35]

The taller Spire believed itself more representative of God's mind than the Dome. The unifying power of its presence in the West and the divisive effect of its power-struggle with the East only accentuated the tragedy of the split mind of God.

Neither the rational-symbolic nature of the spire-like mind nor the abstract-mystical nature of the dome-like mind was adequate by itself.

NOTES

1. Magoulis, BYZANTINE CHRISTIANITY (n.4/5), 88.

2. Ibid., 82.

3. Brown, "Eastern and Western Christendom in Late Antiquity" (n.4/5), 20-21.

4. Brown, "The Rise and Function of the Holy Man" (n.4/5), 95.

5. Brown, THE WORLD OF LATE ANTIQUITY (n.5/1), 148.

6. Leff, MEDIEVAL THOUGHT (n.7/1), 25-26.

7. By virtue of political accident the pope acted as a secular ruler. For instance, Pope Gregory the Great (590-634) wrote in a letter: "It is now seven and twenty years that we have been living in this city beset by the sword of Lombard. How much we have to pay them daily from the Church's treasury, in order to live among them at all, it is impossible to compute. I will merely say that, as at Ravena the emperor has a paymaster for the First Army of Italy, who defrays the daily expenses as need arises, so at Rome for such purposes I am paymaster" (quoted by Magoulis, BYZANTINE CHRISTIANITY [n.4/5], 89). The popes functioned politically to maintain the social order.

8. Brown, "Eastern and Western Christendom in Late Antiquity" (n.4/5), 20-21.

9. Every, MISUNDERSTANDINGS BETWEEN EAST AND WEST (n.4/5), 65.

10. Brown, THE WORLD OF LATE ANTIQUITY (n.5/1), 148.

11. Peonitentiale Theodori, ed., A.W. Haddan and W. Stubbs, Councils and Ecclesiastical Documents

relating to Great Britain and Ireland, 1871, iii, 173-203, cited in Southern, WESTERN SOCIETY AND THE CHURCHES IN THE MIDDLE AGES (n.7/1), 56-57.

12. The Nicaen-Constantinopolitan Creed stated that the Holy Spirit proceeded from the Father. As a result of bitter controversy in Spain in the sixth century, the Council of Frankfurt inserted into the Creed what is called the filioque formula: " . . . the Holy Spirit, the Lord and lifegiver, Who proceeds from the Father and from the son (filioque) . . ." The East claimed claimed this clause upset the balance of the Holy Trinity because the Spirit was sent into the world by the Son although it proceeded eternally from the Father, who begat the Son eternally. The West, it was argued, no longer viewed God the Father as the summit of an isosceles triangle but instead had inverted the triangle by creating two principles from which the Spirit proceeded. The result of the insertion and, therefore, the inversion, was an overt act of defiance against the authority of the Church Fathers meeting in ecumenical councils. The Latins argued that they were not altering or adding to doctrine, only amplifying it (Magoulis, BYZANTINE CHRISTIANITY [n.4/5], 97, 101-102).

13. The East regarded the use of unleavened bread (azyma) as Judaistic, whereas leavened bread (enzyma) symbolized the Holy Spirit as the Giver of Life and was so witnessed to by the Apostles and the ecumenical councils. In 1231 thirteen Greek monks were martyred on Cyprus for refusing to use azyma (unleavened) bread in the Eucharist. The Latins argued that "if the oblation of unleavened bread (azyma) is not the true body of Christ, then the Latin Church is deprived of eternal life" (Magoulis, BYZANTINE CHRISTIANITY [n.4/5], 112--113).

14. Following bitter humiliation in his visit of 968 to Constantinople, Liudprand, Bishop of Cremona (961--972) and representative of Otto I, the Saxon King

of Germany who had been coronated Holy Roman Emperor by Pope John XII in 962, attacked Emperor Nikephoros II Phokas (963-969) and all that was Byzantine. His derisive characterization ranged from ruling titles (e.g., Otto I as "august emperor of the Romans" versus Nikephoros as "the emperor of the Greeks") to dress, food, and personality. For instance: "The King of the Greeks has long hair and wears a tunic with long sleeves and a bonnet; he is lying, crafty, merciless, foxy, proud, falsely humble, miserly and greedy . . . The King of the Franks, on the other hand, is beautifully shorn, and wears a garment quite different from a woman's dress and a hat; he is truthful, guileless, merciful when right, severe when necessary, always humble, never miserly . . ." (quoted by Magoulis, BYZANTINE CHRISTIANITY [n.4/5], 107-108). At the time of the Second Crusade, when Byzantine messengers met Louis VII of France in Greece, Godfrey, Bishop of Langres, interrupted their lengthy and stereotyped expressions of affection to complain: "Brothers, do not repeat 'glory,' 'majesty,' 'wisdom,' and 'piety' so often in reference to the King. He knows himself and we know him well. Just indicate your wishes more briefly and freely" (quoted by Magoulis, BYZANTINE CHRISTIANITY [n.4/5], 136).

15. Liudprand contrasted Germanic boldness with Byzantine tiredness: "Here [Byzantium], faith is old, not young; works do not accompany it, and by reason of its age it is held in light esteem like a worn-out garment. I know for certain of one synod held in Saxony where it was enacted and decreed that it was more seemly to fight with the sword than to fly before a foe" (quoted by Magoulis, BYZANTINE CHRISTIANITY [n.4/5], 107).

16. For instance, John of Damascus simultaneously affirmed and denied putting the mystical into objective language: "Now, one who would speak or hear about God should know beyond any doubt that . . . not all things are inexpressible and not all are capable of expression, and neither are all things

unknowable nor are they all knowable. That which can be known is one thing, whereas that which can be said is another, just as it is one thing to speak and another to know. Furthermore, many of those things about God which are not clearly perceived cannot be fittingly described, so that we are obliged to express in human terms things which transcend the human order" (John of Damascus, WRITINGS [n.5/1], Book I, chp. 2, 166-167).

17. Philip Whitting, "Byzantine Art and Architecture." In Whitting, BYZANTIUM (n.4/12), 141-142, 146.

18. For instance, Aquinas claimed that sacred doctrine was a necessary science: "But we must realize that there are two kinds of sciences. Some of them, such as arithmetic, geometry, and the like, depend on principles known by the natural light of reason. Others depend on principles known through a higher science . . . Sacred doctrine is a science (such as music which depends on principles known through arithmetic), depending on principles known through a higher science, namely the science of God and the blessed. Just as music accepts the principles given to it by arithmetic, so does sacred doctrine accept the principles revealed to it by God" (Aquinas, Summa, I, Question I, Art. 2 [Fairweather, NATURE AND GRACE (n.7/82)]. Cf. Aquinas on "Whether Sacred Doctrine Should Use Metaphors": "We know what God is not, better than we know what he is" (I,Q,I, Art. 9, Fairweather, NATURE AND GRACE [n.7/82]).

19. Whitting, BYZANTIUM (n.4/12), n.17 above.

20. Jonas, PHILOSOPHICAL ESSAYS (n.4/5), 26.

21. Baynes, THE BYZANTINE EMPIRE (n.5/1), 93.

22. Tillich, A HISTORY OF CHRISTIAN THOUGHT (n.1/44), 149ff.

23. Jonas, PHILOSOPHICAL ESSAYS (n.4/5), 26.

24. The primacy of faith was mostly true for the ontological approach which stretched from Augustine through the Franciscans. God was the basis of the quest for God. "When I have found the truth, there I have found my God, the truth itself," to quote Augustine. "God is most truly present to the very soul and immediate knowledge," to quote Bonaventure (both quoted by Tillich, "The Two Types of Philosophy of Religion," THEOLOGY OF CULTURE, edited by Robert Kimball [New York: Oxford University Press, 1959], 12-16; also see Tillich, A HISTORY OF CHRISTIAN THOUGHT [n.1/44], 184-185).

25. The primacy of reason was mostly true for the cosmological approach which Thomas perfected. God was known by inference through "an argumentative rationality" in contrast to "the immediate rationality of the Franciscans." The principles of the higher science of sacred doctrine were not the "uncreated light" of God but the created structure of the mind. "The human intellect cannot reach by natural virtue the divine substance, because, according to the way of the present life, the cognition of our intellect starts with the senses," according to Thomas (quoted by Tillich, THEOLOGY OF CULTURE, [n.24 above]), 16-19; also see Tillich, A HISTORY OF CHRISTIAN THOUGHT [n.1/44], 185-188).

26. Tillich compared the ambiguity of the tension between the Augustinian resolution of faith and reason with the Thomistic dissolution of these. While primarily Augustinian in his emphasis upon humanity's immediate awareness of something unconditional in the very fact of knowing itself, i.e., without inference, Tillich identified the limitation as a "naive identification of immediate evidence with faith" (Tillich, THEOLOGY OF CULTURE [n.24 above], 19). He claimed he was "closer to Aristotle than to Augustine or Plato, because the idea of the living structure of an organism is Aristotelian, whereas the atomistic, mechanical, mathematical science is Augustinian and Platonic" (Tillich, A HISTORY OF CHRISTIAN THOUGHT [n.1/44], 111).

27. Samuel Laeuchli, RELIGION AND ART IN CONFLICT (n.0/8), Chp. 6, "Icon and Idea: Aquileia and Nicea," 111-134.

28. In phrases such as the Son of God was "begotten not made, being of one substance (homoousios) with the Father, by whom all things are made," the polemic and accompanying anathema implicit in the Creed were directed against Christians, not outsiders, which resulted in the splintering of one heretical movement after another (ibid., 127). Sallie McFague identifies less of the partisan nature of the Creed and more of its mixture of narrational and abstract language. In contrast to The Apostle's Creed with its metaphorical quality (e.g., "maker of heaven and earth," "descended into hell"), the Nicaean formula tended more toward conceptual and less imagistic language (e.g., "God of God," "begotten, not made") (METAPHORICAL THEOLOGY: Models of God in Religious Language [Philadelphia: Fortress Press, 1982], 111-114).

29. In the mosaics the symbol of Jonah, for instance, is originally Jewish even as it symbolized the resurrection of Christ (Laeuchli, RELIGION AND ART IN CONFLICT [n.0/8], 127-128).

30. Pope Paschal, quoted in W. Norden, Das Papsttum u. Byzanz., 1903, 94n, and quoted by Southern, WESTERN SOCIETY AND THE CHURCHES IN THE MIDDLE AGES (n.7/1), 77.

31. Chronica Majora (A.D. 1237), iii, 448-469; see also v, 191; vi, 336-337, cited by Southern, WESTERN SOCIETY AND THE CHURCHES IN THE MIDDLE AGES (n.1/7), 83-84.

32. Pachymeres, quoted by Magoulis, BYZANTINE CHRISTIANITY (n.4/5), 166.

33. The terms are quoted from a document of Pope Eugenius III, 6 July 1439 (Conciliorum Oecumenicorum Decreta, ed. J. Alberigo and others, 1962, 499-

-504) by Southern, WESTERN SOCIETY AND THE CHURCHES IN THE MIDDLE AGES (n.7/1), 87-88.

34. Orthodoxy continued, even unto today, to claim to be universal. It regards its "Church as the Church which guards and teaches the true belief about God and which glorifies Him with right worship, that is, as nothing less than the Church of Christ on earth" (Ware, THE ORTHODOX CHURCH [n.5/1], 16, emphasis in original).

35. Letter of Pius II to Mahomet II, ed. by G. Toffanin, 1953, 113-114, quoted by Southern, WESTERN SOCIETY AND THE CHURCHES IN THE MIDDLE AGES (n.7/1), 89.

Part III MANY MINDS—MANY MEANINGS

THE ORIGINAL CONDITION

Ear that hears, eye that sees,

Yahweh has made both of these . . .

Proverbs 20:12 (JB)

THE HUMAN CONDITION

. . . their eyes were opened and

they realized that they were naked . . .

they heard the sound of Yahweh God

and hid because they were afraid . . .

So Yahweh expelled them from Eden to till

the soil from which they had been taken . . .

Genesis 3:7-10, 23

THE DIVINE POSSIBILITY

Is the inventor of the ear unable to hear?

The creator of the eye unable to see?

Psalm 94:9 (JB)

When God comes, 'Then the eyes of the blind

shall be opened, the ears of the deaf unsealed.'

Isaiah 31:5-6 (JB)

Chapter Ten

THE ODD MIND OF HUMANITY

I have argued that the working brain reflects the work of theology.

Because I participate in the Judeo-Christian tradition, I take seriously its "classical"[1] expressions: the Bible as interpreted historical experience and theology as a systematic conceptualization of that experience. For the sake of this new form of empirical theology I have placed doctrinal formulations—that is, redemption and creation oriented theologies—second to empirical evidence. Further, I have minimized conventional thematic events such as Exodus and liberation or Easter and resurrection. This shift of focus has been in order for a neurotheological interpretation to take its place along side other interpretations.[2] Here in this chapter I examine two biblical images directly, using the brain as an interpretive tool—Babel and Pentecost.

What characterizes individuals equally characterizes cultures. Moments appear in which the many meanings of what matters cluster like iron filings in a magnetic field. We call these moments little "kairoi."[3] An event occurs. A discernment is glimpsed. A truth declares itself. The multiple meanings of reality crystallize in a single concrete event.

The Biblical drama of redeeming creation is crystallized in the split mind phenomenon of The Tower of Babel (Genesis 11:1-9) and the whole mind phenomenon of Pentecost (Acts 2:1-13).[4] In a word, Babel portrays disturbed and deficient reality—the reality of sin and death, the drag of the past and the dread of the future. Pentecost, in contrast, discloses new reality—the reality of freedom and destiny, the liberation from bondage and the fulfillment of presence.

THE SPLIT MIND OF BABEL

The mind as metaphor points to the ambiguity of all human activity. Our mental processes frustrate community as well as facilitate it. That which unites us equally works to divide us. We fail to use what we have to the fullest.

The Creation, The Fall, and The Flood in Genesis (Genesis 1-8) dramatize the fact that humanity fails to be genuinely human. Even so, in spite of the disruption of self-consciousness (Genesis 3:7-10) and the escalation of destructiveness (cf. Genesis 4:23-24), life's possibilities are not negated. The Flood represents the continual flooding of contaminated and limiting experience,[5] one--sided and exclusive styles. The aftermath represents the continuing possibility of complementary and inclusive processing.

A new order is declared. Nothing prevents its presence. Everything participates in its power. "Be fruitful, multiply and fill the earth. Be the terror and dread of all . . . I give you everything . . . I will demand an account of every[one's] life" (Genesis 9:1-5 JB).

Although peopling the earth is eternally blessed, no age is whole. Humanity invariable is at odds with the natural order. Human beings are everlastingly entangled with each other. Such disturbances may not be "necessary" in the eternal scheme of things, but they appear to be unavoidable[6] and inevitable.[7] The created order stands ever in need of redemption. The immediacy of right mind process inevitably is converted into the observations of left mind conceptualization. Similarly, the abstracting of left mind process unavoidably modifies right mind experience. The story makes the point (Genesis 11:1-9 JB):

> Throughout the earth people spoke the same language, with the same vocabulary . . . (saying) Let us build . . . a town and a tower with its top reaching heaven. Let us make a name for ourselves, so that we may not be scattered about the whole earth.

The image of The Tower of Babel[8] suggests human aspirations for permanence and recognition. Humanity resists being "scattered" and strives for achievement ("make a name"). These twin motivations of belonging and becoming[9] are associated with the capacity to language, that is, to express what matters in publicly ascertainable ways ("the same language, with the same vocabulary").

Yahweh responds to such self-conscious activity:

> Let us . . . confuse their language . . . So that they can no longer understand one another Yahweh scattered them over the whole face of the earth . . . (the town) was named Babel . . . because there Yahweh confused the language of the whole earth.

Rather than explaining the differences in language, the story simply describes widespread misunderstanding. That which is particular (humanity) no longer adequately expresses that which is universal (the pluralistic "us" of God). Primal harmony has been dissolved. The word "Babel" itself derives from the root bll, which means "confusion." God "mixed" the languages so people would disperse because of their misunderstandings. The most basic human attribute—the capacity to symbolize—obscures our humanity even as it discloses it. We fail to understand each other.

Here are fundamental issues of epistemology: how we express what we know; how we know what we know; how we assess what we know; how we value what we know; how we act on what we know; how we compare, clarify, and celebrate what we know. We speak many tongues. English may be the primary language of international exchange, yet it falls short of being the primary language of humanity. To put the issue of Babel sharply: the Queen's English in the King James Bible is not God's language!

I suggest that issues of "original sin" and "sin" include attempts to deal with the centrality and perplexity of language. Creation—uncommitted cortex to use a neurological anchor—is "good," that is, the brain is capable of coordinated functioning for adaptive purposes. Existence, which means the division of labor that emerges from lateralization, is necessary, that is, specialization for all complex mental activity. Though unnecessary, cognitive deficiencies and disturbances seem inevitable. The double brain makes for divided minds: inevitable by virtue of division of labor; unnecessary by virtue of the corpus callosum. But the Garden of Eden turns into the Tower of Babel. Humanity experiences and exercises the tyranny of language.

We can now understand how differentiation contributes opposition. Dichotomies become dualities. Polar contrasts result in polarizations. Human minds turn against themselves, one another, and God.

Many dichotomies stem directly from Hellenic consciousness. Bruno Snell attributed the discovery of the mind to the Greeks.[10] While rationality emerged in Greece, that culture always struggled with irrationality.[11] During the Archaic Period (620-480 B.C.E.), people became conscious of a quasi-independent self. With that the gods grew more distant and dogma declined.[12] As Julian Jaynes has argued, the origin of the self-conscious human being lies in the breakdown of the bicameral, two chambered, mind.[13]

Apollo versus Dionysus . . .

While the Greeks tended toward the abstract, the Hebrews tended toward the concrete.[14] Even so, Hebraic consciousness discloses its own dichotomies.[15] The Covenant and the Law set the Mosaic tradition, with its emphasis upon freedom and responsibility, and the Davidic tradition, with its accent upon order and obedience, against each other.

Varieties of Christian experience can be read as indicators of a divided mind of the double brain: reason/revelation, agape/eros, law/gospel, didache (teaching)/kerygma (proclamation), diaconia (serving)/koinonia (sharing). Without oversimplifying, such contrasts suggest manifestations of the mind of God in creating versus proclamations of the mind of God in redeeming.

The persistence of split-brain consciousness means that we develop one mind at the expense of the other. Preference for a rational mind-set may atrophy relational input. Or, preference for a relational mind-set may ignore rational input.

The best of Athens and Jerusalem minimized an arid rationalism (left hemisphere) and/or a naive empiricism (right hemisphere). Yet, as I have elaborated above, by the Byzantine period forces were at work fusing and splitting intellect and intuition.[16] Western culture and Christianity lost the Eastern element—the imaginative and the mystical, which appear linked to an all-at-once processing. Eastern culture and Christianity lost the western element—the intentional and the historical, which seem associated with a step-at-a-time processing.

With the split-mind of Babel people fight about the many maps of meaning. Here is madness of a common kind: confusion over manifestations of the mind of creation in humanity's being and conflict over proclamation by the mind of redemption in humanity's becoming. Two isolated processes generate clashing realities.

THE ONE MIND OF PENTECOST

Even though Babel abounds, Pentecost appears!

Our several languages—whether of tongues* or representational systems—and our double brain do not always divide. There are moments—happenings—events—unexpected contacts—disclosures—in which we hear and see and feel the mediated-immediacy of The Way Things Are. In such events the mind of God appears in humanity's two minds as singlemindedness.

Acts 2:1-12 symbolizes the full mind of reality:

> People from every corner of the earth were gathered in one place.[17] Suddenly, the heard something, that is, a sound like the rushing of a mighty wind; they saw something, that is, like tongues of fire over each person's head; they felt something, that is, like the power of the Holy Spirit inside them. Everyone was speaking in his or her own language, yet each understood the others. Some observers asked what it meant, while others laughed it off by saying the participants had been drinking too much.

Here is "madness" of a different kind. I regard the experience as divine-human "sanity." The event called Pentecost[18] provides a paradigm of disclosing and declaring the full mind of reality. People both knew and knew about divine truth. People both knew and knew about each other. People received the gift of standing-under the world in ways that matter most to what is real in the universe and right in society.

I examine two features in the Pentecost account: the deep structure of language, namely, Primal Word below every word, and the deep structure of participation, namely, Primal Community below every group.

Odd Languaging: words and Word

Consider first the "odd" languaging[19] disclosed in the story.

Languages are what transformational-generative linguists call surface structures.[20] These surface structures are transformations of the deep common structure of humanity's capacity to conceptualize. The misunderstanding of Babel-like experiences arises whenever the complete, logical, semantic re-presentation, and referential anchor fails to appear in the surface structure. Information which is either deleted or distorted obscures the content which is specific to the context. What is said mis-re-presents what is publicly available. The primacy of language itself, what in a biblical-theological formulation refers to The Word which is Truth and Power, generates every tongue and dialect.

I contend that that deep structure bears divinity. The Word which is "always-already" becomes flesh—and humanity is Word.

Each surface structure emphasizes some aspects of Word and obscures other aspects. Perception and re-presentation are active processes, shaped by the constraints of individual nervous systems, the social filters of cultural inheritance, and each one's own unique history.[21] "Reality" is a social[22] and individual construction. We live in an open system which gives evidence of emerging from inorganic to organic to living forms.[23] As St. Paul described this: we see reality through a glass darkly (1 Corinthians 13:12a). Pluralism is real.

In brief, people experience differently, observed and conceive differently, express themselves differently,[24] and follow different maps of meaning differently.

All languages—cultural and technical—are potentially accessible to everyone. Every tongue arises because of the mind. No tongue continues without the functioning of the mind. No language has a monopoly on expressive capacity. Every language explains and shapes experience. While each conceptualization can be fruitful, no conceptualization is final. Surface structures themselves are insufficient to generate language, yet surface structure is necessary for language to appear. <u>We only access deep structure through surface structures.</u>

Surface structures are collective and individual expressions of deep structure. In the experience of humanness we find that which eludes direct description. At the same time we find that which is most immediately concrete. Existence in its full subjectivity, whether personal or communal, is primary reality.

In other words, there is no demonstrably identifiable, particular, spatial, temporal object that is "consciousness" or "I" or "we." Consciousness of humanness is not an entity, yet it has reality. In pointing to human consciousness we discover "something which is all of these (particular) facts and more, and (that consciousness) is <u>not</u> a more that will ever be covered by more of the facts."[25]

C.S. Sherrington is quoted by brain physiologist J.C. Eccles to the effect that there is no "centralization upon one pontifical nerve cell." Eccles went on to claim that "the antithesis must remain that our brain is a democracy of ten thousand million nerve cells, yet it provides us with a unified experience."[26] The many surface structures of humanity constitute the primary reality from which all else derives, namely, the full subjectivity expressed in the structure of language itself.

Yet deep structure manifests itself just as elusively and just as immediately as surface structure. Deep structure is an undifferentiated ever-present context.

Polanyi pointed to this indwelling "given" when he spoke of knowledge as personal. There is a "tacit dimension"—a grounding—that is inarticulate and inarticulable.[27] That realm of deep structure provides the material for what is sensed, seen, and spoken. Yet that realm is so infinite we can never adequately say what we know or understand the implications in what we say.

We experience but a fraction of the environment. The image of an animated cartoon, with the tiniest details projected with incredible speed, suggests the immensity of pattern responses spreading through the neural pathways in the brain. This background "noise" supports the activation of attention necessary to maintain consciousness. Yet we must distinguish this background activity from foreground attention.

We direct our attention to only a very select part of sensory input. Yet without this complicated neuronal input of raw data we could not respond with awareness, recognition, comparison, value judgments, correlations with other experiences, aesthetic evaluations, and so on.[28] Polanyi regarded this subcortical activity of "subsidiary awareness" as the basis of all explicit knowledge.[29] Surface structure, which means conscious knowledge, can never be made "wholly explicit." In the subsidiary awareness of deep structure we discover an order that goes beyond our ability to create or understand fully.

In brief, consciousness reflects the active, rational left mind with its surface structure of proclamation. Similarly, awareness refers to the receptive relational right mind with its deeper structure of manifestation.

Beyond the observed and the experienced—each of which are surface structures but of different orders—lies an "other" or a "more." "More" is not quantitative, for no addition of numbers can equal it. "Other" is indescribable, for no definition can contain it. That "other" or "more" is analogous to the two hemispheres of the one mind. Think of the deepest structure, otherness or moreness, as the mind of God. Ian Ramsey labeled our encounter with that as "cosmic disclosure," "an awareness of objective transcendence," the circumstances in which "the universe 'comes alive,' where a 'dead,' 'dull,' 'flat' existence takes on 'depth' or another 'dimension' . . . and in it the whole universe confronts us . . . a single individuation expressing itself in each and all of these disclosures. In other words, from any and every cosmic disclosure we can claim to believe in one (reality) . . . precisely because we talk of there being 'one world,'"[30] even as we refer to "one brain." Deepest structure transcends the immediacy of right hemisphere process and the abstracting of left hemisphere process.

"God," as Clement of Alexandria (ca. 150-215 C.E.) put it, "cannot be embraced in Words or by the Mind."[31] And Nicholas of Cusa (1401-1464) insisted that God is seen only "beyond the coincidence of contradictories . . . and nowhere this side thereof." In other words, God is not one of the poles of any pair of contrasts. "The opposition of opposites," contended Nicholas, "is an opposition without opposition."[32] God can neither be reduced to left mind abstraction nor contained in right mind immediacy. As Augustine confessed: God, thou art not the mind itself; "For thou art the Lord God of the mind."[33] Thus, Clement rightly spoke of this reality as "the Depth" because it contains and fosters all things, "inaccessible and boundless."[34]

Tillich termed this "the God above the God of theism."[35] In the God above God we avoid "the loss of (ourselves) by participation." The explanations of the left hemisphere depend upon the indwelling immediacy of the right hemisphere. Likewise, in the God above God we avoid "the loss of our world by individualization." The experience of the right hemisphere depends upon left half intentionality.

In other words, within us lies "an affinity for making contact with reality."[36] That in which we dwell comes to us from outside, from beyond, as manifestation. It is wholly other, beyond our imagining and apart from our intending. It is mystery disclosing itself meaningfully. That of which we speak appears to us as from inside, from within, as proclamation. It is from us, within our consciousness and a part of our mastery. It is meaning declaring itself intentionally.

The odd languaging of Pentecost fused the deep structure of God with the deep structure of humanity and the surface structures of many languages. The mind of God informed the mind of humanity. As neurolinguistic programming explains, we re-present reality via input systems—the major ones being seeing, hearing, and sensing.[37] We take in raw data through our eyes, ears, and body, translating that into usable information. This is called map-making. Our minds make maps of the territory, and we live according to our maps rather than according to the territory.

In Pentecostal reality all systems are working: seeing, hearing, and sensing, that is, the occipital lobes, the temporal lobes, and the parietal lobes. The many maps overlap to disclose that which is both real and right.

What is "odd" about Pentecostal language is that it combines metaphorical and analytical language.[38] The metaphorical opens up and brings to light the deep structure of experiencing. The analytical shapes and makes explicit the surface structures of expression. The use of all representational systems guarantees fuller contact with reality, and that reality is more awesome than the limited and limiting maps of our own making.

Pentecostal language is different from ordinary language. The word "Babel" means "gate of the god" as well as confusion.[39] Language is not only the gift of God, but language is the gate to God! The mind connects us to God by virtue of its re-presenting God's mind. Odd languaging is re-presenting, con-ceiving, thinking, and communicating in uncommon ways. We experience, exegete, translate, and interpret every surface tongue as a transformation of deep structure.

Our words convey the Word.

Odd Participating: communities and Community

Consider now the odd participating described in the story.

Social interactions are what I call surface structures. Comparable to the transformational view of language, these interactions are transformations of the deep structure of humanity's capacity for attachment and belonging.[40] The scattering alienation of Babel-like experiences appears whenever the individual and communal fail to be mutually enhancing. The primacy of participation itself, what in a biblical-theological formulation refers to the Kingdom of God (that is, the realm and reign of God),[41] generates every community.

I contend that the deep structure of humanity bears the true image of divinity. Presence which is "always-already" becomes participation—and humanity is Community.

Each social interaction affirms community and limits it. Patterns of participation are active processes shaped by the neural, social, and uniquely historical constraints parallel to those of perception and re-presentation. A left minded individualism differs even as does a right minded contextualism. We live in limited and contained systems of reality.[42] They close off possibilities for an inclusive Community. As the Book of Revelation put it: the kingdoms of this world are not the Kingdom of our Lord and of His Christ (Revelation 11:15). Parochialism is real and rampant.

In brief, no one is born or lives apart from some community context, yet no community context exists apart from individuals participating in its dynamics. Some surface interaction is necessary for human life, yet no such interaction is sufficient in itself to generate "the farther reaches" of humanity.[43] However, we only access deep community through surface communities.

Surface interactions are collective and individual patterns of deep structure. When the deeply communal is lost in surface societies, a split occurs. Individual identity and social identification compete for dominance. The more of one, the less of the other.[44] Me-ism versus us-ism. The authoritarian collective swallows up the individual or else the autonomous individual denies the corporate basis of its existence.

At Pentecost, participation meant presence—the presence of the communal-in-the-personal. Each derived from and enhanced the other. Diverse seekers gathered in one place at one time with one intent. People from every nation translates into what anthropologists call cross-cultural presence. New Reality—the true mind of God in the mind of humanity—disclosed a cross-cultural imperative. Race, gender, age, class, and ethnic differences make the emergence of human evolution more varied than anyone imagined.[45] Freud's Vienna of 1890 is no more the norm of humanity than is Marx's classless society. The Human Community includes and transcends every community.

Contextual sensitivity is another way of expressing the meaning of odd presence. We are sensitive to the rainbow of values, emphases, approaches, communities, cultures, mind-sets. People, in truth, operate on different assumptions, hold different values, and act with different intentions.[46]

More precisely, odd presence translates into radical individuality. No communal structure can adequately manifest The Way Things Truly Are, yet no particular individual can adequately proclaim what is really real. Every sensitivity to the specifics of cultural context requires humility in the presence of the single solitary individual.[47] Every concrete moment of meaning calls for discernment about persons-in-community and communities-in-persons. Thus, we have to assess:[48]

> what aspects of this situation are cultural-and--communal?
>
> what aspects are personal-and-individual?
>
> what changes and what continuities are necessary in the person? in the setting?

what changes and what continuities are transactional between person and setting?

In the language of behavioral research the issue of odd participation is this: which actions, by whom, to whom, for what ends?[49] The search for meaning is both more individual and more contextual than we can imagine.

Insistence upon odd presence emphasizes personal identity when we live too much through the lives of others. At the same time it encourages identification with others when we hold too tightly to ourselves alone. Mutuality <u>and</u> aspiration; interpersonal sensitivity <u>as well as</u> intra-psychic exploration; intimacy <u>and</u> individuation; attachment <u>and</u> autonomy.

Pentecostal presence is different from everyday society. God-presence demands that we stand with, apart from, and against one another as well as with, apart from, and against our several communities. In odd participation people find the courage to be as themselves and the courage to be part of the whole.

Our various communities give us glimpses of Human Community. God does work in and through the odd mind of humanity.

NOTES

1. I agree with David Tracy's definition of the meaning of "classic": ". . . what we mean in naming certain texts, events, images, rituals, symbols and persons 'classics' is that here we recognize nothing less than the disclosure of a reality we cannot but name truth" (THE ANALOGICAL IMAGINATION [n.1/43], 108).

2. Conventionally, interpretive approaches have been either hermeneutics of redescription (retrieval) and thereby sympathetic affirmations within a tradition or hermeneutics of suspicion and thereby critical inquiries from outside a tradition. Freud and unconscious motivation, Marx and socioeconomic determiners, and Nietzsche and the will-to-power constitute the major hermeneutics of suspicion. Historical and literary criticism have arisen within the biblical tradition over the last 200 years. In the last quarter of the century, hermeneutics of suspicion have appeared within the theological tradition. For instance, liberation theology calls for and celebrates liberation from oppression, especially male chauvinism and western whiteness. Black and Third World theologies criticize the western whiteness of ultimate meaning and mystery (e.g., Jose Miguez Bonino, DOING THEOLOGY IN A REVOLUTIONARY SITUATION [Philadelphia: Fortress Press, 1975], James H. Cone, A BLACK THEOLOGY OF LIBERATION [Philadelphia: J.P. Lippincott, Co., 1970], Gustavo Gutiérrez, A THEOLOGY OF LIBERATION [Maryknoll, NY: Orbis Books, 1973]). Feminist theology calls into question the masculinization of ultimate meaning (e.g., Judith Plaskow, SEX, SIN AND GRACE: Women's Experience and the Theologies of Reinhold Niebuhr and Paul Tillich [Washington, D.C.: University Press of America, 1980]; Elisabeth Schässler Fiorenza, IN MEMORY OF HER: A Feminist Theological Reconstruction of Christian Origins [New York: Crossroads, 1983]; and Rosemary Radford Ruether, SEXISM AND GOD-TALK:

Toward a feminist theology [Boston: Beacon Press, 1983]).

3. The Greek word "kairos" or "space of time" refers to "the decisive" event or "the essential point." In the New Testament it refers to the decisive experience of the Church to God's full disclosure of righteous love in Jesus-as-the-Christ. See THE INTERPRETER'S DICTIONARY: R-Z (n.1/36), "Time," 642-649; Paul Tillich, THE PROTESTANT ERA. Translated and with a concluding Essay by James Luther Adams (Chicago: The University of Chicago Press, 1948), 32-51.

4. I assume the biblical record reflects experiences primarily of communal origins, understood through shared reflections and conceptualizations. Historical-critical and literary-critical methods deal with issues of textual reliability and variations. A neurotheological approach brackets issues of textual certainty and historical occurrence. I take what is given as a whole, with its diversity and pluralism (see Ashbrook and Walaskay, CHRISTIANITY FOR PIOUS SKEPTICS [n.0/9], 101-115. The analytic metaphor provides an understandable basis for diversity and pluralism in specifying the conditions for intelligible pluralism in the several mind-states. It does not establish any particular conviction and commitment as primary, except for its built-in assumptions of integration of the hemispheres and the adequacy of representational systems. Some of the ideas in this chapter originally appeared in James B. Ashbrook, "Babel - Legion - Pentecost," Journal of Pastoral Care, June 1982, 118-124.

5. For a critical, historical, and literary discussion of The Flood, see THE INTERPRETER'S DICTIONARY: E-J (n.1/36), 278-284. Folk recollections of actual flood experiences combined with legends, which reflected schemes of cosmic cycles independent of traditions of actual historical inundations, to explain and interpret catastrophic transitions between epochs. For contemporary flood parallels, see liter-

ature on The Age of Aquarius such as Marilyn Ferguson, THE AQUARIAN CONSPIRACY: Personal and Social Transformation in the 1980s (Los Angeles: J.P. Tarcher, Inc., 1980). Just as two independent accounts of creation reflect the earlier Yahwist (Lord) J tradition and the post-exilic Priestly (God) P tradition, so two somewhat inconsistent, parallel, and continuous stories of the flood are identified: J in Genesis 6:5-8; 7:1-5, 7, (8-9), 10, 12, 16b, 17b, 23-24; 8:2b, 3a, 6-12, 13b, 20-22; and P in Genesis 6:9-22; 7:6, 11, 13-16a, 17a, 18-21, 24; 8:1-2a, 3b-5, 13a, 14-19; 9:1-17. I associate the "imaginative, charming tale, containing the picturesque incident of sending out the raven and the dove" with a right mind style. The "formal, precise, and calculated" P account correlates with a left mind style. I use the existing conflated account, which contains both sources (also see PEAKE'S COMMENTARY ON THE BIBLE. Edited by Matthew Black & H.H. Rowley [New York: Thomas Nelson and Sons Ltd., 1962], 183-185). This line of interpretation reflects a "narrative logic" in contrast to a "linear logic." The former incorporates both sources because together they bring forth "mutually complementary implications of the narrated event," thus giving readers "a complete imaginative account" of events (Robert Alter, THE ART OF BIBLICAL NARRATIVE [New York: Basic Books, Inc., 1981], 138).

6. Paul Tillich, SYSTEMATIC THEOLOGY: Vol. Two (London: James Nisbet & Co. Ltd., 1957) 33-51.

7. Reinhold Niebuhr, THE NATURE AND DESTINY OF MAN. I. Human Nature (New York: Charles Scribner's Sons, 1951), 251-260.

8. The Tower of Babel story also reflects two separate literary strands, but these are "fused into a single narrative" (PEAKE'S COMMENTARY [n.5 above], 185, XI:1-9; also see THE INTERPRETER'S DICTIONARY: A-D [n.1/36], 334).

9. Cf. such variations of the motivations of being and becoming as Freud's criteria of maturity, to love and to work; David McClelland's achievement motivation, which results from the interaction of need-affiliation and need-power (THE ACHIEVING SOCIETY [New York: Irvington, (1961) 1976]; William Glasser's the need to love and be loved and the need for a sense of worth which comes with responsible behavior (THE IDENTITY SOCIETY [New York: Harper & Row, 1972]). See John W. Atkinson and David Birch, AN INTRODUCTION TO MOTIVATION Second Edition (New York: D. Van Nostrand, 1978) for "a contemporary view" of motivation as well as "historical perspective" on the topic.

10. Bruno Snell, THE DISCOVERY OF THE MIND: The Greek Origins of European Thought. Trans. T.G. Rosenmeyer (Cambridge: Harvard University Press, 1953).

11. E.R. Dodds, THE GREEKS AND THE IRRATIONAL (Berkeley: University of California Press, [1951] 1973); W.F. Otto, DIONYSUS: Myth and Cult. Trans. with intro. R.B. Palmer (Bloomington: Indiana University Press, [1965] 1973).

12. J.H. Finney, FOUR STAGES OF GREEK THOUGHT (Stanford: Stanford University Press, 1966).

13. Julian Jaynes, THE ORIGIN OF CONSCIOUSNESS IN THE BREAKDOWN OF THE BICAMERAL MIND (n.0/13).

14. Erich Auerbach, MIMESIS: the representation of reality in Western Literature. Translated by William R. Trask (Princeton: Princeton University Press, 1952), 3-23. The Homeric style "externalized description" by making everything explicit in "the foreground," whereas the Old Testament style was dominated by the suggestive influence of "this unexpressed 'background' quality, multiplicity of meanings and the need for interpretation" (23). Hellenic concrete descriptiveness actually meant conceptual abstraction. Hebraic suggestiveness actually

meant immediate (concrete) personal and communal experience. According to Thorlief Boman, HEBREW THOUGHT COMPARED WITH GREEK (Philadelphia: Westminster Press, 1960), Greek thinking was visual, with attention on objective appearance; Hebrew thinking was auditory, with attention to subjective impression. The former is knowledge <u>about</u> and the latter knowledge <u>of</u>. See also Arendt, THE LIFE OF THE MIND, <u>Vol</u>. One Thinking (n.1/56), the Greeks and the eye encouraged objectivity by allowing (a) distance and (b) one's own initiative (56, 80, 92, 110-112, 120-121), while the Hebrews and the ear encouraged obedience because the listener was pulled in to listen and learn what is by waiting for it to come (111-112, 119).

15. cf., George E. Mendenhall, "Law and Covenant in Israel and the Ancient Near East," <u>The Biblical Colloquium</u> (Pittsburgh, 1955).

16. Guerdan, BYZANTIUM (n.5/1).

17. The list of nations may be based on an astrological catalogue in which each country was allocated one of the signs of the Zodiac. The description symbolizes all the nations, proceeding from East to West, starting with Rome's great rival empire, Parthia, which represented the eastern ends of the earth, and "going through Asia Minor as far as the province of Asia, back along the southern part of Asia Minor to Egypt, omitting Syria and Palestine, where a Galilean could not need a special gift of tongues to make himself understood, and thence to Cyrenaica, and to those Jewish visitors to Jerusalem who were, like Paul, Roman citizens and might be Greek-speaking or Latin-speaking" (PEAKE'S COMMENTARY, [n.5 above], 888, II 9).

18. Pentecost is the Greek name for the Jewish Feast of Weeks which came 50 days after the Passover ceremony of the barley sheaf. Since the experience of the gift of the Holy Spirit to the Church occurred on the day of Pentecost, Christians reinterpre-

ted the meaning of the event (THE INTERPRETER'S DICTIONARY: K-Q, [n.1/36], 727). Also see PEAKE'S COMMENTARY (n.5 above), 887-890, II.

19. Ian Ramsey, RELIGIOUS LANGUAGE: An Empirical Placing of Theological Phrases (New York: Macmillan, [1957] 1963), and John Macquarrie, GOD-TALK: An Examination of the Language and Logic of God (New York: Harper, 1967).

20. See Richard Bandler and John Grinder, THE STRUCTURE OF MAGIC I: A Book About Language and Therapy (Palo Alto, CA: Science & Behavior Books, Inc., 1975), Chp. 2 "The Structure of Language." See LANGUAGE AND LEARNING: The Debate Between Jean Piaget and Naom Chomsky. Edited by Massimo Piatelli-Palmarini (Cambridge, Mass.: Harvard University Press, 1980), for controversy about whether cognitive structures are innate or learned.

21. Bandler and Grinder, THE STRUCTURE OF MAGIC I (n.20 above), 4-13.

22. Peter Berger and Thomas Luckmann, THE SOCIAL CONSTRUCTION OF REALITY: A Treatise in the Sociology of Knowledge (Garden City, NY: Anchor Books, 1970); Mary Douglas, IMPLICIT MEANINGS: Essays in Anthropology (London: Routledge & Kegan Paul, [1975] 1979).

23. See Pierre Teilhard de Chardin, THE PHENOMENON OF MAN. With an Introduction by Sir Julian Huxley (New York: Harper & Brothers Publishers, 1959).

24. Roger J. Williams, YOU ARE EXTRAORDINARY (New York: Random House, 1967).

25. Ian Ramsey, CHRISTIAN EMPIRICISM. Edited by Jerry H. Gill (London: Sheldon Press, 1974), 62. This section on empirical referents of deep structure is adapted from Ashbrook and Walaskay, CHRISTIANITY FOR PIOUS SKEPTICS (n.0/9), 118-125.

26. Eccles, FACING REALITY (n.1/1), 80.

27. Polanyi, PERSONAL KNOWLEDGE (n.1/10); idem., THE TACIT DIMENSION (n.1/10).

28. Eccles, FACING REALITY (n.1/1), 72-77, 161.

29. Polanyi, PERSONAL KNOWLEDGE (n.1/10), x, 64.

30. Ramsey, CHRISTIAN EMPIRICISM (n.25 above), 66, 130.

31. Clement of Alexandria, Stromateis, V, 12. Alexander Roberts and James Donaldson, eds., THE WRITINGS OF THE FATHERS (1869), William Wilson, trans., 267.

32. Nicholas of Cusa, THE VISION OF GOD. Trans. by Emma Gurney Salter, and Introduction by Evelyn Underhill (New York: E.P. Dutton, 1928), 44; also see John A.T. Robinson, EXPLORATION INTO GOD (London: SCM Press, 1967), 139-140.

33. Augustine, CONFESSIONS AND ENCHIRIDION, ed. and trans. Albert C. Outler (Philadelphia: Westminster Press, 1955), Bk. Ten, XXV, 223.

34. Clement, Stromateis (n.31 above), 269.

35. Paul Tillich, THE COURAGE TO BE (New Haven: Yale University Press, 1950).

36. Polanyi, PERSONAL KNOWLEDGE (n.1/10), 403.

37. Grinder and Bandler, THE STRUCTURE OF MAGIC II (n.2/80), Part I "Representational Systems - Other Maps For The Same Territory," 1-26.

38. Cf. Sallie McFague, METAPHORICAL THEOLOGY (n.9/28).

39. PEAKE'S COMMENTARY (n.5 above), 186. "While Babylonian tradition explained the name as 'Gate

of God' the biblical author substituted a satirical play on words: Babylon is only confusion" (THE TORAH: A Modern Commentary, by W. Gunter Plaut (New York: Union of American Hebrew Congregations, 1981), 80, Genesis 11:9.

40. John Bowlby, ATTACHMENT AND LOSS, vols. I-III (New York: Basic Books, Inc., 1969, 1973, 1980).

41. See THE INTERPRETER'S DICTIONARY: K-Q, (n.1/36), 17-26.

42. See n.22 above.

43. Abraham H. Maslow, THE FARTHER REACHES OF HUMAN NATURE (New York: Viking Press, 1971).

44. Cf. Sigmund Freud, CIVILIZATION AND ITS DISCONTENTS. Standard Edition, (London: Hogarth Press, 1961), 21:64-145.

45. H.C. Triandis, ed., HANDBOOK OF CROSS-CULTURAL PSYCHOLOGY, 6 vols. (Boston: Allyn & Bacon, 1980-81).

46. Florence R. Kluckholn and Fred L. Strodtbeck, VARIATIONS IN VALUE ORIENTATION (Westport, CT: Greenwood Press, [1961] 1973), esp., 1-48, 340-346, 363-367; Arnold P. Goldstein, "Evaluation Expectancy Effects in Cross-Cultural Counseling." In CROSS-CULTURAL COUNSELING AND PSYCHOTHERAPY, edited by Anthony J. Marsella and Paul B. Pedersen (New York: Pergamon Press, 1981).

47. Soren Kierkegaard, PURITY OF HEART is to will one thing. Translated from the Danish with an introductory essay by Douglas Steere. Rev. ed. (New York: Harper, 1948).

48. J.G. Draguns, "History, Issues, Current Status." In Marsella and Pedersen, CROSS-CULTURAL COUNSELING AND PSYCHOTHERAPY (n. 46 above), esp., 19-22.

49. Goldstein, "Evaluating Expectancy Effects" (n.46 above), 87.

Chapter Eleven

CONCLUDING AN UNSCIENTIFIC PROMISE

You will recall the montage of the brain, the dome, and the spire at the beginning of the book. It illustrates what I have written.

In front is the human brain. From research in the neurosciences I have gathered evidence as to how the mind works. Mind serves as a bridge between physical processes and broad social, cultural, and cosmic patterns. In back are central symbols of classical Christianity—the dome of St. Sophia and the spire of Chartres Cathedral. By means of these architectural archetypes I explored Byzantine Orthodoxy and Medieval Catholicism. Together with brain research, they suggest images of humanity's approaches to meaning—an all-encompassing, dome-like responsiveness and a precise, spire-like vigilance. These overlay even mind itself. Just as mind can be understood as the human meaning of the brain, so God can be understood as the religious meaning of mind.

Initially, I asked whether brain research could contribute to theology. I further wondered whether the specialized activity of the left and right brains corresponded to patterns of belief, especially those of proclaiming what is right and manifesting what is real. I turned to architecture to explore the fruitfulness of such speculation. Finally, I extracted implications for understanding the many minds of humanity. As I draw this effort to a close, I review what I have done and then suggest what it has come to mean.

GATHERING UP THE EVIDENCE

This has been a cross-disciplinary venture, bridging the behavioral sciences and the humanities. In writing on THE NATURAL HISTORY OF THE MIND, Gordon Rattray Taylor cited Aldous Huxley's conviction that "one ought to be able to talk about a mystical experience simultaneously in terms of theology, of psychology, and of biochemistry."[1] The "same" data calls for a constellation of understanding which can only come with interdisciplinary dialogue. No one specialty has the only word; every speciality contributes a necessary word.

More pointedly, Taylor marshalled evidence for what he called "The Omega Effect." The Omega Effect consists of "vivid personal experience . . . such fancy trimmings as a sense of identity, a sense of humor or a sense of deity." Identity—humor—deity: these "trimmings" make up the core of human presence. They are the human side of scientific investigation—vivid personal experience of physiological processes.

Levels of Analysis

Without retaining the term "omega effect" I have pursued the suggestion. In the loose interface between personal experience and physical data, that space identified as mind, I have looked for clues to the human meaning of human presence. In connecting the brain and belief I have used mind as an analytic metaphor. This is a way of thinking about human experience in terms of behavioral evidence. Mind points us in two directions: downward into the organized regularities of the brain and outward toward the emergent features of human purposes. Because of this the brain focuses the meaning of mind even as mind enlarges the significance of brain.

Table 13 outlines these levels of organized discourse. As we move from the more physical to the more cosmic, the fit between evidence and inference grows increasingly loose and more speculative. The most objective level, that of the closed system of brain regularities, uses the language of the neurosciences. It deals with neural and endocrine activity, understanding mind as The Primal Mind or The Reptilian-like Brain, as Paul MacLean termed it.[2] At this subcortical level we also deal with The Old Mammalian-like Brain or The Emotional Mind. Here in the limbic system we find motivational drives, a combination of adaptive behavior for the preservation of the species and aggressive behavior for the survival of the individual.[3] Approach and avoidance, a part of the environment and apart from the environment, sociability and self-assertion, relaxation and tension, responsiveness and vigilance—these are the polarities of activity.

At the next level of analysis the precision of the scientific model is modified. Here in the language of behavioral sciences, we deal with the brain-mind itself, what Luria termed "the working brain" and MacLean referred to as The Rational Mind. This new brain is characterized by a division of labor between its left and right halves.[4] Each side handles information differently.

These cortical areas are extensions of subcortical, sensory (thalamic) relay centers. In other words, the new brain—the neocortex—is an outgrowth of the old brain.

Table 13. **Levels of Organized Regularities and Types of Analysis**

Level of Analysis	Language of Analysis	Structural Organization	Suggested Brain-Mind Type
regularities	neuro-sciences	biochemical	chemical brain
		subcortical:	Reptilian-like Brain & Primal Mind*
		-sensori-motor -limbic pre-sentational	Old Mammalian-like Brain & The Emotional Mind*
			The Working Brain**
Model			
	behavioral-sciences	cortical: -re-presentational	The Brain-Mind*** The New Brain & The Rational Mind*
emergent features		-asymmetrical re-presentational behavior & consciousness	The Purposive Brain****
Metaphor purposeful patterns	social sciences humanities	cultural: -language -social organization -history	Human Mind (rational/relational)
	philosophy theology	cosmic: -world-views -religion	Divine Mind (redeem/create) (proclaim/manifest)

There is a change in logic, language, and relevant information at each level. Analysis includes examination of: (i) form, e.g., typologies or themes, and (ii) process, i.e., descriptions of interactions and/or feedback/feed-forward.

* Paul MacLean, "The Triune Mind."

** A. Luria, "The Working Brain."

*** T. Bever, "Cerebral Asymmetries In Humans Are Due To The Differentiation Two Incompatible Processes: Holistic and Analytic."

**** Ragnar Granit, "The Purposive Brain."

310

Thus, higher cortical functions have lower anatomical connections. What is significant, even though it complicates using the brain as a model, is the lack of correspondence between cognitive activity and specific brain regions.

These massive cortical connections create such an intricate system that all complex activity draws upon all parts of the cortex. At the subcortical level the brain exhibits organized regularity. At the cortical level it presents functional configurations. Rather than specific areas, we find patterns of association. Mind is more than brain.

This asymmetry, lateralization, and unequal activity of the new brain marks the influence of emerging universes of influence. Instincts alone no longer determine approach and avoidance. Now the mind-set, the world as perceived and conceived by the double-minded brain, influences everything that happens. Even the effects of medication must be monitored to take account of individual reactions. With lateralization of functions an active organism interacts with an active environment.[5] The Rational Mind actually reflects The Purposive Brain.[6] We act on the basis of what we expect and what we intend.

Research on the brain shows that two patterns distinguish the way our one head works. The left half proceeds item-by-item and step-by-step. It is rational, sequential, analytic. This narrow analytic style admits only "a few members to any given category" and attends "to detail and small differences."[7] The right half functions all-at-once and by leaps of imagination. It is relational, simultaneous, holistic. This broad integrative style groups "a wide variety of similar objects or concepts together, paying little attention to detail or differences."[8] Neither hemisphere functions alone. Each depends upon what the other contributes. Together they make for unified consciousness and integrated behavior.

Mind As Metaphor

In the Hellenic tradition, the human mind was viewed as an analogue of cosmos—the meaningful universe as ordered and sustained by God as Mind. As I cited in the Introduction, the second century document Poimandres interpreted humanity's being created in the image of God in terms of Mind. Our capacity to experience—to see, hear, and sense—was understood as "the Logos of the Lord," "the Mind, God, both male and female." In contrast to Poimandres' gnostic pessimism about the material world, yet in line with its vision of Mind as "the archetypal form," "the world-creator," I regard brain as a central clue to correlating the human mind and the mind of God.

Since mind is not reducible to the brain, to speak of mind is to speak of it metaphorically. My intent has been to explore the human meaning of the physical brain, the suggestive possibilities of that which is mind-like and yet not-mind. Though the approach is discounted by some neuroscientists,[9] at the very least it has generated extensive research.[10] To speak of the left brain as an analytic mind and the right brain as an intuitive mind[11] is to leave hard science behind.

The level of analysis, therefore, shifts from the organized regularities of the behavioral sciences to the cultural level of the social sciences and the humanities. Here mind provides a metaphor with which to explore the reaches of human activity.

A left minded approach shapes life rationally. It observes, organizes, and explains everything systematically. Two substrategies contribute to this conceptual patterning: one "names" or distinguishes objects; the other "analyzes" or connects them according to basic principles (Table 5). This left brain way is always "on alert," ever vigilant in isolating and mastering what needs to be taken into account in accomplishing human purposes.

The right minded approach processes information relationally. It assumes a web of connectedness which blurs differences and emphasizes similarities. Two sub-strategies make up this more contextual patterning: one is an "immersion" in an immediate context; the other engages in "leaps of imagination" (Table 5). This right half constantly interacts with the environment, responding without definitive labels and so always according to personal meanings.

Brain research further refines these minds or mind--sets. I described how the sensory representational systems contribute to how we understand reality. We take in raw data, transform that into maps of reality, and then act according to our maps (and not the territory itself). Seeing, hearing, and sensing are the major sensory systems, supported by smelling, tasting, and touching. Just as humanity exhibits a right-side bias, so we exhibit preferences in our use of sensory systems. Some of us depend more upon our eyes (visual re-presentation), others on our ears (auditory), and still others on our body (kinesthetic). Over time we tend to rely more upon one system, to the neglect, and even exclusion, of other systems.

These rational and relational strategies and representational systems characterize dominant and variant ways of ordering life and life together. Further, mind-like is more than mind itself, which is why I use it as a metaphor rather than a model. The human mind cannot contain itself. As Augustine put it: "I do not myself grasp all that I am. Thus the mind is far too narrow to contain itself. But where can that part be which it does not contain?"[12] Mind is neither its own origin nor its own destiny.

So to deal with mind points to emergent and purposive features that transcend mind itself: the social and cultural contexts of conventional space and time, the cosmic context or universes of significance in which mind finds itself. Again as Augustine described the experience: "I will seek thee (God) that my soul may live. For my body lives by my soul, and my soul lives by thee."[13]

Here, then, we find the cumulative contribution of the other levels of analysis. The regularities of the brain are transformed by the semi-autonomous mind of meaningfulness, a leap of faith if you will, as to what is real and what is right. The way we are made reflects the way we are meant to be. We are to become the way we are.

The presence of humanity provides the focus of this new form of empirical natural theology. Stephen E. Toulmin, the eminent philosopher of science, articulates postmodern science's return to the issue of cosmology, the meaning of the universe as found in and through its origin, processes, and structure. We live in a "world that has not yet discovered how to define itself in terms of what it _is_, but only in terms of what it has _just-now-ceased-to-be_."[14] We are so inescapably participants in what we know that we can ignore neither ethical issues of how we act nor ecological issues of the environment in which we live. Neutrality about life—its purpose and processes—is no longer an option.

Instead of the old scholastic approach of arguing from sense data to faith commitment, and instead of the older theological liberalism which asked what we can know about God from science, I am part of the current probings that asks "What can we know about God by our own natural lights?"[15] Mind connects us to the context in which we live and the purposes for which we are to live. Once again Augustine provided a description: "The mind itself is not hidden from the truth, but the truth is hidden from it . . . When I found Truth, then found I my God, who is the Truth."[16] "Where, then, did I find thee so as to be able to learn of thee—save in thyself beyond me. Place there is none. We go 'backward' or 'forward' and there is no place. Everywhere at once, O Truth, thou guidest all who consult thee, and simultaneously answereth all even though they consult thee on quite different things."[17]

I turned to brain research to discern within it its theological promise. I found that theology presents parallels to the brain's regularities and mind's emergent properties. Two family resemblances or trajectories of belief distinguish the ways in which people have expressed their experience of God, their pursuit of Truth. One is the hermeneutics of proclamation. What has been experienced in historical events (such as Exodus and Easter) is interpreted as that which makes explicit the significance of human life. The other trajectory is the phenomenology of manifestation. What has been experienced apart from formal language elicits wonder and participation.

To use the evidence of brain research for understanding human life is to use mind analytically and not simply metaphorically. The empirical data curtail wild speculations and often clarify uncertain associations. Though the approach is minimized by some historians and theologians, at the very least to juxtapose these realms of discourse generates intense reflection.[18]

The trajectory of proclamation reflects the rational strategy of the left mind. To make right what is real requires deliberate intention, step-by-step processing. It demands obedience to the articulated God-of-the-universe, the logos of order and ordering. This mind-set may rely more on "naming" or "analyzing," but regardless, it always draws upon relational processes. Its dominant feature is the logic of explicit, rational explanation. In proclamation people hear the truth and the imperative to act on the basis of that truth. This is a redemption oriented theology.

The belief pattern of manifestation exhibits the relational strategy of the right mind. Experiencing the wholeness of life comes as people are in touch with both inner and outer reality in immediate ways. It elicits trust in the manifesting God-of-the-cosmos, the eros of creating and unifying. The mind that manifests itself anywhere and everywhere may rely more on "immersion" or "imagination," but regardless, it always draws upon rational processes. Its dominant feature is the meaningfulness of whatever is and whatever is imaginable. In manifestation people experience the fullness and holiness of the real. This is a creation oriented theology.

The ways in which mind works, therefore, suggest (by analogy) two ways in which God works: step-by-step in making straight the way life is to be and all-at-once in showing forth the way life is. The pattern of proclamation—theologies of redemption—makes explicit what is implicit in the way our mind works, namely, intense vigilance. Similarly, the pattern of manifestation—theologies of creation—keeps vivid the way reality is, namely, expansive responsiveness.

To use mind as an analytic metaphor, therefore, combines brain research and belief patterns. This allows us to identify and assess how functional various mindsets are.[19] An exclusive reliance upon either rational proclamation or relational manifestation prevents a full use of our minds and thereby restricts our knowing the mind of God. Competing processes make for disturbed activity. A house divided against itself cannot stand (Matthew 12:25). In contrast, with every sensory system contributing both relationally and rationally, we are most fully and truly human. In the words of the biblical imperative we love God, our neighbors, and ourselves with all that we are (Mark 12:28-34).[20]

Yes, mind is a metaphor. But as a metaphor it gives us more than simply an imaginary flight of fancy (which is not really the proper use of metaphor) or simply an aid to memory. It organizes evidence and connects distinguishable spheres of investigation in coherent and comprehensive ways. It permits appraisal of various levels of analysis in terms of both their contributions and their limitations. Since mind shows us to be more than we are, an understanding of how it works provides ways by which we can be what we humanly are.

Architectures of Mind

To use the brain to investigate theology I searched for constellations of experience. Two questions shaped the task:

> Are there central tendencies or commonalities within cultural expressions which

allow for discernible and reasonable groupings?

Can these commonalities be understood in terms of how the mind works?

When constellations emerge, I believe we have clues to coherent forces within a culture. These forces stabilize society. Where contrasts are apparent—either in deficient or disturbed processing—I believe we find divergent forces at work. These upset cultural equilibrium, setting loose activity that can be destructive and creative simultaneously. Central tendencies, therefore, are dominant strategies of consciousness, ways of processing experience and explanation. They shape historical periods even as they shape individual psyches.

Living within a certain time and place, people participate in a collective ethos. I link such an ethos with strategy of processing or mind-set. The mind-set reflects the common cosmos or order of human meaning which shapes the character of that society. Constellations of time, place, and strategy help us understand the varied ways humanity has experienced and expressed its place in the world.

Once I identified our several mind-sets, actually, strategies of the mind of humanity and, by inference, a way of understanding God's ways of being God, I applied the analytic metaphor to ways in which western Christians expressed their perceptions of the mind of God. Architecture provided the focus. In building their places of worship, Christians gave us architectures of mind, outward and visible images of inward and spiritual mind--sets. The great dome of St. Sophia and the stretching spire of Chartres Cathedral are central symbols of the human meaning of mind.

Byzantine Orthodoxy visualized triumphant splendor, Christ as the Light of the World and Ruler of the Universe. God's presence showed itself anywhere and everywhere. Thus, the dome hovered over the known world gathering all under its embrace. The place of the holy was unpredictable because it was everpresent, everywhere. Presence—real, authentic, available—created a world transparent to its Creator.

In contrast, Medieval Catholicism called people to a pilgrimage to the place of revelation—Christ crucified on the cross in the Holy Land and sacrificed on the altar in the Church. God's power was borne by the popes as representatives of the kingdom of heaven and in a lesser way by the emperors as rulers of the kingdom on earth. Thus, the spire directed a bewildered and broken world to the only place in which the holy could be found, the altar. The place of the holy was known because it had been specified. Power—authoritative, ordered, specialized—redeemed the world.

Each of these mind-sets exhibited its own grandeur.

The dome hovered in brilliance for a thousand years. And the dome-like quality of God manifesting God unpredictably still quickens the eye of faith. It reminds us of the expansiveness of relational process. It inspires us by its all-at-once and all-around responsiveness. Similarly, the spire stretched heavenward for a thousand years. And the spire-like quality of God redeeming humanity intentionally still calls to the ear of faith. It directs us to the intensity of rational process. It informs us by its piece-by-piece and step-by-step vigilance.

The analytic metaphor not only organized the patterns of belief but also assessed their contributions. The dome proved deficient in drawing upon rational process. It perpetuated a precarious vision. And the spire struggled against relational process to the detriment of both.[21] It established a precarious inquiry. The two patterns collided and collapsed—their grandeur gone, their continuation but a caricature of their originating power.

Whenever one way is not only preferred but relied upon exclusively, the contribution of the other is neglected, if not negated. But that information is not lost. It simply goes underground, reappearing in disruptive and destructive forms. This applies to the deficiency of relying on only one mind-set or to the disturbance of strategies competing with each other for attentional dominance. In contrast, the theological conviction of the oneness of God calls for humanity to use both processes of its one mind.

This conclusion is not new. I did not come to it as a result of seeking theological promise in brain research. I, like others, struggle with contrasting ways of meaning, the polarities which have been identified so often and in such varied forms. But neuropsychological investigation helps us understand how these contrasts arise and how they persist. It reinforces the necessity to keep them together as functional variations of a unified whole.

The dome and the spire serve as central symbols of religious belief. In themselves they provide images of the pattern of manifestation, which is ever responding to and including what is real, and the pattern of proclamation, which is always intensifying and specifying what is right. When these symbols are linked with the brain by means of the concept of mind, we have archetypal patterns of human meaning. The relational strategy of the dome-like makes for diversity. The rational strategy of the spire-like contributes to clarity. Whether we enter the realm of reality, the heavenly city, the new Jerusalem, through the gate of the rational or the gate of the relational, once there we need all that we are.

A dome-like mind, whether Byzantine mystery or as found in various patterns of manifestation, opens before us the unavoidable experience of relating to everything and everyone, for God is all-in-all. Here is the presence of God in the midst of the absence of God, mystery beyond intelligibility, the "loving immanence" of life as a gracious gift.[22] We immerse ourselves sensitively within each context. We open ourselves imaginatively to unsuspected possibilities. A right mind wholeness affirms reality because it is accommodatingly responsive. It keeps us mind-ful of all that is.

And a spire-like mind, whether Medieval mastery or as found in various patterns of proclamation, confronts us with the invevitable task of interpreting what is happening and what we are to do about it. Here is "judgment upon all human pretensions," a recognition that "the gracious God can never be taken for granted," a reminder that "the Hidden and Revealed God disclosed in the crucified One [is] the God-forsaken One"[23] who takes upon Himself responsibility for all. We name each part as uniquely itself and analyze what matters most—that is, schemata of what is, rationally and logically—for God acts to bring to life that which God intends for life. A left mind explanation directs us to what is right. It sets boundaries. It specifies obligations. It is adaptively vigilant. It keeps in mind what is to become of us.

Many Minds, Many Meanings—One Humanity

The Pentecost event provides a paradigm of the odd mind of humanity. Deep structure, which is our most immediate connection with the God-like, expresses itself through the surface structures of our many languages and communities. These are our representations of what God intends for humanity. The oddness of humanity witnesses to one mind working in many ways. The more truly our mind works the more fully our lives disclose what we are meant to be.

Experts in the neurosciences, theology, history, and architecture have pressed me about what they regard as my sweeping generalizations. They acknowledge the central tendencies I have identified but insist that exceptions are the rule. In fact, some argue that exceptions are more plentiful than patterns; for them, analysis dominates synthesis. In a less doctrinaire fashion, most of my critics urge caution, for the evidence is ambiguous.

Because I continue this unscientific promise of discerning theological promise in brain research let me cite some of the ambiguity in both brain research and belief patterns.

We know more about the location of language in the brain than any other complex activity. That is why for the last one hundred and twenty-five years the left hemisphere has been called "dominant" or "major" and the right hemisphere "nondominant" or "minor." The left brain talked, the right brain kept its contribution to itself.

But consider the evidence more closely.

True, the incidence of speech in the left hemisphere is dominant (95.5%) among right-handers suffering from damage in that area. But in left-handers the location of speech in the left hemisphere appears in only 61.4% of those so damaged. Further, in the remaining group, speech is equally divided between being located in the right hemisphere (18.8%) or represented in both hemispheres (19.8%)(Table 14).[24]

Popular views of left and right brains assume a reciprocal relationship between language and spatial abilities. That is, if speech is located in the left half, then spatial ability is in the right half. Such clarity of structure and function shows a less than perfect fit. Among right-handers, slightly more than two-thirds are estimated to have spatial ability lateralized in the right half. Further, among left-handers, only about forty percent show the same pattern. The remaining percentage divides between a left half lateralization or a bilateral distribution across both halves (Table 15).[25]

Table 14. **Incidence of Left, Right, and Bilateral Speech Representation Derived from Unilateral Brain Injury Data (%)***

	Speech Lateralization		
	Left	Bilateral	Right
Right-handers	95.5	—	4.5
Left-handers	61.4	19.8	18.8

Note: Data from Segalowitz and Bryden (forthcoming)

*From Bryden, LATERALITY, Table 10.5, 170

Table 15. **Incidence of Left, Right, and Bilateral Representation of Spatial Abilities (%)***

	Lateralization of spatial abilities		
	Left	Bilateral	Right
Right-handers	30.7	—	69.3
Left-handers	28.1	29.3	42. 6

Note: Figures derived from Table 10.8 in text.

*From Bryden, LATERALITY, Table 10.9, 175.

When gender is added to handedness as a variable, the generalization between left and right brains becomes even more questionable. Generally, male brains are more lateralized than female brains. Verbal and spatial processing are more sharply divided between the two halves for men. But evidence points to women being more lateralized in nonverbal auditory processing and less lateralized in visuospatial perceptions.[26] The most accurate summary of the literature on gender differences and lateralization is that it is "rife with inconsistencies."[27] Although we cannot speak of gender-specific differences, we can identify gender-related differences (Table 16).

Linguistic processes are more prevalent in the left hemisphere of males (95%) than of females (80%). Further, males show greater specialization of spatial processing in their right hemispheres (75% vs. 60%). Women, on the other hand, tend to rely more on verbal strategies to solve spatial problems. The import of the evidence is that "men and women differ in the pattern of cerebral organization, rather than in the degree of lateralization."[28] Because of the specialization in men of linguistic and spatial processes, they are more likely "to show complementarity of specialization."[29]

Hypothesized extrapolations of the data show that about three-quarters of men (72.5%) engage in balancing the two strategies. At best, left and right are complementary; at worst they compete for dominance. A similar complementarity or competition is hypothesized for slightly more than half the women (56%) (Table 16). By inference, then, slightly less than half of women (44%) and slightly more than a quarter of men (27.5 %) depend primarily on the same hemisphere for "both language and spatial processes." The result is a restricting effect on spatial ability.

Table 16. **Hypothetical Percentage Distribution of Sex Differences in Cerebral Organization***

	Cerebral Lateralization					
	Language		Spatial		Complementarity	Noncomplementarity
	Left	Right	Left	Right	(LR & RL)	(LL & RR)
men	95	5	25	75	72.5	27.5
women	80	20	40	60	56.0	44.0

*From Bryden, LATERALITY, Table 14.3, 240

The way the brain works may not be a precise typology to characterize either individuals or cultures.[30] Factors of socialization, mutation, chance and accident, all influence personal and communal patterns. Every generalization can—and must—be modified by the ambiguity of evidence. For this reason I have used mind as a suggestive metaphor rather than the brain as an exact model.

I have identified "naming" and "analyzing" as strategies of rational proclamation. In addition, I have associated "immersed" and "imaginative" with strategies of relational manifestation. These distinctions have been useful in organizing and relating date to separate spheres of knowledge and levels of analysis. Groupings can be discerned and defended. Both individuals and cultures present dominant and variant preferences. To correlate brain processes and belief patterns clarifies similarities-within-differences.

LIVING WITH THE INFERENCES

More than the ambiguity of the evidence, however, I have been shocked by ramifications of the evidence.

Consider again the dispositional tendencies of men and women. The brains of females are predisposed to mature earlier than those of males. That results in the division of labor—lateralization—between the rational left and the relational right being less pronounced. Verbal and nonverbal processes intertwine. Polarities are never as sharp for women as for men. Even the distinction between the intensity of the spire-like mind and the inclusiveness of the dome-like mind suggests a male-related way of thinking. Contrasts dominate in lateralized processing, while intertwining prevails in bilateral processing. Specialized male-related minds and generalized female-related minds are shaped by family patterns and societal influences, that is all too true, but the tendencies originate in biochemical predispositions. These shape the social shaping.

Furthermore, as feminist critics of culture have argued, dominant male-related minds have dictated cultural paradigms. The male mind has created sharp boundaries, clear hierarchies, and fixed patterns of belief. Most blatant gender differences appear with the onset of puberty. By then the effects of socialization are well established. What is genetic and what is cultural are difficult to separate. Nevertheless, regardless of origin, gender-related differences are discernible.

Research on life cycle development, for instance, calls into question the supposedly normative pattern.[31] Freudianism described the paradigm of psychosexual development (that is, oral, anal, genital, Oedipal) as based upon father-son competition for the favored woman (wife or mother). Eriksonian identity issues shifted the paradigm to psychosocial development based on a sequence of individuality moving through the stages of trust-mistrust, autonomy-shame and doubt, initiative-guilt, industry-inferiority, identity- role diffusion, intimacy-isolation, generativity-stagnation, and integrity-despair. In sum, the paradigm identifies the task of becoming human as moving from undifferentiated intimacy to differentiated individuality. Difference is an achievement.

Piaget, in cognitive development, and Kohlberg, in moral development, built upon that basic paradigm. Carol Gilligan was actively part of the Kohlberg research. In the process she began to discern pattern differences between men and women.[32] Male socialization gave few experiences of the care and nurturance of others. She noted that the normative theories neglected morality as being matters of responsibility and care. Further, they neglected attachment as the primary value and differences as the given. Her paradigm suggests the mother-infant bond rather than the father-son struggle. In the normative paradigm one becomes a person in one's own right <u>before</u> one can lose oneself in intimacy and generativity. Or, in the language of belief trajectories, one must be redeemed. Life must be straightened up in line with basic principles.

The sequence of identity-then-intimacy does not fit female reality. Gilligan's investigation of pregnant women resolving moral issues (that is, aborting, putting the baby out for adoption, or keeping the unborn infant) indicated a different pattern from that of male oriented principles. For them identity-and-intimacy were intertwined; in fact, they were inseparable. Whereas the males focused upon principles and justice, aspiration and achievement, the female focus included responsibility and care, inclusiveness and relatedness. For them one becomes a person <u>only</u> in one's connectedness. Only in and through relationships does one become oneself. Again, in the language of belief trajectories, people are created whole. Life unfolds in terms of a web of caring relationships.

In an admittedly simplified speculation, I infer that learning for early maturers, who are primarily women, [33] involves a context sensitive approach rather than a field independent one.[34] Thus, men tend to abstract and simplify, even as I am doing, while women tend to see complexity and insist upon contextual understanding in making critical decisions. The male-related paradigm has tended toward the splits of either-or dichotomies, including left brain/right brain processes and interpretive proclamation/phenomenological manifestation belief patterns. The female-related paradigm is calling for a reality beyond dualism.[35]

The cognitive precariousness of western reality, and of our theological assumptions as well, can no longer be obscured. At best, cognitive extremes create unnecessary difficulties; at worst they are dysfunctional. In our present ecocultural and ecological crises we are, paradoxically, colliding with an incredibly finite and an amazingly infinite universe. Instead of the previously dominating competitive, abstract, principled, rational, and independent strategy, the human situation calls for a more inclusive, cooperative, concrete, relational and interdependent strategy.

Melvin Konner, a biological anthropologist, cites the cross-cultural evidence for male-related aggressive dominance and female-related affiliative patterns.[36] Despite differences among cultures, the direction of difference within any culture is always the same—boys show greater egoism and/or greater aggressiveness than girls. He concludes from this that "speaking of averages there is little doubt that we would all be safer if the world's weapon systems were controlled by average women instead of by average men."

Whether we deal with this shifting paradigm on the level of socialization stereotypes,[37] or on the supposed superiority of androgeny in which both masculine and feminine attributes are combined (that is, "high self-esteem, high achievement-motivation, superior parenting attitudes and the like"),[38] or on the recognition that male and female are not "absolute categories of reality" but "in fact (are) dynamic rather than static phenomena,"[39] we are called to learn about and know a reality vaster and deeper, more complex and elusive, less explainable and more mysterious, than anything we have thought or imagined.

The relational strategy is not the exclusive pattern of women nor is the rational one exclusively male. The distinctions are always tenuous and even questionable. Furthermore: when does one name? how does one analyze? when is one context sensitive? how does one engage in leaps of imagination? The mind-sets, strategies, emphases, processes, belief trajectories—call them what we will—never answer the question of who does what, when, where, how, and for what end?

The elusive issue of how we make real what is right has emerged in the late twentieth century as a third trajectory of belief. Theologian David Tracy calls this "historical" or "prophetic" action. Resemblances in this family include political and liberation theologies.[40] Here is protest against that which cripples and oppresses humanness. Here also is promise of that which liberates and fosters community. I regard the political theologies of protest as extensions of the trajectory of proclamation—that rational strategy of working for that which is just and right. Similarly, I regard the liberation theologies of promise as extensions of the trajectory of manifestation—that relational strategy of making community genuine. The prophetic trajectory focuses on practical activity to transform "what is" in the light and power of "what is to be."

Conflicts and contradictions in the dominant culture are exposed more explicitly than previously. Concern shifts from "alienation to oppression; an oppression enforced by means of all the life-killing structures—economic dependency, sexism, racism, classism, elitism."[41] Exodus and Easter provide primary symbols that represent "God as the God of the oppressed who suffers and works with all peoples for their fully human—their personal, political, societal, cultural, religious—liberation."[42]

To see the manifestation of God and to hear the proclamation of God finally means to act according to the promises of God. Representational systems overlap--visual, auditory, kinesthetic. Primary processes intertwine—relational and rational. Subsidiary strategies coalesce—naming and analyzing, immersing and imagining. We are to act in concrete situations.

The correlates of brain and belief are too varied for summary. Lists of left and right mind activities make the world more orderly than it is. Descriptions of manifestation and proclamation can turn God into a split-mind deity.[43] The dialectic between created world (nature and history) and redeeming power (God) comes together in the human mind, that which struggles to make real that which is right. As William James insisted: "Where you have purpose, there you have mind."[44] And where we have mind, there we have meaning—a continually calling forth and calling to that which is genuinely human.

The trajectories of proclamation and manifestation—redemption and creation oriented theologies—are among the strategies which humanity has used to make "reality humanly meaningful . . . a meaningful place for (humanity) . . . a humanly meaningful universe."[45] The spire of Chartres Cathedral and the dome of St. Sophia provided central symbols of humanity's making its presence intelligible to itself in western civilization.

The dome-like and spire-like, however, are not restricted to the West. In the Gulbenkian Museum of Oriental Art at the University of Durham, England, for instance, one can see two mid-17th century maps of the cosmos (Figure 8). One consists of rectangular, box-like, heavy lines, which are remarkably similar to the rational step-by-step process of the left mind and the spire-like. The other is characterized by wavey, snake-like patterns, which are remarkably similar to the relational all-at-once process of the right mind and the dome-like. Here we see the language of space with its distinctions between the curving and the straight ways by which humanity orients itself to reality. Such a mapping reflects mind-sets, mental processes, that people find in themselves and which they take as reflective of the universe of meaning. Cross-cultural similarities of this kind, while beyond the scope of this work, warrant further investigation.

Since the dawn of the modern period, the sacramental sense of both Byzantine and Medieval belief has receded. In correcting the precarious imbalances, enlightenment rationalism spawned its own tyranny. Only in this last half of the twentieth century are we beginning to regain a glimpse of humanity's humanity in the midst of humanity's inhumanity.

Apart from specific religious convictions, both popular and serious concern with "right brain" wholeness emphasize diversity, relatedness, and creativity.[46] Within traditional belief systems attention to metaphorical theology emphasizes second naivete and imagination[47]—right mind ways of processing. Within ethnic groups communal reality[48] and soul [49] emphasize pluralism and spontaneity—again, right mind responsiveness.

These contemporary counter-re-reformations need not lead us into a new tyranny, this time from an unbalanced immediacy. Brain research demonstrates the necessity of both rational and relational processes. Belief patterns testify to the necessity of proclamation and manifestation coming to maturity in prophetic action. Each must be faithful to its own expression on "behalf of the fully concrete reality of all."[50]

Theological promise in brain research is more inferential than factual.[51] The evidence describes primary structures and functional processes. Yet the scope of science is expanding to take account of inner experience. As Sperry argues: "Human values are inherently properties of brain activity."[52] More than simply the human species or its societal dynamics, we are compelled to "include the welfare of the total biosphere and ecosystem as a whole."[53] Tracy states the same point theologically: "Love, and love alone, is the surest clue to who God is and thereby to what reality, in its ulti-

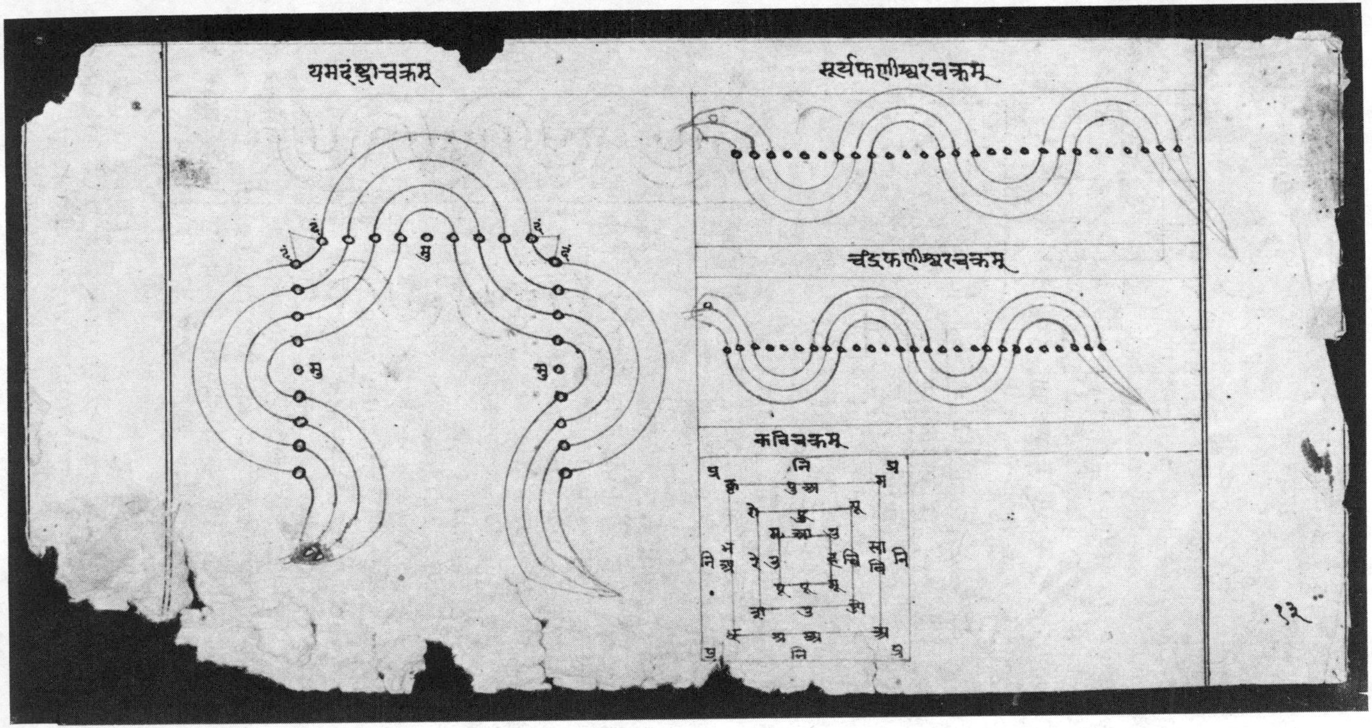

Figure 8 17th Century Map of the Cosmos (India) (Curved Lines)

Figure 8 17th Century Map of the Cosmos (India) (Straight Lines)

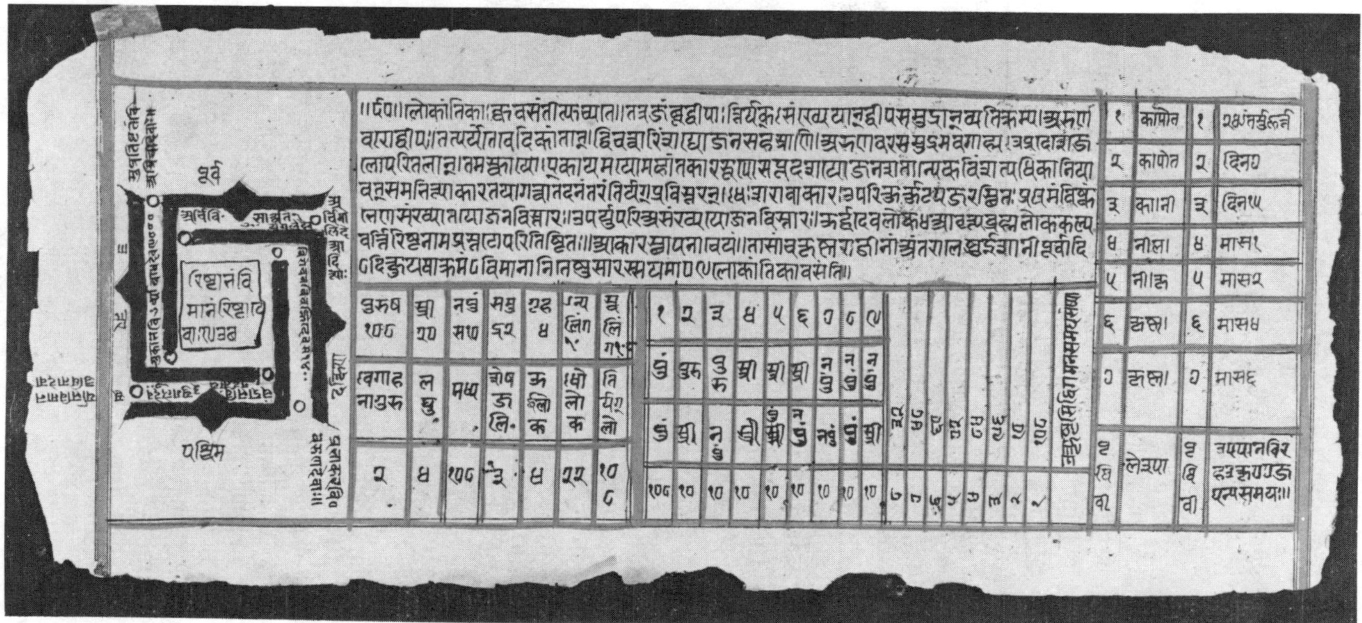

mate meaning, in spite of all else, always-already is."[54]

There are many gates or cognitive entrances into New Reality (Revelation 21:22). Ecological inquiry[55] requires, on the one side, a relational understanding that comes with our being a part of reality, and, on the other, a rational explanation which arises from our being apart from that reality. We face the task of making sense humanly of our human presence. Just as there are many gates into loving action, so there are many mansions, dwelling places, for human living (cf. John 14:2).

My exploration has carried us toward New Reality, a shift in paradigm, and so brings us back from the Holy City at the end of history to Pentecost in the midst of history. In the paradigm of Pentecost I find pluralism and relativism, the universal and the particular—every people, from every place, with every tongue. In the promise of Pentecostal presence we catch our breath at the possibilities of ecocultural fullness and ecological fruitfulness.

A Pentecostal paradigm reverses the regressive processing of a Tower of Babel paradigm (Table 6). Idolatry, that mind-set which takes a limited expression of reality as the whole of reality, distorts and mis-represents reality (cf. Psalms 135:15-18). Lack of faithfulness is linked with misuse of the primary re-presentational input systems. Jesus speaks in the "odd" language of parables[56] precisely because people "look without seeing and listen without hearing or understanding" (Matthew 13:13). He cites the prophecy of Isaiah (6:9-10) in support of this assessment (Matthew 13:14-16 RSV):

> You (Israel) shall indeed hear but never
> understand, and you shall indeed see
> but never perceive.
>
> For this people's heart has grown dull,
> and their ears are heavy of hearing,
> and their eyes they have closed,
> lest they should receive with their eyes,
> and hear with their ears, and under-

> stand with their heart, and turn for
> me to heal them.

And the full disclosure and proclamation of God's being all-in-all came when the major processing systems functioned as one: people saw, heard, and felt (Acts 2:1-12) —rationally and relationally. In the words of the hymn: ". . . mystic harmony, linking sense to sound and sight."[57]

Here is a different reality. Faith confronts us with the demand of wholeness because of the reality of wholeness (Mark 12:30 RSV):

> Hear, O Israel: The Lord our God, the Lord is one; and you shall love the Lord your God with all your heart, and with all your soul, and with all your mind, and with all your strength . . . (and) your neighbor as yourself.

The divine imperative unifies two mind-sets with one spirit. Love (in Greek "agape") means intelligent, outgoing concern for others' well-being apart from our own. As such, it is an intentional strategy of proclamation. Heart (in Greek "kardia") identifies inner nature and character. As such, it is a strategy of participation. Soul (in Greek "psyche") implies living being. As such, it is primary experience. Mind (in Greek "kianoia") refers to intentional purpose. As such, it is conceptualized direction. And strength ("ischuous" in Greek) emphasizes the ability and power of the person to carry through the imperative.[58] With left mind rationality we are to intend right mind attending, that is, we seek that which is right because we know what is real.

St. Paul characterized the process: ". . . be transformed by the renewal of your mind . . . "(Romans 12:2RSV). Mind (in Greek "nous") implies the whole person. Similarly, transformed (in Greek "metamorphous") suggests "a revolution" in one's thinking which brings about a new sensitivity in morality.[59] It is yet-to-be realized, even as it is something that has been always-already, "something which has existed since the beginning, that we have heard, and . . . seen . . . and touched . . . the Word, who is life" (I John 1:1 JB).

A FINAL WORD

The question is asked many times: of what use is the juxtaposing of the brain and belief? What is gained? Quite simply, clarity.

Knowledge of how the brain works helps anchor belief in an empirical foundation. Such a grounding adds precision to the patterns that are associated with belief trajectories. We can see more clearly what is missing and identify more accurately what needs attention.

And, in reverse, knowledge of belief helps give perspective to the evidence of neuropsychology. It sets the findings in larger cultural and cosmic patterns, showing the ramifications of suggested relationships and the compelling intensity of particular information.

In brief, both the brain and belief present corresponding patterns of order, of variety, and of intensity. We are faced with the redemptively responsible task of creatively relating to our environment and to one another.

Whether there is any correspondence between the way the brain works and the way the universe works is left to leaps of faith and paradigms of knowledge. Neurological correlates of consciousness cannot be specified easily.[60] Conscious expression of cerebral activity is distinct and special in its own right, "different from and more than its component physiochemical elements."[61] Life resists typology.

The great British neurophysiologist Sir Charles S. Sherrington described the "functional instability" in results from stimulating the same cortical point in chimpanzees, gorillas, and orangutans. He also found variation from time to time in the same animal. The noted Canadian neurosurgeon Wilder Penfield wrote of the comfort Sherrington's findings gave him. If such variation were present among animals, then he could be less distressed with "the vagaries of response" that he found in the human cortex.[62] Without a doubt there appears to be what one researcher spoke of as "a recalcitrant oddness at the heart of things."[63]

To leave the elusiveness of life at that ignores the more affirmative stance of faith. God is the reality that holds surprises in store for us that we cannot even imagine (2 Peter 3:13; 1 John 3:2). Every identified brain process and belief trajectory must also be understood in terms of their variety and vitality. The Spirit moves where it will, as it will (John 3:8). There can be no single meaning. There is concealment in every disclosure. There is absence in every presence. There is the incomprehensible in every moment of genuine comprehension. There _is_ "radical mystery empowering all intelligibility."[64]

To the mind of faith such elusiveness holds before us the mystery of that power working in us and through us to make human that which is most truly us.

As an analytic metaphor, mind is limited. It helps only to a point. Beyond that life slips out of every cognitive net (2 Corinthians 4:7; cf. also Revelation 20:1-15).[65] Yet I find the use of the metaphor deepening my religious convictions and clarifying my theological understanding. Eight years ago I walked into that lab in the Medical School of the University of Rochester to study neuroscience because of my faith in what Tracy terms "some fundamental trust in reality as constituting an order in spite of all absurdity and chaos."[66]

In the tradition of Augustine, my faith seeks understanding. I direct my reason to what I intuit in my being and in that reality in which I dwell. Just as mind conveys the human significance of the brain, so, for me, God crystallizes the cosmic purpose of humanity.

NOTES

1. Taylor, THE NATURAL HISTORY OF THE MIND (n.1/1), 17-19.

2. MacLean, "A Mind of Three Minds: Educating the Triune Brain" (n.2/53), 308-342; idem., "Brain Roots of The Will-to-Power," Zygon, Vol. 18, no. 4 (December 1983), 359-374.

3. Hampden-Turner, MAPS OF THE MIND (n.1/8), 84.

4. Bever, "Cerebral Asymmetries in Humans Are Due To The Differentiation of Two Incompatible Processes: Holistic and Analytic" (n.2/1).

5. Karl H. Pribram, "Transcending the Mind/Brain Problem," Zygon, Vol. 14, no. 2 (June 1979), 103-124, 117.

6. Ragnor Granit, THE PURPOSIVE BRAIN (Cambridge, Mass.: M.T.T. Press, 1977).

7. M.P. Bryden, LATERALITY: Functional Asymmetry in the Intact Brain (New York: Academic Press, 1982), 222-223.

8. Ibid.

9. Ibid., 278.

10. William Orr Dingwall, LANGUAGE AND THE BRAIN: A Bibliography and Guide. Vol. I and II (New York: Garland Publishing, Inc., 1981). The work provides the beginning student with "a logical step-by-step introduction to the field" (I, ix). It further provides for the researcher "the most complete compilation" up to then of research in the empirical realm, namely, 5746 entries.

11. Robert E. Ornstein, THE MIND FIELD: A Personal Essay (New York: Grossman Publishers, 1976);

idem., THE PSYCHOLOGY OF CONSCIOUSNESS (n.0/5).

12. Augustine, CONFESSIONS AND ENCHIRIDION (n.10/33), Bk. Ten, VIII, 210.

13. Ibid., Bk. Ten, XX, 219.

14. Stephen E. Toulmin, THE RETURN OF COSMOLOGY: Postmodern Science and the Theology of Nature (Berkeley: University of California Press, 1983), 254, quoted by Harold P. Nebelsick, Theology Today, Vol. XL, No. 3, 1983:383, emphasis in the original.

15. Harold P. Nebelsick, "The Return of Cosmology: Postmodern Science and the Theology of Nature." Book Review (n.14 above), 382-384. Science may have a fallen quality, "a basic 'disharmony' or 'irrationality' at the heart of things. If so, a part of our redemptive action vis-a-vis nature may be the articulation of a rationality which nature does not have apart from us or apart from the redemptive activity of humanity for the whole of creation."

16. Augustine, CONFESSIONS AND ENCHIRIDION (n.10/33), Bk. Ten, XXIV, 222-223.

17. Ibid., Bk. Ten, XXVI, 224.

18. See ns.0/5-12, 14; Hampden-Turner, MAPS OF THE MIND (n.1/8); Mary Lou Anderson, "The Vision of Italian Landscapes," "Point-Counter Point," "Order Out of Chaos," and "The Personal Out of the Impersonal" (unpublished articles); Karl A. Johnson, AN INQUIRY INTO HUMAN WHOLENESS (unpublished D.Min. thesis: Colgate Rochester Divinity School/Bexley Hall/Crozer, 1976); James Albert Flurer, THE DEVELOPMENT OF A CHRISTIAN APPROACH TO SPORT MEDITATION (unpublished D.Min. thesis: Colgate Rochester Divinity School/Bexley Hall/Crozer, 1980).

19. See Ashbrook, "The Working Brain: A New Model for Theological Exploration," (n.0/14), for such a tentative assessment of Bernard of Clairvaux and Carl F.H. Henry.

20. Ashbrook, "A Theology of Consciousness: With All Your Mind," (n.0/9).

21. Cf. Tracy, THE ANALOGICAL IMAGINATION (n.1/43), 413: the late Thomistic tradition produced "the neo-Scholastic manuals [in which we find] the clear and distinct, the all-too-ordered and certain, the deadening . . . [it was a] world of the dead analogies of a manualist Thomism, committed to certitude, not understanding, veering toward univocity [only one meaning], not unity-in-difference."

22. Ibid., 431, 436.

23. Ibid., 426, 431.

24. Bryden, LATERALITY (n.7 above), 170.

25. Ibid., 175.

26. Ibid., 232; de Lacoste-Utamsing and Holloway, "Sexual Dimorphism in the Human Corpus Callosum," (n.2/95).

27. Ibid., 238.

28. Ibid., 239.

29. Ibid., 240.

30. Ibid., 268.

31. E. Douran, "Learning to listen to a different drummer." Review of Carol Gilligan, IN a DIFFERENT VOICE. Contemporary Psychology, 1982, 28, 4:261-262.

32. Gilligan, IN a DIFFERENT VOICE (n.2/94); A. P. Arnold, "Sexual Differences in the Brain," American Scientist, March-April 1980:165-173.

33. Waber, "Sex Differences in Cognition: A Function of Maturation Rates?" (n.2/101).

34. Field independent and dependent cognitive styles have been the focus of research by H.A. Witkin and his associates for more than forty years (H.A. Witkin and D.R. Goodenough, COGNITIVE STYLES: Essence and origins field dependence and field independence [New York: International Universities Press, Inc., Psychological Issues Monograph 51, 1981]). The issue is how people process information about the environment. Whether the task requires determining the upright position of a rod in space or discerning simple figures embedded in more complex figures, some people rely upon environmental cues and others prefer their own bodily cues. Boys tend to be more field independent than girls (67). Hormonal influences have been associated with cognitive restructuring tasks reflective of field independence. Although findings are inconclusive, they suggest that some variation in cognitive restructuring may be effected by an X-linked female genetic determinant. These are most closely linked with late language maturers who appear to have greater restructuring ability than early maturers (69). This applies to both sexes, although more boys than girls are later maturers. Some of the research has yet to be replicated (72).

35. L. M. Glennon, WOMEN AND DUALISM: A sociology of knowledge (New York: Longman, 1979).

36. M. Konner, "She & He," Science 82, Sept. 1982, 54-61.

37. J.H. Block, "Conception of Sex-role: Some Cross-cultural and Longitudinal Perspectives," American Psychologist, June 1973:512-526.

38. G. Babladelis, "Accentuate the Positive." Review of J.T. Spence and R.L. Helmreich, MASCULINITY AND FEMININITY: their psychological dimensions, correlates, and antecedents (Austin: University of Texas Press, 1978), Contemporary Psychology, 1979, 24, 1:3-4.

39. Martin and Voorhies, FEMALE OF THE SPECIES (n.2/105), 11.

40. Tracy, THE ANALOGICAL IMAGINATION (n.1/43), 371, 390-398.

41. Ibid., 394.

42. Ibid., 395.

43. Cf., for instance, Peter L. Berger (ed., THE OTHER SIDE OF GOD: A Polarity in World Religions [Garden City, NY: Anchor Books, 1981]), contrasts the monotheistic traditions of the West, which stress a confrontation with an external God, and the great religions of southern and eastern Asia, which stress the interior encounter with the divine within the human soul. Although the typology was sharply questioned, as every typology can be, "there was agreement that the typology, however flawed, did indeed refer to empirically valid phenomena" (viii, 3-27).

44. William James, PRINCIPLES OF PSYCHOLOGY, (n.1/79), 18ff; idem., PSYCHOLOGY (n.3/40), 462-468.

45. Peter Berger, THE SACRED CANOPY: Elements of a Sociological Theory (Garden City: Anchor Doubleday, 1969), 100-101.

46. For instance, Ferguson, THE AQUARIAN CONSPIRACY (n.10/5); James L. Lee and Charles J. Pulvino, EDUCATING THE FORGOTTEN HALF: Structured Activities for Learning (Dubuque, Iowa: Kendall/Hunt Publishing Co., 1978); Richard Sinatra and Josephine Stahl-Gemake, USING THE RIGHT BRAIN

IN THE LANGUAGE ARTS (Springfield, IL: Charles C. Thomas, Publishers, 1983); Bernice McCarthy, THE 4 MAT SYSTEM: teaching to learning styles with right/left mode techniques (Oak Brook, IL: EXCEL, Inc., [1980] 1981).

See also, Howard Gardner, FRAMES OF MIND: the theory of multiple intelligences (New York: Basic Books, 1983). He argues for a multiplicity of human intelligences or cognitive competencies: linguistic, musical, logical-mathematical, spatial, bodily-kinesthetic, and personal in terms of a sense of self and a sense of others. Each of these needs to be mobilized for greater diversity among us and wider social goals. These multiple processes represent a significant reconstruing of what constitutes intelligence.

47. McFague, METAPHORICAL THEOLOGY (n.9/28); Tracy, THE ANALOGICAL IMAGINATION (n.1/43).

48. For instance, M. Ramirez III and A. Castandea, CULTURAL DEMOCRACY, BICONGITIVE DEVELOPMENT AND EDUCATION (New York: Academic Press, 1974); Edward P. Wimberly, PASTORAL CARE IN THE BLACK CHURCH (Nashville: Abingdon Press, 1979).

49. For instance, Alfred B. Pasteur and Ivory L. Toldson, ROOTS OF SOUL: The Psychology of Black Expressiveness (Garden City, NY: Anchor Press/ Doubleday, 1982), especially, Chapter 2 "How Come Blacks Act The Way They Do? A factor of hemispheric confluence and melanin quantity," 15-38.

50. Tracy, THE ANALOGICAL IMAGINATION (n.1/43), 437.

51. See, for instance, Garth Thomas' skepticism "that facts extracted from one level of organization of experience can have anything compelling to contribute to another level" (vii above).

52. R.W. Sperry, "Bridging Science and Values: A Unifying View of Mind and Brain," (n.0/1); idem., SCIENCE AND MORAL PRIORITY: merging mind, brain, and human values (New York: Columbia University Press, 1983).

53. Sperry, "Bridging Science and Values" (n.0/1), 242; Bateson, STEPS TO AN ECOLOGY OF MIND (n.3/38); idem., MIND AND NATURE: A Necessary Unity (New York: E.P. Dutton, 1979); Rosemary Radford Ruether states the issue from a feminist perspective: "Dominant social roles exaggerate linear, dichotomized thinking and prevent the development of culture that would correct this bias by integrating the relational side. Women and other subordinate groups, moreover, have had their rational capacities suppressed through denial of education and leadership experience and so tend to be perceived as having primarily intuitive and affective patterns of thought. . . . What we must now realize is that the patterns of rationality of left-brain specialization are, in many ways, ecologically dysfunctional . . . Linear thinking simplifies, dichotomizes, focuses on parts, and fails to see the larger relationality and interdependence. . . . An ecological ethic must always be an ethic of eco-justice that recognizes the interconnection of social domination and domination of nature" (SEXISM AND GOD-TALK [n.10/2], 89-91).

54. Tracy, THE ANALOGICAL IMAGINATION (n.1/43), 431.

55. J.C. Gibbs, "The Meaning of Ecologically Oriented Inquiry in Contemporary Psychology," American Psychologist, 1979, 34, 2:127-140.

56. Sallie McFague, SPEAKING IN PARABLES: A study in Metaphor and Theology (Philadelphia: Fortress Press, 1975).

57. "Fairest Lord Jesus, Ruler of All Nature."

58. See entries for Love, Mind, Heart, Soul, and Strength in A THEOLOGICAL WORD BOOK OF THE BIBLE. Edited by Alan Richardson (New York: Macmillan Company, 1957), 134-136, 144-146.

59. Peake's COMMENTARY ON THE BIBLE (n.10/5), 949, Romans XIIIf.

60. Cf. the contrasting positions on the functional center of consciousness, e.g., Penfield's integrative cortex (Penfield, THE MYSTERY OF MIND [n.1/4]), Eccles' left frontal cortex (Eccles, FACING REALITY [n.1/1]), Mountcastle's association cortex (Mountcastle, "The World Around Us," [n.2/40]), and Sperry's whole cerebral cortex ("A Modified Concept of Consciousness," Psychological Review [1969] Vol. 76, No. 6, 532-536).

61. Sperry, "A Modified Concept of Consciousness," (n.60 above), 533.

62. Wilder Penfield and T. Rasmussen, THE CEREBRAL CORTEX IN MAN: A Clinical Study of Localization of Function (New York: Macmillan, [1950] 1957), 14.

63. Frank Barron, CREATIVITY AND PERSONAL FREEDOM (Princeton, NJ: D. Van Nostrand Company, Inc., 1968), 302.

64. Tracy, THE ANALOGICAL IMAGINATION (n.1/43), 413.

65. Every typology oversimplifies with the result of (a) collapsing as a clarifying structure in the end, and (b) minimizing significant data for the sake of order. Talcott Parsons and Edward Shils (TOWARD A GENERAL THEORY OF ACTION [n.2/3], 187) correctly identified this oversimplification of empirical reality by "any analytic scheme." The issue, therefore, is "whether the selection of variables . . . is more or less useful than an alternative selection . . . [useful in terms of] fruitfulness in research . . . [and] the relationships of the chosen

set of variables to other variables in a highly generalized conceptual scheme," emphasis in original.

66. Tracy, THE ANALOGICAL IMAGINATION (n.1/43), 410.

A GLOSSARY for THEOLOGY

ANALOGICAL: a way of referring to God by way of concepts and inferences drawn from the natural, finite, created world.

ARIANISM: an approach to the theory of Christ, developed by Arius in the 4th century and declared heretical, in which the Son is viewed as subordinate to the absolute, unbegotten God the Father. Just as it denied the divinity of Christ, so, also, it denied his humanity.

ATTRIBUTES OF GOD: characteristic ways of referring to and defining the nature of God.

CATHOLIC: refers to what is universal, orthodox, true, and shared. Prior to the Protestant Reformation it meant the historical tradition of the Latin West, namely, Roman.

CATHOLIC SUBSTANCE: the phrase of Tillich which emphasizes the concrete expression of Spiritual Presence.

CHRISTOLOGY: the part of Christian doctrine which focuses on the meaning of God's revelation in Jesus Christ.

COSMOLOGY: the "doctrine of the world" or that inquiry which focuses on the origin and nature of the universe.

CREATION: the view that all things are ultimately dependent on the Creator God as the one transcendent reality.

DIALECTICAL: a way of reasoning based on a pattern of logical development and contrast.

EMPIRICAL: an inductive approach to knowledge which looks to and is derived from concrete experience and which in theology involves inferences about God drawn from "facts" in the public domain.

ESCHATOLOGY: that part of Christian doctrine which deals with the final end and purpose of human life in God.

ETERNAL: that which is not subject to time and so is above time and space.

FAITH: one's basic and intentional orientation to life in contrast to belief which involves conceptual assent; basically, the centrality of a whole response of unconditioned trust, most properly, only in relationship to God ultimately.

FILIOQUE: the Christian understanding of the Holy Spirit correlated with the Son in the phrase of the Nicaen-Constantinopolitan creed which states that the Holy Ghost "proceeds from the Father <u>and from the Son</u> . . ."

GNOSTICISM: that pattern of religious conviction in the Graeco-Roman world in the first centuries of the Christian era that viewed salvation as deliverance of the good, immortal soul or spirit from the prisonhouse of the bad, mortal body or world of matter and emphasized the finite capacity to know the infinite, literally, "knowers."

HERESY: that which the Church defined as contrary to its established beliefs.

HOMOOUSION: the Greek word which describes the relationship of the Son and the Father as "of one and the same nature" in order to insure the conviction that Jesus was truly and fully God's act.

KAIROS: a Greek word used in the New Testament to refer to nonmeasurable and meaningful time, e.g., "fulness of time" or "ripe time," in contrast to clock time.

KERYGMA: the Greek word meaning "to proclaim" the good news of the Gospel, i.e., "the preaching" of the Church.

LOGOS: the Greek word for reason, order, or mind of God, which the Church used to identify and understand God's action in Christ.

MANIFESTATION: the constellation of beliefs and practices that has preverbal disclosures of wonder, power, and mystery in and through natural and symbolic expressions as the primary focus of meaning.

METAPHORICAL: a way of thinking which focuses on the surplus meaning in language and by so doing identifies basic similarities between referents even as it recognizes dissimilarities.

NATURAL THEOLOGY: an approach to understanding God apart from special revelation and on the basis of general revelation, i.e., experience and reason.

ONTOLOGY: the inquiry into the rational, coherent, and necessary nature of the universe, i.e., the nature of ultimate Being.

ORTHODOXY: that which is taken to be correct, normative, and right in terms of belief. It also refers to those Eastern Churches related to Constantinople.

PATRISTIC: that period and those theologians ("the Fathers") of the early church between the first and 8th century.

PHENOMENOLOGY: a method of understanding which identifies the basic structure given in the phenomena of experience and brackets assumptions as to causal factors.

PROCLAMATION: the constellation of beliefs and practices that has the centrality of the spoken

Word, instructions and imperatives, as the primary focus of meaning.

PROPHETIC-HISTORICAL: the constellation of beliefs and practices, according to Tracy, that has practical transformative action, that which calls into question existing institutions and ideologies, as the primary focus of meaning.

PROTESTANT PRINCIPLE: the phrase of Tillich which emphasizes the protest against every claim to ultimacy made on behalf of any finite reality.

REDEMPTION: God acting to save or restore the relationship which has been broken with Him because of Humanity's sin and rebellion.

SACRAMENTAL: the view of life that God is present, embodied, and communicated in and through the concrete world. A sacrament is a specific rite which mediates God's grace uniquely, an "outward and visible sign of an inward and spiritual reality."

SCHOLASTICISM: the pattern of Medieval thought that assumed a rational structure to reality and, therefore, self-evident knowledge and which devoted itself to detailed elaboration of that universal rationality based on the authority of the Latin Fathers and of Aristotle (and his commentators).

SYMBOL: an image or object that bears and creates special meaning that is concrete and tangible without being literal and limited. According to Tillich, symbols, in contrast to signs, participate in that which they express.

THEOLOGY: the attempt to discover, define, defend, and share the truth implied by the experience of the faith of the Church. More generally, it is a way of thinking about the nature and meaning of the divine that is both rational and systematic.

GLOSSARY for the BRAIN

ACTIVATION: the arousal process of the brainstem systems.

ADAPTATION: any beneficial modification of the organism that is necessary to meet environmental demands.

AFFECT: emotional response.

ALPHA WAVES: the long, slow, synchronized brain waves (8-13 cycles per second) recorded by EEG during wakefulness which indicate nonattention and relaxation.

ANTERIOR: situated further toward the front of the cerebral cortex, as opposed to posterior.

APHASIA: a class of disorders affecting the ability to translate experiences into verbal symbols rather than actually involving organs of speech.

AROUSAL: the physiological condition of behavioral alertness activating the sympathetic adrenal response of the fight-flight pattern of the autonomic nervous system.

ASSOCIATION CORTEX: those parts of the brain which are neither sensory nor motor but have the function of associating or integrating the incoming sensations with the outgoing motor functions.

ASYMMETRY: a term which refers to structural or functional differences between the left and right hemispheres.

ATTEND: the intentional selection of, and focus on, certain aspects of experience to the exclusion of other aspects.

ATTENTIONAL DOMINANCE: cognitive patterns by which information processing is handled according to the expectancy set either by the left or the right hemisphere.

AUDITORY: involves the sense of hearing.

AUTONOMIC NERVOUS SYSTEM: a part of the nervous system somewhat independent of the central nervous system and so somewhat independent of voluntary control. It includes the sympathetic and parasympathetic systems which regulate breathing, heart rate, blood pressure, intestinal movement, and hormone secretions.

BETA WAVES: the fast, short brain waves reflective of mental activity and arousal.

BILATERAL: each hemisphere is the mirror image of the other structurally and functionally, which means that a function is distributed equally across both hemispheres, in contrast to being confined to one.

BRAINSTEM: the enlarged bulbous area of the upper part of the spinal cord which is responsible for carrying sensory information from the various parts of the body to the thalamus and motor information from the cortex to the centers in the stem and spinal cord. It encases the reticular activating system.

BROCA'S AREA: the area of the brain in the left frontal cortex associated with articulated or spoken speech.

CENTRAL NERVOUS SYSTEM: the brain and spinal cord which are responsive to conscious or deliberate intention.

CEREBRAL CORTEX: the outer, convoluted grey matter of the two hemispheres necessary for higher cognitive activity and constituting the top 80% of the human brain.

CEREBRAL HEMISPHERES: the two large halves of the brain which rest on top of the brainstem. They include the cerebral cortex, the extensive tracts of connecting nerve fibers, and the subcortical areas.

CEREBRUM: the largest part of the brain, which in humans perceives sensory input, organizes thought and memory, and controls voluntary activity. Another name for the cerebral cortex.

COGNITIVE PROCESSES: the mental activity of perceiving, conceiving, reasoning, and judging and includes the additional intellectual aspects of remembering, attitudes, motives, etc.

COMMISSURES: the neural connections between the corresponding areas in the right and left hemispheres, the largest being the corpus callosum.

COMMISSUROTOMY: an operation cutting the connections between the two hemispheres, primarily the corpus callosum and the anterior commissures.

CONVERGENT PROCESSING: the logical cognitive process which creates order and consistency. The opposite of divergent.

CORPUS CALLOSUM: the large group of nerve fibers which connect the two halves of the brain, sending information back and forth and coordinating their activities.

CORRELATES: at the level of the brain, biological events that change as behavior changes; at the level of the mind, cognitive processes that accompany socio-psychological-cultural activities.

CORTEX: cerebral cortex.

DIVERGENT PROCESSING: the fluid cognitive process which generates variety and newness. The opposite of convergent.

ELECTROENCEPHALOGRAM (EEG): a recording of electrical changes in large groups of nerves by means of attaching electrodes to the surface of the scalp.

EPILEPSY: a disturbance of the nervous system in which a damaged area in the brain produces electrical discharges (like a thunderstorm) which can result in seizures or convulsions by spreading through the brain.

FIELD DEPENDENCE: difficulty in separating a stimulus from its surrounding context. The right hemisphere is visually more field dependent than the left.

FOREBRAIN: the two cerebral hemispheres, characteristic of mammalian brains.

FRONTAL LOBES: the front part of the cerebral cortex where initiating, planning, executing, and evaluating behavior originates.

HABITUATION: the process by which a repeated stimulus loses the ability to elicit a reaction.

HEMISPHERE: a lateral half of the cerebral cortex.

HOLISTIC: the simultaneous processing of information in terms of a pattern or configuration of information which is more than the sum of separate bits.

LATERAL EYE MOVEMENT: a shifting of the eyes (either left or right) when responding to a task requiring selective activation of one hemisphere over the other.

LATERALIZATION: the separating of functions between the left and right hemispheres.

LESION: brain tissue damage due to injury, disease, or surgical procedure.

LIMBIC SYSTEM: a group of functionally related subcortical structures of the brain at the border ("limbus") of the stem and the hemispheres associated with emotional and motivational behavior such as hunger, thirst, sex, fight-flight, preservation of the self (the amygdala) and of the species (septum).

MOTOR AREAS: the middle areas of the cerebral cortex directly associated with motor movements.

NEOCORTEX: the outer layer of the cerebrum which is the uniquely human or rational brain capable of symbolization, intellect, and imagination.

NEURON: the basic elements of cortical tissue, i.e., the complete nerve cell which comprises the basic structural and functional elements of cortical tissue.

NEUROSCIENCE: the multidisciplinary study of the structure, chemistry, and the biological and psychological functions of the nervous system.

OCCIPITAL LOBES: the back part of the cerebral cortex that processes visual information.

OLFACTORY LOBES: the sensory parts of the brain which mediate smell and are an extension of the cerebrum.

PARASYMPATHETIC: one of the two subdivisions of the autonomic nervous system and associated with rest and renewal.

PARIETAL LOBES: the top middle part of the cerebral cortex that processes general sensory input from the body itself.

PERIPHERAL NERVOUS SYSTEM: the parts of the nervous system apart from the central nervous system of brain and spinal cord and in contact with the environment.

POSTERIOR: situated toward the back of the cerebral cortex, as opposed to anterior or "toward the face."

PROPOSITIONAL: the capacity of language to create words and combinations of words in an infinite number of sensible statements or "propositions."

REPTILIAN BRAIN: the oldest part of the forebrain which rests on top of the brainstem and involves instinctual behavior.

RETICULAR ACTIVATING SYSTEM (RAS): the system in the brain stem which sends impulses to the thalamus and cortex, resulting in wakefulness and attention as well as giving a constant input of stimulation to maintain the resting potential just below the critical threshold of consciousness.

SENSORY AREAS: the regions in the middle of the cerebrum directly involved in receiving sensory information.

SET: a cognitive orientation or "mind-set" of how to organize and deal with cognitive problems, a predisposition to utilize a certain strategy.

SOMATIC: relating to the body or visceral factors.

SPATIAL: orientation to visualizing or manipulating objects in space, e.g., doing a jigsaw puzzle or drawing from a perspective.

SPECIALIZATION: the location of specific cognitive functions in either the left or the right hemisphere.

SPLIT-BRAIN OPERATION: the severing of the nerve fibers which transport information between the two halves of the brain.

SPLENIUM: the large posterior area of the corpus callosum across which visual and auditory information from each hemisphere is communicated to the other.

SUBCORTICAL: areas of the brain below the cerebral cortex, including the limbic system and the brain stem.

SYMPATHETIC: one of the two subdivisions of the autonomic nervous system which is activated during arousal and stress for purposes of action.

SYNERGY: the enhancement of factors so that the combination goes beyond what can be expected from the mere addition of parts.

TACHISTOSCOPE: an instrument to present visual material for fractions of a second. A subject looks at a dot in the center of the visual field and the device permits presenting images to only one hemisphere.

TEMPORAL LOBES: the parts of the lower level of the cerebral cortex which process sounds.

UNILATERAL: relevant or relating to only one side of the cerebral cortex.

UNCOMMITTED CORTEX: the newly evolved areas of the cerebral cortex which are not specifically predetermined or "committed" to sensory or motor functions.

WERNICKE'S AREA: the region next to the temporal lobe which receives and analyzes auditory information in terms of meaningful comprehension.

INDEX OF NAMES

INDEX OF SUBJECTS

INDEX OF SCRIPTURE

About the Author

JAMES B. ASHBROOK is currently professor of Religion and Personality at Garrett-Evangelical Theological Seminary and an advisory member of the Graduate Faculty of Northwestern University in Evanston, Illinois. Previously, he spent ten years in parish ministry and served twenty-one years on the faculty of Colgate Rochester/Bexley Hall/Crozer Theological Schools in Rochester, New York.

In addition to writing extensively for professional publications and contributing chapters to four books, he has written six, most recently, THE OLD ME AND A NEW i, RESPONDING TO HUMAN PAIN, and CHRISTIANITY FOR PIOUS SKEPTICS. He serves on the editorial boards of The Journal of Pastoral Care and Review of Religious Research.

His education includes a B.A. (Denison University), a B.D. (Colgate Rochester Divinity School), a M.A. and Ph.D. (Ohio State University). Denison University conferred an Honorary Doctor of Laws degree in 1976. He is a Diplomate in the American Association of Pastoral Counselors and a Diplomate (subspeciality clinical) of the American Board of Professional Psychology.

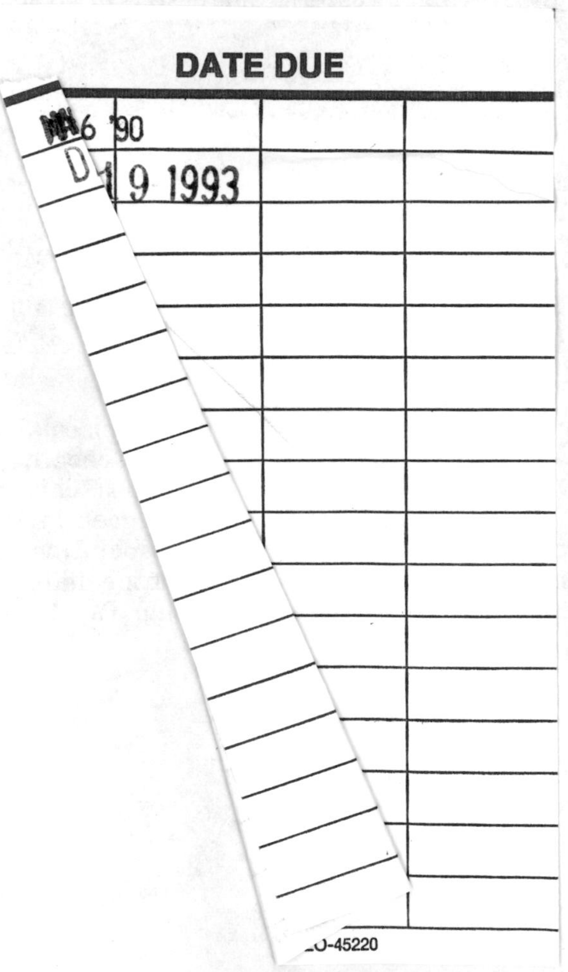

DATE DUE
MA 6 '90
D 1 9 1993
-45220